THE
CARROLL
SHELBY
STORY

THE
CARROLL
SHELBY
STORY

by CARROLL SHELBY

Published by Graymalkin Media LLC

www.graymalkin.com

Previously published as *The Cobra Story*

Copyright © 1965, 1967 by Carroll Shelby and Lyle Kenyon Engel

This edition published in 2020

Book design by Timothy Shaner

ISBN: 978-1-63168-287-2

Printed in the United States of America

1   3   5   7   9   10   8   6   4   2

"As soon as the engine was installed
I really felt that, with some development,
we had a world champion."

–CARROLL SHELBY

A most grateful acknowledgment to the following
for their assistance in completing this book:

John Bentley, Bernard Cahier, George Engel, Bill
Fleming, Donald Frey, David Hebb, Robert Hefty,
Max Muhleman, Jacque Passino, and Stanley
Rosenthall.

My special acknowledgment to the Goodyear
Tire and Rubber Co., whose personal interest and
invaluable assistance at the time I was attempting
to create the Cobra contributed so greatly toward
turning a dream into reality.

Dedicated to those who love the sport of motor racing

CONTENTS

THE
CARROLL
SHELBY
STORY

INTRODUCTION

IN THE COLORFUL postwar period of motor racing, Briggs Cunningham brought back to Europe the blue and white of the American sports car, while a dedicated Californian, Phil Hill, became the first American to take the World's Drivers' Championship title.

Today, Dan Gurney is usually spoken of in the same breath with Jim Clark as the finest all-round driver in the world, and American cars and *pilotes* have established for themselves a formidable reputation on the international racing scene. This is no mere chance—no romantic coincidence; it is plain, demonstrable fact. In looking over the list, however, a proud one indeed of superb achievements by our American friends, I am firmly convinced that Carroll Shelby has, in his own unique way, gone further than almost anyone else to boost United States prestige on the international motor-racing scene.

I think I can claim to know Carroll pretty well. I have followed his career almost since its very beginning and he has at times spoken to me with greater frankness of his hopes, ambitions, and disappointments than perhaps to any other motoring journalist and friend. And, although Carroll never became World Champion, nor was he considered perhaps as tough a driver as Gurney is today, yet the name and image of this tall, lanky, casual, and likable Texan have always invoked in us Europeans an emotion of a very special kind—one with a unique meaning. It is really not too difficult to put into words the image and the emotion created by it, because Carroll Shelby is the typical embodiment of the courageous, intelligent, colorful, and individualistic type of American who, in France

XIII

and elsewhere, excites both admiration and envy. It is this feeling which makes the French sporting public happily exclaim "*Voilà les Americains!*" when Carroll and his Cobras come to Le Mans. "Here come the Americans!"—a greeting spoken with the same friendly, enthusiastic feeling one heard everywhere during those moving days of the Liberation in 1944.

When Carroll first came to Europe, people immediately took to this tall, debonair, Texan driver who looked so typical of his country and of his state, and who also never ceased to evoke smiles when he wore that railroad driver uniform (which he called chicken farming coveralls, or something like that) and that cowboy hat!

It was not long before Carroll became something more than a highly respected driver; he achieved, without seemingly trying at all, a measure of popularity that set him apart from his fellow countrymen in Europe. Soon, as Shelby's bright, warm smile with a touch of roguishness in it began to light up the European racing scene and his engaging personality became part of the racing fraternity's trademark, he gained many friends wherever he went. This was never more obvious than when he pulled off his Big Win at Le Mans in 1959 for the Aston Martin team. You never saw so many happy friends, drivers, journalists, and supporters as gathered around him then, simply because we liked "*nôtre cowboy!*" In truth, we had always wanted to see him achieve the success he did that year and reach the very top; and I must say that on that victors' podium, surrounded by pretty girls, joking, laughing, and drinking with evident pleasure from an enormous magnum of champagne, he looked every inch the handsome and dramatic concept of what an internationally famous racing driver *should* look like! Incidentally, Carroll acquired quite a taste for champagne after that, probably because it seemed to fit his personality so well.

It is not my purpose, in writing this little introduction, to go into the career and highlights of Carroll Shelby's life as a race driver. They are pretty well covered in this interesting and often unique story of his life. But I well remember, some three years ago, when he visited me at the time of the Monte Carlo Rallye. Naturally, I wondered with some curiosity what might be up in that creative mind of his, since I knew that by then he already had given up racing for good. Well, it turned out that Carroll had decided to build his own sports car, which he had appropriately named the "Cobra," as many of the competition were soon to find out!

In 1963, with Ferrari still completely dominating the international Gran Turismo picture, the fact that an American-designed and built Cobra had won the U.S. production sports car championship did not reach Europe with anything like the impact which it perhaps deserved. So matters had to wait another twelve months, and it was 1964 that became "the" year for Carroll and his Cobras. He decided to run for the International Manufacturers' Championship in the GT class, and the story of what happened and how closely he came to snatching the laurels from Ferrari is told in this book with plenty of drama and many interesting sidelights.

Speaking as a European and, I believe, one of Carroll's earliest and oldest friends, I can say that it matters less to the public whether his cars win or lose than it does whether they show up at all! The Cobras are always crowd pleasers and Shelby has become one of the highlights of racing news, regardless of where he may finish. If there were such a title as "Car of the Year" for a competition automobile, the Cobra would win it by an overwhelming majority. Let's not forget his drivers and mechanics, either, who in one season became, as one enthusiast put it, "the most colorful and wanted group in the European racing circle!" Quite a compliment, and one which I heartily endorse.

Tireless during the whole 1964 season, Shelby seemed to be everywhere at the same time; talkative, creative, enthusiastic, diplomatic, and seemingly possessed of all the qualities vital to a successful team manager. Suddenly one began to feel in no uncertain way his stimulating presence on the European racing scene, which had gradually been losing color during the past few years because of a lack of opposition to the Prancing Steed of Modena, especially in the GT class.

In fact, the arrival of the Cobra on the European scene appeared to be "just what the doctor ordered," and now, as I write this at the opening of the 1965 season, everyone in Europe is already asking about Shelby and his Cobras. Any notion that the Cobra team might not appear at a major event would create enormous disappointment. "They"—the public, the press, the race organizers, and even the communities where the team stays—would be disappointed beyond words.

I don't really believe one could offer greater homage to Carroll Shelby, that colorful, swashbuckling individualist from Texas, than to say that he has brought an enormous measure of drama, excitement, prestige, and goodwill to the international world of motor racing.

BERNARD CAHIER

April, 1965
27 Avenue des Grottes
Evian, Haute Savoie, France

– 1 –
A RACE DRIVER IS BORN

IN THE LIFE of every race driver worth his salt there are going to be "those" days. Things will happen that will be impossible to escape no matter how smart you may think you are behind the wheel. The law of averages is against you; sooner or later you're going to come to a violent, unscheduled stop as the result of colliding with a hard object that may be another car, a stone wall, or a concrete post. What happens then is in the lap of the gods, but one thing's for sure: if you live to recall the experience, you'll certainly never forget the date or the place where you got skinned!

I was no exception to this. My worst crash in more than eight years of intensive racing occurred during the second meet of California's new Riverside International Raceway. And, to make matters even worse, I wasn't driving just some ordinary sports car but a brand-new $20,000 Maserati belonging to John Edgar, my sponsor. This magnificent 4.5-liter machine was his pride and joy and he didn't even have the satisfaction of seeing it complete a single lap!

On the very first practice lap of this 3.27-mile rolling course I pulled the biggest, costliest, and most unforgivable booboo of my entire racing career.

It happened at Turn Six, where, I guess, I got just a bit too eager and self-important. The next thing that happened was that I wasn't driving the Maser any more. It was driving me and going like a runaway steam engine—in a straight line—right into an earth bank at pretty close to 80 mph and there wasn't a thing in this world I could do, as the front end had washed out completely.

I guess the term "explosion" would describe what happened next rather better than the ordinary word "collision." But for my

1

seat belt, the chances are that I'd still be flying, probably in orbit.

Turn Six, in those days, didn't have any guard rail and quite a bit of sand had begun to blow across the track even before the start of practice, so that was a convenient and logical thing to blame. Anyway, I got two wheels in that sand and when I slammed on the brakes the wheels didn't slow down at all. They simply locked while the car continued on its merry way.

The collision itself was a tremendous jolt that shook a few teeth out of my head and displaced the cartilages in my nose. I was so badly cut up that I needed seventy-two stitches and some skillful plastic surgery as well. I must have blacked out completely for a few moments, because I have no clear recollection of the impact itself. I do, however, clearly remember, just an instant before I hit, thinking whether this was going to be any worse than, say, being born! Would it hurt more? What was waiting for me beyond?

Imagine asking yourself a question like that! Yet it's often said that drowning men often see the whole of their lives pass in review before them at the last moment. How anyone has ever been able to learn this from a drowned man is more than I can figure out, but the craziest notions do seem to enter your head at moments when you feel pretty sure that the hourglass has run out on you. So, while I think of it, why not start at the beginning and tell you what really *did* happen at the time of my birth and why it's just possible there might be something to this business of astrology and the signs of the Zodiac and what have you.

But let me say something right now that's uppermost in my mind and that'll more than likely crop up again later on in this book. If you're going to walk around thinking about getting killed and what *that's* going to be like, then my advice to you is to give up motor racing. Take up croquet, roller skating, or just plain gardening. That way you get rid of the anxiety.

Maybe I'm not quite like other guys; I don't know. But the thought that was uppermost in my mind as I headed for that earth bank at Riverside and about the worst smashup I ever had in my entire racing career wasn't what it would be like to *die,* but whether entering this world was a more painful process!

* * *

If there had been such a thing as television back in 1923, a well-known newscaster might have said on the evening of January 11, "Well, what kind of a day has it been? It's been a day of unseasonably low temperatures, even for this time of the year—a day marked by an historical event with serious political and international overtones. Today French and Belgian troops marched into the rich industrial area of the German Ruhr and occupied this area to enforce reparations from Germany as the result of World War One."

I doubt, however, whether the newscaster would have added, "Oh, and by the way, this was a day when a son named Carroll was born to Mr. and Mrs. Shelby of Leesburg, East Texas, a little town with a population of about two hundred people, located one hundred twenty miles northeast of Dallas. . . ."

Carroll Shelby (or should I say I) set up a lusty squawk for such a puny babe and, I'm told, grabbed his first bottle as though he was trying to shift gears with both hands.

The year of my birth produced a number of interesting automotive landmarks. Passenger cars for 1923 reached a new high of nearly 3,800,000 units; Dodge came out with an all-steel body, the four millionth Ford rolled off the assembly line, and the Ford Motor Company (in those days no one had thought of calling it FoMoCo) announced a "weekly purchase plan" for its undying Model T, which you could buy in any color so long as it was black. Four-wheel brakes began to come in as a regular production item, the most notable being from Captain Eddie Rickenbacker, who threw his hat in the ring with a medium-priced model that had these brakes. A guy named "Cannonball" Baker drove an Oldsmobile with gears locked in high all the way from New York to Los Angeles in twelve and a half days. Some twenty-eight new makes appeared on the market that year, none of which was fated to survive for very long.

There were some American sports cars back in 1923—makes like Templar, Stutz, Mercer, Duesenberg, Marmon, Daniels, Biddle, and others, all of them hand-built and costing an arm and a leg, so that only a few rich kids could afford them.

The population of my home town, Leesburg, has long since shrunk to a mere fifty souls. My father, Warren Hall Shelby, and my mother, who was born Eloise Lawrence, were strictly local people—

both were born about twenty miles away in Mount Vernon, Texas. I have one sister, three years younger than myself, whose given name was Anne and who was also born in Leesburg. She got married, as might be expected, and is now Mrs. W. E. Ellison.

My father profoundly influenced the eventual path of my adult life. Dad was a rural mail carrier, but contrary to what one might think, he made out pretty well at it. My earliest recollection is that he got around in a buggy with a couple of horses, delivering mail in East Texas, but it wasn't too many years before he switched to an automobile. Delivering mail was pretty hard work, of course, and driving along the rutted lanes that passed for roads was not exactly easy on one's kidneys, either. My dad would be out from early morning until late at night, but deep down he always had a love for cars and I'm certain that my own love of cars was a matter of association. I had gone along when my dad was delivering mail with the horses and buggy, but this made far less impression on me than my first car ride on the mail route, which seemed like an exciting and reckless adventure.

The first automobile my father drove was a used Overland touring car, a 1925 model. I can even remember the first time he drove home with the Overland, late in 1927, which made me less than five years old. My mother and I stood watching as Dad drove up to our frame house and pulled up sharply, racing fashion. He was wearing a big grin and, boy, that Overland really was something. Even though it was already a couple of years old, whoever had owned it before must have taken very good care of it. It was a dark-green touring car with a folding top, black fenders, and wheels of natural hickory wood that still held their varnish. They had those demountable rims that let you change the tire without taking the wheel off and the spare was mounted on the back. Of course I was the first to jump in and the cushions had a nice springy feel about them—enough bounce to make a kid happy. I didn't know it at the time, but this was a four-cylinder job that cost somewhere around $495. However, in those days there wasn't much difference to me between a million and a dime. What interested me most was that after a while my dad let me sit on his lap and hold the steering wheel and make like I was driving the car. The engine would chug along cheerfully and strongly, and even though the Overland squeaked a bit on those rough roads, I don't ever remember that it broke down on us. Just the same, Dad used to love to open that hood and stick his head into the vitals and tinker around like he was making adjustments, which maybe he was. All that machinery under there was a mystery to me then, but I'd watch him, fascinated, and wished I knew as much. One thing I did copy, though: whenever Dad washed the car, that would be a good time for me to give my tricycle a thorough hosing down. Strangely enough, a couple more things about that Overland have stuck in my mind—it had a wood-rimmed steering wheel and a stick shift with a long floor-mounted lever. Seems we've come full circle, haven't we?

"Well," Dad said proudly, rubbing his palms together, "that's it, son. No more hosses. From now on we ride behind the hosses under that hood. Thirty of 'em."

"Thirty hosses, Dad?"

"Well, they're a different kind, of course. They don't eat oats, but they do the same kind of work, you might say."

I think my mother, ever practical, asked what kind of a model it was and I seem to remember Dad saying it was a "touring car," a Model Ninety something. Anyway, as I was saying, being a rural mail carrier in the 1920s was a pretty-well-paid occupation for people who lived in the country. You didn't get rich on it, but you got by all right at a time when farmers in this particular area either raised black-eyed peas or a couple of hogs or maybe a little bit of corn. Thing is, no matter how hard you have to work, you don't feel too bad if you can eat well, and that we were always able to do.

My interest in cars began to be whetted at a young age by the frequent stream of automobiles that would come down the newly surfaced highway in front of our house. The cars were of every type and size and were not really racing each other at all, yet seeing bunches of them go by at varying speeds, much as one might on a race track, must have triggered off some emotion deep inside me. Of course the cars that went the fastest and the ones that made the most noise held my special attention.

Then there were the airplanes that came over once in a while. When I'd see one zoom past in the sky my allegiance would switch for the moment to wings and I would fancy myself sitting up there in the cockpit, an intrepid flyer doing all kinds of stunts.

At the age of six, even if you're a bright kid, you just don't pigeonhole your likes and dislikes the way an adult can. In this respect I was completely normal because I didn't yet have what you might call a consuming interest nor did I have any special hobby. I was about seven years of age when we moved to Dallas in 1930. By then I had had two years of grade school in East Texas and I had another five to go in Dallas before I moved up to high school.

A couple of years before, in 1928, I remember my dad came home one day with a brand-*new* Overland Whippet and it had wire wheels. That was what really stuck in my mind—not the color, which seemed a rather drab gray, but those wire wheels. That and the fact that the Whippet had a four-door body, high and boxy, called a coach. Then there was that new-car smell, which is the sweetest perfume in the world. Its a subtle blend of new paint, rubber, metal, and wood that blends into an intoxicating scent you can never really mistake or forget.

Truth to tell, I never really lost interest in cars, neither in grade school nor high school, and couldn't wait to get one of my own, which I did when I was fifteen years old. When I talk about having owned a car at that age, I'm kind of overstating the case, because it wasn't legal and they never would have given me title. Actually it was my dad's car, but he let me spend so much time with his invest-ment that I got to thinking of it as my own. I really learned to drive a car when I was only fourteen, which would make it 1937, and that was in a 1934 Dodge that needed work; but with my dad's help and a local mechanic's we made it go.

There were three other cars that I remember driving around: a Model T Ford, a Model A Ford—which in my opinion, and I'm not alone, is one of the finest automobiles ever built in America—and a 1938 Willys. With the exception of the Model T, you had to be able to shift gears properly in those days because there was none of that synchromesh and automatic stuff. You had to know about double clutching, the way truck drivers still do today, and if you made a mistake and clashed a gear—brother, they could hear you three blocks away!

By the time a kid gets to high school, he generally begins to get some pointers as to his special aptitudes. I was an apt student all right, but only in the subjects that I liked, such as history and geography—things that could be said to tie in with travel and adventure. But what kind of adventure? I certainly wasn't apt in math or English, and to this day I don't much care about them, though I can manage to put two and two together when it comes to anything that concerns automobiles. So in high school I think it could be said that my consuming interest *was* automobiles—unfortunately not a subject on the curriculum and therefore not one that could indicate to my teachers what I was cut out to do. I used to spend every spare moment reading about automobiles, and airplanes, too, although my interest leaned more toward cars. Getting to an airport meant that you had to spend considerably more time and effort, but as a matter of fact I did manage to hang around airplanes, too, often during 1936 and 1937, sweeping out hangars and so forth—anything to get to sit in a cockpit, hear an engine start, and sometimes even get a short ride.

Going back a bit, again, the reason why we moved to Dallas was that my dad was transferred from being a rural mail carrier to the job of postal clerk in the Dallas post office. From that time on, I can say that he really began to encourage my interest in automobiles because he went further than just talking about them, getting me to recognize the different makes, or letting me pretend I was driving. He used to take me to what we called the "bull rings," the small, oval, dirt tracks where stock-car and sprint-car racing had their beginnings. But my dad went even further. There were times when he would allow me to go to those races on my own as I grew older, and this gave me a chance to get in free by doing any job where they happened to need help. I guess it's long enough ago now to admit that some of these outings to the races were at the expense of high school time, but my education never got beyond high school anyway, so what's the difference?

"Son," my dad would say to me with a sly wink and the air of a conspirator, "there's no man born with a drop of red blood in his veins that doesn't enjoy a race of some kind. If you happen to like automobiles, that's okay with me. I like 'em too. Trouble is I was born just a bit too late. Now, while I look the other way, you slip out and watch some of those drivers spin dirt. Some day—who knows?—you might want to do the same yourself. But don't breathe a word of this to your mother! She wouldn't approve of it."

Both my parents were regular churchgoing folk who never missed a Sunday service at the local Baptist church, but for all that I don't think my dad had any qualms about winking a blind eye while I sneaked off to the "bull rings." Mother had a raft of common sense, and when it came to this racing bit, her comment was brief and to the point.

"Skidding automobiles around dirt tracks don't make much sense to me," she'd say. "There's nothing to be learned from that and precious little to be got, except maybe some broken bones!"

The main auto racing competition we had, back in those days in that part of the country, was only a bunch of backyard bombs powered by four-cylinder Ford blocks or some 228-cubic-inch Chevy blocks with a strange variety of cylinder heads, some of them pretty ingenious, yet the "bull fights" were quite exciting as the cars skidded on the loose dirt, trying to claw their way round the turns under full throttle. This was the kind of thing that really fired me up and made me want to become a race driver. Some of the names I recall from those days around the Dallas area were Gene Frederick, Hershel Buchanan, Oscar Coleman, and Tex West—all of them long since forgotten. But in those days they were all outstanding men on this type of circuit. This was before the era of the Midgets set in, which was not until three or four years later. The term "sports car" seemed to have come and gone in the United States, but in Europe things stayed pretty busy in that department. That was when George Eyston was running a team of blown MG's in the Mille Miglia and stuff like that.

There came a time when, obviously, we could no longer hide from my mother the strong interest I had developed in automobiles and racing, but, as I say, although she disapproved and couldn't see what it was all leading up to, she didn't give me too much static about it.

My physical condition wasn't particularly good for many years. When I was nine or ten years old the doctor spotted a heart murmur and I was told to take good care of myself and give my body a chance to build up. The thing that irked me most was having to rest for several hours every afternoon. Any time I neglected to do this I got tired very easily and then I'd be forced to sit down and rest, whether I liked it or not, much in the same way that I take care of my heart condition now.

However, as time went on I got bigger and taller, I gained strength and seemed to grow out of most of this heart trouble. In fact it never again showed up until three or four years ago, when I had to get out of racing because of it.

Physically, I grew tall and slim like my paternal grandfather Shelby. In fact, at one time or another, I've been called just about everything by not-too-polite buddies and other people. Things like Craggy Face, Skinny Texan, and Gangle Gut are among the more printable ones, but I'm a believer in the notion that it's better to have people say even uncomplimentary things about you than nothing at all.

Now, when a guy writes a book about himself, an autobiography like this one, it's maybe not a bad idea to lead in with a few clues to his character and general psychological makeup. You'd be surprised how many people seem to set store by this business of astrology, and oddly enough, though I'm not one of those who subscribe to it, I've found so many things in a book about Capricorn folk (my sign of the Zodiac) that seem to apply to me, that my horoscope might not be a bad place to start from. For instance, it says about money that "this is your strongest point and you apply yourself to achieving monetary gains. Of all the signs of the Zodiac, yours imparts the greatest desire for security."

Can't argue much with that. In three years, starting from nothing—and I mean nothing—I've built up a $16-million business with what might be termed a unique specialized product in the automotive field, an all-American high-performance automobile that can match anything they have in Europe.

About home life, this books says, "Although you yearn for the security of a home, domesticity does not hold the appeal for you that it does for others. Yet you feel the responsibility of parenthood very heavily." Another bull's-eye.

In friendship, quoting from this little gem, "You are a person who has a wide circle of acquaintances but very few close associations. You value your friends highly, though, and those who really get to know you also appreciate your friendship." I hope so. "On the other hand, though you steer clear of argument and like to keep the peace, if you're pushed too far you blow up." And how! Ask the guys who work for me.

Then there's the bit about romance. "You are intellectual rather than emotional in your approach to romance, and your heart is governed by your mind. The Capricorn husband is seldom a good emotional companion for his wife, and although he falls readily enough into the domestic scheme, he adds little to its spiritual success. Still, he's a good provider, for he is very ambitious and successful in business most of the time."

As the father of three kids and the former husband of a very fine gal, I think I know what this guy is driving at; but I can't help wondering whether he ever got the yen to drive a race car. That urge is a thing that burns like a bright, unquenchable flame which nothing can put out. You have it or you don't. If you have it, you live in a world apart, and I guess it's the thing that's just a little bit ahead of whatever comes next. So I guess the guy who wrote that horoscope was never a race driver. Race drivers do marry and sometimes it works out just fine, but most often the cars get in the way. I'm sorry to say that's what happened with me.

Take the substance of what it says in that little book, the chase for a buck, home life, friendship, romance, and marriage, and you've got a pretty good character portrait of one Carroll Shelby.

– 2 –
GOOD-BY, EXCELSIOR

DURING MY HIGH school days in Dallas, a couple of other things got to me—flying and golf. Flying was a hobby obviously beyond my means, so I came in the back door by learning to be an airplane mechanic of sorts. It was the same thing with automobiles, by the way. I just didn't have the money to hire someone who could do the work for me, so the next best thing was to find out how to do it myself. Don't imagine that I was or ever became a clever mechanic who, when he can't find what he wants in a parts store, goes back to his shop and makes it on a lathe, and things like that. No, sir, at best I never got beyond being a so-so mechanic, whether on airplanes or automobiles. I haven't the patience to fool around for hours with bits and pieces, measuring this and checking that. When something technical interests me, I can grasp its working principles as quickly as the next man and learn to take it apart and put it together again, but still, to this day, I don't care to fool with anything that stands in the way of something I really want. There are experts in carburetion, ignition, suspension, and braking. I use them.

In 1939—when World War II broke out in Europe—I started going out with the girl I eventually married, the mother of my three children. I'll give you several guesses as to where we met. *We met in church!* As I've already said, my folks were staunch Baptists who regularly attended church on Sundays, but getting me to do the same was quite another matter. I would think up all kinds of excuses to beg off at the last moment, knowing that neither Mother nor Dad would insist beyond a certain point. But a Sunday came when I couldn't very well get out of going with them, and I don't doubt that was the way it was meant to be. For that Sunday I happened to notice an uncommonly attractive girl, a pert brunette with velvety brown eyes, rich brown hair, and a trim, 115-pound figure that was helped by the fact that she was not very tall, only about five feet four inches. Her name was Jeanne Fields, I soon found out, and she came from Dallas, of course. When Jeanne smiled, which was often enough in those days, her face lit up in a way that could make even the heart of a Capricorn skip a beat!

Sure enough there was the local drugstore in those days, and the movies, too, but we didn't go in much for that kind of thing. More for walks and drives and visiting each other at our homes. Our love grew gradually, you might say; it certainly wasn't one of those sudden flash-of-lightning things, but I definitely fell in love with Jeanne when still quite a young fellow and one day I finally did pop the question.

"Guess you know about me and cars and airplanes and all that stuff?" I told Jeanne.

"I should, by now." She smiled.

"It's not going to bother you too much?"

"I'll get used to it."

That meant "Yes," and I was a mighty elated guy, though we had to wait until December, 1943, when I was nearly twenty, before we finally got married. Still, the fact that our engagement, you might say, survived a wait of nearly four years and a goodly part of the nastiest war in history showed that we had something pretty much worthwhile going for us. And for a long time, despite all my racing and my evergrowing absences and the many times when Jeanne couldn't go with me because of the kids, it worked out unusually well. Unfortunately I've never heard of a conflict between a wife and a racing automobile in which the wife got the better of it, no matter how fine she might be. It just doesn't work that way, especially when the kids start to come along. This tended to keep Jeanne ever closer to home, while, on my side, racing trips seemed to take me ever further afield.

During those Dallas years before I signed on with the Air Corps, in spite of other and more pressing interests, I was very far from losing my love of automobiles. Not for one moment did that happen. Once the car bug gets into your system you never really shake it off, no matter what.

Those high school years passed quickly, and suddenly I was seventeen and in reasonably good health, though still pretty thin and nowhere near as tall as I am now. By then I had decided I wanted to be a race driver, but since I didn't have any money the only way open to me was the same as that taken by countless others—to start as a racing mechanic and show my wares and work up to where I wanted to get: in the driving seat. This looked to me like it was going to take much too long, and having just graduated from high school, there was nothing left to me but either to go to college (which my parents couldn't afford) or to start earning a living in earnest. But doing what? Sweeping out airfield hangars to burn free rides? Not much future in that. So I did some fast thinking and decided that for the time being I'd better shelve the race-driver idea and maybe try to become a pilot instead. The only problem was how to go about it. At first sight it seemed just about as difficult as carving out a career racing automobiles. I soon found out that you had to have a minimum of two years of college before you could get into the cadets for special training as an airline pilot, but there was nothing to stop me from joining the Air Corps, anyhow.

Looking back now, the way I came to that decision is rather amusing. At this time there were four of us waiting it out till we got to be eighteen, the minimum age for enlisting into the armed forces. We earned some money by delivering packages for a drugstore at a nickel a package—cigarettes, prescriptions, newspapers, and so forth—and I used a little English motorcycle called an Excelsior for this purpose. Along with the James, it was the first foreign motorbike imported into the U.S. in quantities, and I had bought it for a dollar down and a dollar a week. It certainly paid for itself, because I could earn ten bucks a week without too much trouble, and that would buy you as much as twenty-five a week would today. Not bad money for a kid.

But sooner or later, I guess, it had to happen. I was on one of those runs of about five or six miles to deliver some stuff when I got in a skid and the motorcycle went out from under me, in a dead-end street, luckily. Not so luckily, my behind hit the curb an awful whack and the bike ended up on top of me, after which it seemed to gather momentum again and continue on its way alone until it finally crashed. I was too sore to go after the darn thing and pick it up, and also too mad at the world and myself, so I just left it there and hobbled back to the drugstore and told them, "That's it. I'm quittin'. I'm all through."

The manager's jaw dropped. "What for? Have a spill or somethin'?"

"Yeah, I had a spill and that decided me. I'm joining the Army."

"Well, buddy," the guy said, "that's your privilege, I guess."

I asked the other boys if they too were ready to join up and they said "Yes"; so the next morning we went down to the recruiting office. At least, three of us did, and we were told to sit down and wait. Then the recruiting sergeant came in, a tough, muscular, red-faced guy with a back like a ramrod, and looked us over in a manner that indicated he wasn't too much excited.

"You guys want to join up?"

We nodded yes and he said, "Well, the only openings we have now are with the infantry in the Philippines."

"That's a long way from Dallas," I said. "Too far for me."

The sergeant looked me up and down as if to say, "Boy, are we going to have to go to work on you to build you into something!" But all he said was, "You're kiddin'," and didn't add anything to that. He waited for me to make up my mind.

"I'm sorry, Sarge," I said, "but there's two things wrong with your offer. First, I don't want to get in the infantry. I'm interested in serving in the Air Corps. And second, I'm not interested in the Philippines, no matter what the service."

"Son," he says, just a little more softly this time, "we just don't have any openings at all in the Air Corps, so are you going to the Philippines or not?"

I told him "no," and, boy, was I glad later that I hadn't signed my name on that piece of paper. The two fellows with me did sign up for the infantry and the Philippines—Hughes and Cook were their last names—Ace Hughes, I remember; and one of them survived the infamous Death March, only to get blown up in a submarine, later, on his way to Japan.

But the sergeant didn't give up on me quite so easily.

"Tell you what, son," he says, "if you want in the service, you'd better sign up today anyway. You never know what may happen tomorrow. If there's a war you don't have any choice."

"Looks like I don't have any choice now, either."

I started to leave and got as far as the door when the sergeant called after me. "Now are you *really* interested in joining the Air Corps?"

"Yes, I sure am."

"Well, okay then, I'll give you a call when we have some openings—*if* we have some openings!"

It didn't take him long to find what he thought was the right slot. He called me the very next day. "Carroll Shelby?"

"That's me."

"Sergeant Smith, here. Just heard we've got some openings, just a few, in New York State, son. How would you like to go to New York, eh?"

"Thanks, Sarge, but no thanks," I said. "New York's still an awful long way from Texas."

I don't think he expected this reaction, but he took it better than I expected, if rather pityingly. "Well, okay, son. I don't guess you know a break when you see one, but I'll keep in touch if anything nearer home happens to come up."

Sure enough, three days later he called again.

"Better get ready to sign," he said. "You can go to Randolph Field, right here in Texas, if you want to. Air Corps and all."

"That's for me, Sarge," I agreed. "Thanks and I'll be right over."

So Randolph Field was where I wound up, and that was the start of nineteen different places in Texas—nineteen different specialist jobs!

When it came to actually saying good-by to my parents, I must admit I had an uncomfortable moment. I guess it always hurts a bit to leave a good home. Our financial condition in Dallas wasn't actually as good as it had been in East Texas, even though my father made about the same amount of money, but that was because the Depression was on and it cost more to live in a big city, anyway. Our house in Dallas was actually smaller than the one in Leesburg, but there was enough to buy the groceries and make sure we all had turkey for Christmas.

Anyway, I passed my physical without much trouble and signed on and got shipped off to Randolph Field, which was quite a break for those days. They were quite willing to sign you on, but if you lacked the required education they automatically shoved you into the infantry. Also, there was no such thing as a choice of specialized training, the way you have today.

Anyway, my flying experience, even as a trainee of any kind, could be reckoned as nil at the time I joined the Air Corps. No one had ever tried to teach me to fly, and the most I'd been allowed to do was hold the controls for a moment in flight, in return for sweeping the hangars and stuff like that.

Going back a minute, my very first flight in those days when I hung around airfields was in a Ford Trimotor. I want to tell about it because when you get right down to it I wasn't so sure then that I even had the guts it took to go up in an airplane. I'd been bugging my father for months to take me to Lobb Field, where those Ford Trimotors took you up for a buck and circled the city of Dallas in a flight that lasted about ten minutes. One Sunday afternoon Dad suddenly gave in and took me to the airport.

"Okay, son," he says. "Now you're going flyin'."

"Fine!" I said, but, I remember, as I started walking toward the airplane, the old Ford Trimotor, I told myself, "Boy! I think maybe you made a mistake here."

When we got to the airplane I couldn't hold it back any longer. "Dad," I said, "I'm not so sure that I want to go after all."

My father's expression didn't change a bit. "Look, son," he says, "you've got just about two seconds to make up your mind. You're going or you're not. Which is it?"

So I thought, "Well, if I've got to die young it might as well be now. We've got this far and I can't chicken out."

"It's go, Dad!" I said, gritting my teeth.

As it turned out I thoroughly enjoyed the flight after the first two or three minutes and was sorry when it ended. The next airplane that I flew in, when I was about eleven years old, was a Curtis Junior, a pusher-type airplane where you sat out front. Then I had a few trips in the old Aeroncas around Hampton Place Airport in Dallas. The pilot would let me hold the stick once in a while but not really fly it as a student taking instruction. The Aeroncas had all that wire bracing on top and a peculiar-looking A frame, but they flew pretty well, just the same.

–3–

THIRTY-FIVE-MILE WALK

THE FIRST THING they did with me when I finally joined the Air Corps was put me on a train with seventy-five other recruits (Sergeant Smith must have been a master of understatement!) and ship me out to Randolph Field, Texas. We arrived about five o'clock in the afternoon in the middle of a downpour, and they shoved us into some tents that were far from dry. Next morning we were awakened at five o'clock with our mess kits and given breakfast. Then they gave us mops and told us to go to work in the hangar.

Basic training had begun—the same old stuff that every new recruit has to go through. "About face! Forward march! Look lively, there!" It was just a routine way of busting you down so you got to say "Sir" and salute like an automaton. You also quickly learned that if they said "Right shoulder arms!" they meant like now, or you were liable to get two weeks of KP. What it amounted to was teaching you to think the way the Army wanted you to, or, in other words, not at all. They did feed us as well as anyone ever got fed in the service, and as a result of all this healthy living and forced feeding I grew another six inches during the first half-year of my stint in the service, though I didn't put on much weight.

When basic training came to an end, I assumed, as did many of the other recruits, that we'd all be assigned as aircraft mechanics, or at least be given something to do with aircraft. But that's not the way the service mind works. Instead, I was assigned to a detail hauling chicken manure from an old abandoned chicken farm to various flower beds around Randolph Field. Strange to relate, although I later got into the chicken raising business by one of those quirks of

17

fate, chickens were not at this time a particularly fascinating subject so far as I was concerned. Much less was I interested in that part of them they set us to hauling.

You'll hardly believe it, but this detail continued for three months and came to an abrupt halt only because an ole boy from Tyler, Texas, and I decided that we'd rather spend a little time in the guardhouse than shovel any more of this dirt. I can't remember his name, but we worked out a nice little plan that would land us where we wanted to go without breaking any specific regulation. You see, there's no regulation that covers the digging of a hole, except the 96th Article of War that covers any offense not specifically taken care of by all the other articles.

So there we were, this guy from Tyler and I, sitting around in the little pile of chicken manure, waiting for a character who was known as the Toro Kid. He was called by that name because that was the name of the tractor he used for hauling the chicken manure. Now, the Toro Kid also happened to be the sergeant in charge, and that suited us fine. This was a real veteran with twenty-five years of service—an ole master sergeant who used to turn his cap around backward so he could push the tractor along faster, and in addition wore goggles to protect his eyes from a possible overdose of chicken manure.

What was more natural than that we should decide—while waiting for him to return and pick up the next load—to dig just a little hole in the ground. Along the part over which he would be driving, of course. Anyway, we covered the hole neatly with Johnson grass, meaning to give the Toro Kid just enough of a jolt so we'd be put under arrest. Unfortunately that hole was a bit deeper than we'd meant it to be, with the result that the tractor keeled over on its side and the Toro Kid got a pretty rough shaking up. Sure enough we made the guardhouse, though for longer than we'd expected. They kept us in there for five days.

Still, it was worth every moment spent in confinement, because after that there was no more hauling of chicken manure for Private Carroll Shelby. Instead, I became a fireman and was given the privilege of sitting on what we called the Flying Line for eight hours at a time. They were putting the cadets through their basic training just about then, and Randolph Field became a busy place. I drove a crash truck as a fireman for about three months, and during this period they passed a new regulation that those of us in the Air Corps who had finished high school and were anxious to get into flying could become flying sergeants, provided of course we passed the necessary physical and qualified in other respects. The reason for this was that the shooting war had just started for Americans and there was an immediate lowering of requirements for those who wanted to serve as air crew. Still, there was a minimum weight limit for fellows of a certain height and I happened to be about ten pounds under that required weight, with no hope of making it in time by any normal means. So I had no alternative but to stuff myself with bananas and milk and suffer for three hours until I could get it pumped out after the physical.

Anyway, I made it in November of 1941 and was at once sent off on a course of preflight training which, it was hoped, would later enable me to become a pilot. I moved about fifteen miles across San Antonio to Lackland Army Air Force Base, which they had just opened as a preflight center. About a million men must have gone through it since, and it's still there today. As I say, I didn't learn to fly at Lackland, but instead began to learn what flying was all about. This included courses in navigation, radio, engineering, and the whole bit. Everything, in fact, short of actual flying. Average time was from four to six weeks and there was some math involved, but nothing very complicated.

Preflight over, we moved to a primary flying school which was located close to a little town called Cuero, Texas, about eighty miles east of San Antonio. This course lasted about ten weeks and it was here that you learned to actually fly an airplane. I happened to be assigned to a Fairchild PT-19 and was lucky enough to have an instructor named Glennon, an experienced civilian pilot before the war. He was the man who taught me to fly, and I doubt whether I would ever have graduated from this first phase without his help. I caught pneumonia and was in the hospital for two weeks, and it was only due to my instructor's patience and perseverance that I managed to catch up with the others. Sure, they had lowered the requirements to get into the Army Air Force, but the same old spirit still prevailed with those in charge of flying schools. They were still thinking in terms of how many guys they could wash out, rather than trying to see how many they could help to pass. There's this to be said for the present-day Army: when they find somebody around who isn't especially competent, they try to save him by giving him special direction and guidance. But it seems that in those days the Air Force wanted to see how many guys they could flunk and took pleasure in making things as tough as possible for you. A polite term for this, I suppose, would be a "highly selective type of training," but there are other, shorter, and more descriptive words for it.

Anyway I put in approximately nine or ten hours a day before I was ready for my first solo, and that seemed about par for the course. If you failed to solo within a certain number of hours, no matter how competent your instructor might be, they just threw you out. By this means, the Air Force destroyed the egos of countless men who could eventually, with a little more patience and understanding, have been useful to them. Instead, these guys ended up with their morale broken by a stupid system that simply added up numbers, regardless of what kind of training you were getting. Apparently the competence (or lack of it) of your instructor didn't mean a thing. Of course the preflight navigation training I had received at Lackland, along with preflight mechanics and a lot of other stuff, helped no end in preparing me for the actual flying, but I still don't believe any man who tells me that he wasn't a bit nervous on his first solo and that it came easy. You're always nervous the first time you get up in that grabber by yourself with nobody there to tell you what to do if something goes wrong. The first time I went up solo I shot three or four landings in probably ten to fifteen minutes.

The next step consisted of flying intermediate-type aircraft, either pursuit or twin-engine types.

I took my basic flight training at Sherman, Texas, and—by the way—here's one that you won't come across too often: I courted Jeanne more by airplane than any other way! She lived out on a farm north of Dallas and I used to fly over and throw her notes in my flying boots. Love letters, too, and that was our courting correspondence! I was always a terrible letter writer and didn't seem to be able to remember what the mails were for, so I'd fly out low over

Jeanne's house and drop the boots right in her yard with the letters in them!

Around September, 1942, at Ellington Field, near Houston, Texas, they made me a sergeant—a flying sergeant—and then commissioned me in December of that year. I went through what was called air students' training, instead of air cadets', the difference being that the Army Air Force "students" didn't have the college requirements and had to go through special classes first to become flying sergeants. The commission I got was that of a second lieutenant, but I never rose any higher, nor tried for further promotion. I was much more interested in flying and having fun during those days than in getting a promotion that would bring a lot more responsibility with it. As I've said before, though I loved to fly, I never did take to military discipline. Some guys are just not made that way and I'm one of them.

An amusing thing happened when I was courting Jeanne by air, an incident that I didn't really contrive, it just happened that way. Early in 1943 I had flown into Dallas to pick up some airplane parts. They told me it would be three or four hours before the parts were ready, so I decided to do a little barnstorming on my own. I flew to a small airport near Jeanne's home and got her on the phone.

"Come on down, honey, and I'll give you and your mother an airplane ride."

"Carroll, you're just kidding me. It's another of your little jokes!"

"Come on over and find out, why don't you?"

"You mean you've really got the plane there, waiting?"

"Sure do, ma'am, but it's not going to wait forever. I have some parts to pick up in a few hours."

"All right. I'll tell Mother and we'll be over right away."

"Swell."

As I was about to pop the question to Jeanne anyway, I thought this would be a pretty good way to make time with both Jeanne and her mother. Impress them—you know. So they came out, sure enough, and got in the AT-11, the good old Beechcraft twin-engine job, and I took them full circle over Dallas, looking at everything, going up, then coming down, so they could really get a good idea of what their own city looked like from the air. I shuddered for a long time afterward, thinking of what might have happened if I'd gotten caught. I would have been court-martialed out of the Air Force, lost my wings, my commission, and the whole bit, no doubt, as there wasn't any possible excuse for doing a thing like this, especially in wartime. But when you're in love, I guess you don't stop to worry about little things like that. Also, I got a big kick out of seeing how much they enjoyed the flight—every minute of it. With a little coaxing I got my future mother-in-law to sit up in the nose of the airplane, where the big domed plexiglass nose was, and where we used to drop the practice bombs from. She wasn't a bit nervous and thought the view just wonderful. It was a clear day with a visibility of several miles and the clouds well above us, so she felt like someone sitting in a private grandstand, I guess, getting a marvelous view of all that went on below. Jeanne also got a big charge out of it, and that day the Carroll Shelby stock went up several points!

I finished twin-engine training at Ellington Field, and after there started flying bombardiers and navigators at San Angelo, Texas, where I stayed for a few months. My usual ship was a twin-engine Beechcraft AT-11, with an occasional B-18 thrown in. Then I moved on to other bombardiering schools and flew B-25's and 26's, finally winding up in a B-29 at Denver, Colorado. That was when I got out of the service in 1945. I had by then been in the Army Air Force four years and six months and had never left the country except to fly out over the Gulf of Mexico once in a while. That's the twelve-mile limit. I never did any operational flying, but instead—acting as an instructor—flew students, and also took on the job of test pilot. This was not as glamorous as it might sound. I didn't actually test new aircraft, but after the routine maintenance of existing types I would take them up and test them out before they went back into service.

Sure, I would have liked to fly combat. I'd say at least 35 per cent of the instructors I worked with wanted to go into combat, primarily so they could get the war over with. I know that was exactly my feeling, especially after several narrow escapes when I was a test pilot and a couple of wheels-up landings. I remember one time especially, when my twin-engine Beechcraft caught fire over the Matador Ranch in Texas, at night of all times. It was an electrical fire that came up under the control pedestal, where the throttles and propellor controls were located. Pretty soon the cockpit was full of smoke and stench and sparks and I couldn't figure out where the heck it was all coming from. I was the pilot that time and we didn't have a bombardier instructor. The only guys with me in the aircraft were a couple of cadets who were about ready to graduate as bombardiers and were doing their stuff solo. One was a little bitty guy and the other a great big husky specimen. I'll never forget their names—although that doesn't matter here.

"Better get the hell out," I told them over the intercom. "This crate's on fire."

"Okay, skipper," says the little guy without hesitation. He didn't even ask any questions.

He salvoed the door and got ready to jump, but then he began to have trouble with the big guy.

"Hey, skipper," the little one says. "That dumb bastard won't go! I've tried—"

My hands weren't burning yet but things were getting pretty hot and I was anxious to get out, too. "Now you get the hell out—both of you sonovabitches!" I shouted.

That did it. The little guy put his GI brogan squarely in the seat of the pants of the big one and hauled off. I heard a scream as the big lunk started falling through the night, and then the little guy jumped out as nimble as a squirrel. Well, we had lost a lot of altitude during this discussion, and when I finally ran back to jump out I didn't even have time to fasten both leg straps, so my parachute opened upside down and pulled the big collar up over my ears. I didn't know where I was or what was going on by the time I hit the ground, but thank heavens the chute opened just in time. The other two guys made out okay. Both their chutes opened fine and they started walking toward the lights of a town only two miles away. As luck would have it, I never saw them at all, nor did I catch sight of those lights. When I came to a fork in the road where they had taken the left turn, I took the right fork and had to walk thirty-five miles clear across the largest ranch in all Texas, if not the world.

Believe me, thirty-five miles at night on a totally deserted road is quite a long way, especially after you've bailed out of a plane. You'd like to talk to someone, but the only talk I heard was the voices of coyotes sitting up in the hills. I was barely twenty years old and hadn't seen much of West Texas and I didn't know that coyotes only make a spine-chilling noise but never actually bother you. On top of it all I had one hip slightly injured by that fall and it got to hurting more and more as I walked; but I wouldn't have stopped for anything in the world—not with those howling coyotes out there.

After a while it started to get colder than the inside of an ice-box, but luckily I had on heavy flying clothing and that kept me from freezing to death.

As I trudged on, thinking of this and that to keep my mind alert and at the same time forget about the pain in my hip, I got to figuring I must have bailed out at about five hundred feet, which was rather too close for comfort at night, especially when you have only one leg strap fastened. Anyway, bleary-eyed and exhausted, I watched the sun coming up over the horizon and as the prairie came into relief, it only served to emphasize in what a vast and lonely place I'd landed. It wasn't until nine o'clock the next morning that I finally stumbled into one of those small outlying cattle stations, so beat I could hardly put the words together to tell them what had happened.

By then, of course, the other two guys had reported in and I was presumed missing and Jeanne already knew about it when I called her. We were still many months away from getting married, but she cared more than I had ever imagined.

"You okay, honey?" her voice quavered. "Is it really you? I thought—"

"It's the good ones that get killed off!" I quipped, trying to cheer her up, but it didn't do much good. I could hear her starting to cry.

"Listen," I said. "What are you worrying about? Guys like me have a straight line to hell—and that's where I'm calling you from! So how about it?"

The tears turned into laughter then, because she knew that if I could talk the way I usually did, it really must be me and I wasn't much hurt.

The next pleasant little episode of this kind was a vapor lock that hit both engines of my AT-11 at the same time. One moment we were purring along, sweet as a nut, and the next—blonk, blop! No more engines. Something had gone whacky with the fuel system. I had two cadets with me in this Beechcraft bomber-trainer, but this time it was daylight and we could at least see what was coming toward us by way of landscape. There was nothing we could do but make an emergency wheels-up landing on someone's farm in West Texas, which luckily was flat enough for this purpose. When we started sliding along on the ships belly the bomb bay doors were tom clean off and great clouds of dust started boiling up inside the airplane. I was certain we were on fire in a big way and liable to blow up at any moment, so while those two cadets were wondering there in the back end what the heck was going on, I beat them both right out the door. None of that hero stuff for me this time! Which just goes to show that once in a while if something hits you wrong, you can forget all about your responsibilities. That's sometimes called a yellow streak up and down your back. Matter of fact I'd banged my nose hard on the instrument panel as we slid to a stop and the impact scrambled my brains so that I was dazed and didn't know what the heck was going on.

Jeanne and I got married, on December 18, 1943. I continued to fly and had a daughter named Sharon Anne born September 27, 1944, by which time they had transferred me to Denver, Colorado, where the climate was very nice. I stayed there with my newly acquired family until August, 1945, when V-J Day came and the war, at long last, was over for keeps.

At this point I wanted out. I hadn't actually seen any overseas service but I'd had more than a bellyful of the whole business. When I made a formal request for my release, a courteous major received me with an ingratiating smile.

"Wouldn' t you sooner switch to the Army Air Force Reserve?" he inquired. "It offers many benefits, plus the fact that you can continue to keep up with your flying. One soon forgets, you know."

"I know that, sir, but I've no civilian ambitions as a pilot."

"Still, the Reserve—"

"Well, I've accumulated enough points to get out, haven't I?"

"Yes, of course." He gave me a smile of annoyance. "But that's hardly the point. We still need trained men against any possible future emergency. Especially men like you, who can train others."

"Maybe, but switching to the Reserve isn't the same thing as getting out altogether, is it?"

"No, not exactly. You'd have to show up a couple of times a month for a meeting and such. But against that you'd be able to draw some useful pay."

"Negative, sir," I told him. "Just let me get out altogether. I don't care for any more of this life and the pay of a Reserve pilot doesn't tempt me enough."

"As you wish," the major said and sighed. He had done his best and failed, and he knew it. "I'll have your papers processed without delay."

I saluted and walked out, and that was about the last I saw of the Air Force.

−4−

ROUGHNECK−LIMBERNECK

AFTER V-J DAY, the moment they gave me my release, Jeanne, Sharon Anne, and I returned to Dallas, and for a couple of weeks, while I was looking for a house, we stayed with my wife's parents. I had a nice welcome and all that, but what does a young fellow do who's not far off twenty-three and totally untrained for anything except flying airplanes? After some searching I found just the right house for my family, but the problem of how to make a buck still remained unsolved. It was pretty difficult making this readjustment to civilian life, more so as I had no formal education and yet faced the immediate need of supporting a family. Frankly, the idea of becoming a commercial pilot didn't appeal to me at all and I never gave it more than a passing thought.

Then suddenly, as things were beginning to look bleak, a lifelong friend of mine, Bailey Gordon, came up with a bright idea that immediately appealed to me.

"What say we get into the dump truck business together, Carroll?"

"Dump trucks?" I said. "What do I know about them, except that they have wheels?"

"Well, I know something about them." Bailey grinned. "And you can soon learn. There's money in it, too."

"Now you're talkin'."

"As you know," my friend went on, "I already own a truck and what started me was my father-in-law, who's been a very successful trucking contractor. He said I couldn't go wrong and I believe him. In fact I'm getting more business now than I can handle. So why don't we start a partnership. You get a truck, too, and we're in business."

Luck was with me this time and I didn't have much trouble in raising a good down payment, especially with that kind of collateral. Bailey Gordon found me a Ford that was in topnotch shape and didn't need any money spent on it, and away we went, driving our trucks twelve hours a day. Things went so well with us, hauling to the ready-mix concrete places in and around Dallas, that within a few months we were able to add several more dump trucks to our little fleet. These included Internationals, Diamond T's, and more Fords. The work was hard, but those dollars came rolling in on the truck wheels, and both Bailey Gordon and I were soon making a nice living out of it, which was a pretty tough thing to do for a couple of boys with very little background and no money, fresh out of the service. Because, if the truth be told, our initial starting capital in this business added up to a great big zero dollars.

Well, anyhow, that was the way it went, and my son, Michael Hall, was born November 2, 1946, while Bailey Gordon and I stayed in the ready-mix concrete business all during 1947. At this point I started to branch out on my own and got into the hauling of lumber. This meant a further expansion to my trucking fleet, with different vehicles, of course, and again things went well. I started hauling lumber for East Texas to keep pace with the housing boom that had sprung up not only in Dallas but all over the country. Still, it seemed fairly obvious that the housing boom, and consequently the lumber-hauling business, couldn't continue forever and I began to get scared I might be caught with a fleet and nothing more to haul.

It was my father-in-law who really put into words what had been a growing sense of uneasiness at the back of my mind.

"Son," he says, "there's no use fooling yourself. You're doing all right at present, but how long is this housing boom going to last? And what do you do when it ends?"

"What would you suggest, sir?"

I asked that question, knowing that my father-in-law had valuable interests in the oil business.

"I'd suggest that you drop this trucking business, get rid of your fleet and the liabilities that go with it, and get into the oil business."

"Sounds great," I agreed. "But how do I do that?"

"Well, one thing's for sure," said my father-in-law, "you don't learn about the oil business by starting at the top. You start at the bottom, the way I did, as a roughneck, working in the oil fields. Then, if you've got the right stuff in you, someday you become an oil tycoon."

"I'll certainly think about it, sir," I told him.

I went home and talked things over with Jeanne. As usual, she said, "You must do whatever you think best, honey."

So I did what I thought best and took my father-in-law's advice. All during 1948 and part of 1949 I worked in the oil fields, putting in a lot of hard labor and getting little pay in return. So little, in fact, that the day came when I couldn't go on being a roughneck any longer. I couldn't afford the luxury. My father had passed away back in 1943 from heart trouble, but my mother was still alive and at this particular time very ill. This meant a raft of hospital bills on top of having my own family to support, so I had to give up on the idea of someday becoming an oil tycoon.

The car bug had never left me, it had only lain dormant during those war years. When I found out that some of our employees raced their old junk cars on a local half-mile track near Dallas, I went out to have a look. I wound up driving those heaps about half a dozen times and I seem to remember winning a race one time during that period. As for sports cars, they were nonexistent in Texas at that time and only just beginning to seep through, back East, from Europe. When I became a roughneck, however, my only contact with race cars was when Jeanne and I took a couple of trips to Indianapolis in 1948 and 1949 to watch the famous 500. We were strictly spectators and I had no connection whatever with Gasoline Alley or any of the builders, entrants, or drivers of that time. I do recall, though, that a Blue Crown Special won the race both years. It was a front-drive job that seemed to handle better and go faster than any of the competition, with Maurie Rose getting the checker (and a huge jackpot) one year and Bill Holland doing the same thing the next. I don't know how I'd have made out as a driver at Indy, or whether I would have made the grade at all. Particularly back then, the Indianapolis 500 was a truly incredible race. The cars, most of them, were simply not good enough at that time for what the drivers were trying to make them do.

Today, of course, with these ultramodern, lightweight, rear-engine jobs, much better suspensions, and more scientific weight distribution and streamlining, it's another story altogether.

But let's get back to 1949. When I quit the oil business, some bug got into me to take an aptitude test to find out what I was *really* cut out for—if anything. You may not believe it, but this aptitude test came up with the answer that I was very adaptable to raising any kind of animals. Yep, that's a fact. It also proved to be the start of one of the worst financial setbacks I ever encountered in my life. Unfortunately, I didn't know it then. A lot of things convinced me I ought to make a start in the chicken raising business. At this time, raising broilers as a business occupation, rather than just something down on the farm, was getting going in a big way down in Texas, and there was the added inducement that this was about the only business where you could get started with credit. Raising broilers was an occupation approved by Uncle Sam, who was willing to lend you all the money you needed. In addition to that, the feed companies were also anxious to help finance you and let you have their products on the cuff. So that was how and why I wound up as a chicken farmer.

Believe me, I didn't fool around with this thing, once my mind was made up. I started raising twenty thousand chickens at a time and really worked at it. Unfortunately, the very first group of chickens I raised netted me a profit of somewhere between $4000 and $5000, so I thought, "Well, here's a real easy way to make money. Just a simple occupation and pretty soon you can start your own bank!" Actually it took only ten to twelve weeks to raise a batch of these broilers, so I almost got to worrying about what I was going to do with that steady twenty-five grand a year those chickens would earn me.

But naturally, as you might have expected, it didn't work out that way. My second batch of chickens suddenly caught a fatal disease that had long been known in Texas as "limberneck," but which the learned guys started calling Newcastle's Disease. Whatever you called it, once a chicken got that disease it usually died within two or three days at most. Anyway, when this thing hit my broilers, I lost nearly twenty thousand of them within a day or two, and almost overnight, there I was completely bankrupt.

I don't know how much worse you can do in business than go bankrupt and find yourself in debt up to the eyes, and I'm not anxious to find out, ever again.

Roughneck, limberneck—it's about time we got to cars. The embers of my enthusiasm for automobiles were still smoldering, awaiting, it seemed, the right moment to flare up.

After the chicken disaster, I was pondering what to do next for groceries, when I met an old childhood chum of mine, Ed Wilkins. Ed and I used to go to the dirt track races along with my father in the old days, and we'd also shared an interest in airplanes and automobiles at a very young age. Well, at this time Ed had a couple of cars, one of which he had built himself, and the other an MG-TC. The home-built special, which so far as I recall didn't have any name, interested me quite a bit. It featured a ladder-type frame of quite modem concept, 1932 Ford V8 suspension, including the solid front axle, a flathead Ford engine, and a homemade body similar to those you see on our sports cars today—I'm talking about the home-built specials, of course. Still it was a nice job, well put together and reflecting a lot of work and time. I told Ed so, and suddenly he turned to me with a straight face and asked, "Would you like to drive the thing for me?"

"Drive it?" I asked. "Where?"

"There's a drag meet in a few days [it was January of 1952 by then] at the Grand Prairie Naval Air Station, between Dallas and Fort Worth."

"You mean just straight dragging on a strip?"

"Yeah," he nodded. "It's a quarter-mile and I'd sure like to see how this baby goes."

"You just got yourself a driver," I laughed.

As things turned out, there wasn't much to it. My opposition consisted mainly of a bunch of sports cars, nearly all MG's, and I just ran away and hid from them. When you consider what I had under the hood, it's not exactly surprising, but the nice thing was that Ed's Special handled just fine and did nothing unpredictable.

It seemed to me that Ed got a charge all out of proportion to what I had done, but then he had built the car himself and worked all those Ford bits into the design and come up with something that actually ran pretty well. So I guess he was entitled to feel happy. I was happy too with almost the next thing he said to me.

"I think you've got the touch, Shel. Would you like to have a go with the TC in a real sports car race—I mean one with corners and all that?"

"Why not?" I asked.

"Then we might as well start preparing the car without delay. There's a race in May at Norman, Oklahoma, if they don't scrub the thing by then. Anyway that's when it's scheduled for."

"Okay. But what's this bit about preparing? We're not equipped to do any serious work on your MG, other than just check out to see everything's tight and the timing is right and the plugs gapped properly and so forth."

"That's just what I meant," Ed assured me. "No modifications. Just a routine checkout."

Well, we did that, and in those days, since I wasn't working regularly but just making out on a little of this and a little of that—odd jobs and buying and selling bits and pieces—time wasn't of any real importance.

The course at Norman turned out to be triangular and easy to drive, even though it was one of the first stabs taken in the southwest at a real road circuit. What we were running on was actually a huge concrete and gravel airplane parking area that had not been used since the war, and someone had dreamed up the idea of using three pylons to mark each of the angles of the triangle. Each lap was about a mile or a mile and a half, I'm not sure which, but enough to work up a little bit of speed. The first race, as I recall, was for MG's only, and I don't think I had a very good starting position. I was someplace in the middle of a pack of fifteen or twenty identical automobiles—not the best place to pop the clutch in. And so far as Ed's car was concerned, it really was as stock as the day it had left the factory. The windshield was on, the spare tire and the whole bit. I remember that I wore a helmet, but I haven't any idea what number our car carried on its side.

What I do remember was watching for that flag to start dropping. Then I let in the clutch, pushed the throttle down, and squeezed through a series of gaps by no more than the thickness of the paint. This didn't put me in the lead by any means, but at least it gained me a few places to make up for that lousy spot on the grid. I also remember that one guy in a car that looked exactly like Ed's drove a pretty good race and gave me a lot more trouble than I had expected for a couple of laps, before I finally got by him and into the lead. I just waited for him to make a mistake and let his tail end come around a bit too much, and under the pressure of pursuit he did just that. It's never much fun having someone breathing down your exhaust pipe, because you don't really know whether they're fully extended or playing a cat-and-mouse game. The pursuing driver has a much easier time of it.

There's not much more to tell about my first true road race except that I seem to have won it by a good margin, with the rest of the field strung out. Ed Wilkins was tickled pink at having his car win, so when they started lining up a bunch of XK 120's for the next event and one of the officials came up and asked us if we'd like to run the MG, as I had won the previous race, Ed jumped at the offer. Then he turned to me a bit sheepishly and asked, "Think you can make it, Shel? I mean, you don't have to start with those Jags unless you want to, you know."

"What can we lose," I told him, "besides some tire tread? Sure, I'll run."

I don't have to remind anyone, even today, that an XK 120 was an entirely different breed of cat from an MG-TC, but back of my mind was an idea—maybe something I'd read or seen someplace—that those Jags didn't corner half so well as a lot of people were led to believe. They had a thing called understeer where, when you try to take a corner really fast, and the corner is sharp enough, the front end starts to wash out on you. But against this they had tremendous speed and about twice as much acceleration as the little TC. So it was probably the drivers, because I ended up by winning that race, too, although not nearly as easily as the previous one. It didn't take me long to figure out that if I was going to skunk those XK's, I had better do it on the turns and not wait for them to gobble me up along the straights. Pretty soon I worked out a pattern of going wide, at full bore in a kind of drift that converted the triangle into a rough circle. I had to use the full width of the runway and the pylons ceased to have any meaning, except as rough guides, but this idea paid off. It paid off just fine and I got the checker after a very enjoyable drive that taught me several useful things.

Not to take anything away from the opposition, I guess I must have had a little bit of ability or something and didn't recognize it at the time, because I don't mind admitting that no one was more surprised than Carroll Shelby when he beat those Jags.

Anyhow, this was about the time when I really got hooked on the sports car racing business, and I don't know what I would have done about it if some offers hadn't started to come in. But that's the way it goes, luckily. You win a couple and some of the owners get to thinking maybe they've dug up a new Fangio, and pretty soon a lot of people are offering you rides.

The next race after the one at Norman was along about August or September of 1952 at a place called Okmulgee, Oklahoma, a county seat about twenty-five miles south of Tulsa, in case you're interested. That time I drove an XK 120 and beat a bunch of other XK's to win without too much trouble. Though my wife Jeanne has religiously kept hundreds of clippings about my drives and wouldn't part with them to anyone that wasn't bonded, I just can't remember the details of all those early races, or even of many of the later ones. So if you expect a kind of blow-by-blow recital, you're headed for a disappointment. My experience is that if a driver can't remember a race, then it probably wasn't anything very outstanding and it doesn't matter; and if he can't remember a race that *did* matter, he had better get his head examined. You just don't forget the really worthwhile ones.

Before the Okmulgee race (I had to look up the spelling of that one on the map!), a Louisiana sportsman, Charles Brown, had asked me if I'd drive his Cad-Allard for him and I had agreed to do this. In those days, you know, the Cad-Allard was a mighty powerful beast with a lot of pep, even though it owned the craziest front end you ever did see on a racing automobile; so I guess my being asked to drive this baby could be taken as a compliment.

So the next important race I drove as a novice was at Caddo Mills, Texas, in November of 1952, wheeling Brown's well-prepared Allard. This, by the way, also happened to be the very first race that Masten Gregory ever drove in, and I must say he had an awful lot of guts, cutting his teeth as a race driver in a Cadillac-powered Allard. Quite a crowd turned out to watch that one, because it was one of the early SCCA (Sports Car Club of America) races and the course was laid out right close to this little town of Caddo Mills, about forty miles from Dallas. Also there seemed to be quite an array (for that time) of powerful and expensive machinery.

Masten gave me a good battle and would have finished second, but unfortunately his throttle linkage broke. It was a funny thing: I think Masten and I had less experience in driving this hairy stuff than any of the other drivers, yet somehow I ended up winning the race and, as I say, Masten lost second through no fault of his own. Driving a brute like that Allard for the first time in a race, you had to feel your way a bit carefully at first. It was rather like walking across a floor strewn with marbles.

When Christmas came around, and the end of 1952, I had run in, I think, four races and won them all and had begun to collect a few little trophies at the same time. In those days it was unthinkable for a gentleman to accept any money for his racing, and sure enough I didn't earn myself a cent. Only the boys at Indy or a stock car or midget driver would soil his hands with money in this noble sport. At least, that was the popular misconception of the times.

Don't mind if I jump back and forth a bit during those early racing days, but I've just thought of a rather funny episode in connection with that Special Ed Wilkins built—the one he let me drive in the Grand Prairie Drag Race. After we won, Ed got the idea he wanted to drop a Chrysler mill into that rig to replace the little Ford, and we decided to do the job in my garage. It was a handy place to work in, and that way I was able to put in more time at home and not leave Jeanne alone so much. Well, Ed Wilkins was one heck of a good mechanic when it came to the Detroit stuff; he really knew his way around like a bat in a cave and he could overhaul engines with the sure touch of a mechanical artist. But, still, this business of trading engines got to be pretty hectic because it entailed a lot more detail changes to the car than we had figured out at first. Among those detail changes was some extensive revamping of the body-work, and here, too, Ed was an expert. He could bang away with a ballpeen hammer like nobody's business, but when it came to that, plus our kid-raising job, Jeanne couldn't stand any more of it. The whole business had been grating on her nerves for days and finally we got the ultimatum: "Either Ed goes, or both you and Ed can go together!"

Needless to say that Ed packed his things quietly and left; and while I wasn't exactly happy at this situation, I could see Jeanne s point of view as well. She wasn't opposed to my racing activity, but she didn't want it right on her doorstep! Also I forgot to mention that there had been some complaints from the neighbors, who told my wife we were ruining their sleep.

–5–
YEAR OF THE ALLARD

THE TITLE OF this chapter is, I think, appropriate, since that year—1953—I drove Allards almost without exception. Those cars gave me many a good ride and practically a hundred per cent total of wins, but I'm not going to quarrel with anyone who might feel like calling this machine a hairy brute. It was that fine British driver, Tommy Cole, who unfortunately lost his life at Le Mans that same year, to whom credit must go for first dropping a hopped-up Cad engine into the Allard. Man, I sometimes wonder if Tommy realized just what he had unleashed! In those days, for a car to break six seconds from zero to sixty was really something; but when you pump that kind of performance plus a top speed of about 150 mph in a chassis designed for hillclimbs, you've really got yourself a jet-propelled kiddie kar! I've already mentioned the Rube Goldberg geometry of the Allard's front end, due to its peculiar split axle, but the chassis also had some strange quirks. Rigidity definitely was not one of its virtues. In fact, the durn thing had so much whip built into it you could get the doors to fly open if you cornered fast enough! Any novice who tried to race an Allard and forgot to tread those opening laps with a wary foot stood a good chance of becoming a statistic—a memory. Several guys did just that; yet the car enjoyed great popularity in America during 1952 and 1953, and once you got to understand its temperament and master some of its oddball traits, it took something costing twice as much to beat you.

That was my feeling, at any rate, and when Charlie Brown of Monroe, Louisiana, offered me another ride in his Cad-Allard at Caddo Mills, Texas, during January, 1953, I looked forward to a lot of fun and a continued association that would benefit both of us. My last race for Charlie had been at Caddo Mills in November of the previous year, when I had won fairly handily, so I didn't have much to learn about that course. I won again this time, but what followed was a great disappointment. Early in March Charlie Brown called to tell me he had just sold his Allard, so I had better look around for something else. He had no immediate plans to continue racing.

This left me in about the worst possible condition for a race driver. There I was, badly bitten by this racing bug, confident of my ability, yet with little to do but worry about the future. By then I knew that people were beginning to notice Carroll Shelby a little bit, although I hadn't accepted any money for driving during 1952. Not one cent. I had just managed to keep my head above water from a very small income made up mainly of payments still due me on some trucks I had sold and things like that, but I was getting uncomfortably close to the bottom of the barrel, while my family showed no signs of losing their appetite. Somehow I'd managed to salvage a few splinters from the wreckage of that chicken farm venture and I was now raising some Irish setters and pheasants, but not on a scale you could call a living.

Right then it seemed to me that if I was really going to make a career out of motor racing I'd better do something about it right quick, or else forget the whole thing. Then at a moment when I was sitting around wondering what the heck to do, a phone call came through from Jacksboro, Texas, and a familiar voice inquired, "That you, Carroll?"

"Yep."

"Know who this is?"

"Sounds like—let me see—Roy Cherryhomes, isn't it?"

"Right the first time. It's several months since we met, but I'm calling you on the off-chance you might not have any serious racing commitments for this season."

"You're talkin' to the right party."

"Okay, then, how would you like to drive for me?"

"I'd like it fine," I said without hesitation, "but what happened to Roy Scott, your regular driver?"

"He's found himself another ride," Cherryhomes explained. "In fact it was Roy who suggested that I call you."

"He sure had the right idea," I said, trying to keep from sounding too eager.

"Tell you what, then," Cherryhomes said, "I'll be in Dallas in a couple of weeks. Let's get together then and talk things over."

"Suits me," I agreed. "What's it to be—your Cad-Allard?"

"What else?" he laughed. "You seem to have a way with those babies."

From then till we met, two weeks later, I was walking on cloud nine. I didn't know Roy Cherryhomes at all well. We'd met at one of the races and chatted awhile and I'd had the feeling, right away, that here was a guy who didn't fool around. Chances were that if he said something, he meant it. I also knew he was a motorcycle collector, but that was about all. When we did get together, there was no written agreement or anything like that, nor any firm commitment in terms of time. You don't do anything like that down in Texas. They offer you a ride and if you're good enough to hold it, well, you get to stay on. If you aren't, then you're out. The only understanding we had was that I would drive strictly for expenses, but even so I was pretty much thrilled. In the southwest, good rides were mighty hard to come by in the sports car field, especially in those days. And suddenly there I was with the latest equipment—a car I knew well—and a competent mechanic to care for it, and not a cent to lay out. It sure was a good start, and just to make it stick I won my first race for Cherryhomes at Omaha, Nebraska.

But there was another reason why I got a big charge out of the agreement to drive for Roy Cherryhomes. Until then, Masten Gregory had been winning just about everything in our part of the country. He would show up with some pretty good equipment—always the newest and fastest—and it seemed that there was no one who could stay with him, no matter how hard anyone tried. "Well," I thought to myself, "maybe we can put a stop to *that*—always in a friendly way, of course."

I remember that I drove two or three more races in Texas out of a total of eight or nine with the Cherryhomes Allard that year, but I don't recall losing any of them. Then there was this event at Eagle Mountain Naval Station, Fort Worth, Texas, and that one I'd like to talk about a little because it was the first time I showed up wearing those striped farm coveralls that sort of became my trademark. It was a very hot day in August and I'd been working on the farm, or what remained of it, when I realized I'd have to hurry over to the naval station if I was going to get in any practice. This was on a Saturday morning, so I took off just the way I was, and when I got in the car I realized how much cooler those coveralls were than the regular driver outfits. Well, seems like everyone got a big laugh out of that and my picture appeared in the papers and I got more publicity because of those doggone coveralls than I did for winning the race. "What the heck," I thought, "might as well stick with them." And I did, from then on.

I'll grant you it did look kind of silly showing up at these sports car races in what people used to call my farmer's overalls, when drivers like Gentleman Jim Kimberly made a great thing of color schemes and immaculately tailored driving suits and all that jazz, but the thing stuck and I guess no one would have recognized me if I'd shown up dressed any other way for racing.

Getting off this coverall kick for a moment, I want to answer a question here that I've been asked dozens of times, seemingly because I cut my teeth on big-bore machinery, and didn't do too badly at it. People are always quoting something that Briggs Cunningham is supposed to have said a long time ago: "You can't beat cubic inches." And do I agree with that? Well, you have to qualify the thing, of course. You *can* beat cubic inches with a highly sophisticated engine—twin overhead camshafts and all that—which is another way of saying you can beat cubic inches with a big bundle of dollars. Obviously, when we talk about cubic inches, we're thinking of those big-bore, pushrod-type American engines that come in so handy for hauling along big American cars; and, well, if you look at the FIA International Manufacturers' Championship, our Cobras won in 1965 and the way the Ford GT rewrote the record books at Le Mans against the fastest Ferraris ever built, who can argue with that? I guess if you want real performance at a realistic price, then the answer is that you can't beat cubic inches and Briggs was right and we were right.

But we shouldn't lose sight of the fact that if the European engine has developed along different and more sophisticated lines and has come to rely on very high rpm to get the power, that's because

European automotive needs and problems are entirely different from ours. Our gasoline, for instance, is not only of high quality but is by far the cheapest you can buy in any country, so this economy bit doesn't mean much to the average American owner. Another reason is that you find many more winding roads in Europe and everything is on a smaller scale, so what would be the point of having big cars? Then, too, many European countries tax their automobiles on the size of the engine or the weight of the vehicle, or some such thing. So it was quite natural for the British and French and Italians and Germans to look toward small, high-performance engines, not only in touring but in racing.

Another thing that ties in with this big-bore stuff and people too often forget about, is that when in 1949 European-style road racing started picking up momentum over here, none of our chassis were worth the powder and shot to blow them to hell. The European makes had it all over us for roadability, braking, and handling, and about the only thing we could counter with was a big-bore engine. Well, under those conditions, that often wasn't enough. I think Lance Reventlow was about the first one of the new crop of serious American designers who realized this and did something about it.

Today we're in a very different position, even though we seem to have been a bit slow to learn about chassis, or at least to apply the theoretical knowledge that was available. But now, other things being equal, and by this I do mean chassis design, why heck, you can't beat cubic inches, especially on a dollar basis.

Okay. Now that we've got that straight, let's go on to talk about Argentina at the start of 1954, because I reckon that was really the turning point of my racing career. In January of 1953, just a year earlier, John Fitch and Jim Kimberly had raced in Argentina, and Kimberly had decided it would be nice to donate a trophy. There would be a challenge race every year in Argentina between an American and an Argentine sports car team, regardless of who else might be running or of things like overall results. So, in January of 1954 the Automobile Club of Argentina paid for shipping over to Buenos Aires four cars to be raced by American drivers. This had already been decided the previous December, and the drivers picked included Phil Hill, Masten Gregory, Bob Said, and me. There were a great many Argentine drivers, all in all, but I don't recall offhand who had been chosen as our four opposites. I do remember, of course, that we Americans were the gentlemen representatives of the Sports Car Club of America and that we had co-drivers, but in spite of all this I must say we made a pretty poor showing. Phil Hill and David Myskes, whose 4.1 Ferrari, though a little tired, at least looked impressive, quit with transmission trouble after only thirteen laps. Bob Said and David Moffat in an OSCA 1350 didn't even last that long. It took only five laps for their transmission to call it a day. Dale Duncan, who was down on the program to co-drive with Masten Gregory in the C-Jag, switched over to driving with me, which was perhaps just as well for him, and turned out to be a break for me. Masten's car started okay but ended up by covering only seventy-nine laps at an ever slower speed, its engine sputtering and missing and no one able to find out why, despite some pit stops and a lot of head shaking. The real trouble was that the trouble was just too durn simple. People sometimes forget about little, unimportant things like a battery, and batteries have a nasty way of failing or going dead just when you need some work out of them. That was Masten's problem.

So that left Carroll Shelby and Dale Duncan in a two-tone Cad-Allard No. 6 which belonged to Roy Cherryhomes, who wasn't even there to see it run. Not that he missed anything by staying away. On the contrary, I'd say he spared his feelings.

But as I told just now, the way things turned out I was a lucky cat to have Dale Duncan from Kansas City as my co-driver. This guy not only was good behind the wheel but was also a regular air-lines pilot with Braniff who had the bug the same as the rest of us. The only reason either Dale or I was able to make it was that our expenses were paid over there and Dale, being a pilot, could also get a pass. Those, I guess, were the economic factors that caused us to team up, and we made out okay in the end, but I'm sure it was Dale who saved the day. The fenders flapped and flew off, and after several flat tires we were reduced to running without a spare. Then the engine caught on fire, but my co-driver's presence of mind in the pit has probably never been equaled, let alone topped. When he saw what was happening, he raised the hood and tinkled straight into the carburetor without a moment's hesitation, putting out the fire and at the same time relieving a rather pressing problem. Some alert photographers caught him right in the act and we still have some priceless prints, but that didn't faze Duncan a bit. He kept right on at it until the fire died out. Anyway, I think the old Cad engine was so surprised—so taken aback by this strange and rather humiliating way of putting out a blaze—that the last ornery streak died out of it and it started up without giving us much of a hard time.

We had to hand it to that big-bore 5.5-liter job, though. It just chugged right along, taking us to a tenth-place finish with a total of ninety-six laps before the race ended. It was an event with a real mouthful for a name, I remember: Mil Kilometros de la Ciudad de Buenos Aires; but the 5.8-mile course with its peculiar shape, and the thirty-seven bright-hued starters, mostly in expensive machinery they didn't really know how to handle, justified it all, I guess. Part of the circuit was made up of a longish section of plain road on the outside of the regular grounds, and it was called, I believe, Avenida General Paz. Don't ask me about General Paz. I couldn't tell you who he was.

There was the usual Le Mans start with the cars lined up at an angle and the drivers on the other side of the track sprinting across to their machines when the flag dropped. Right away, three blue Ecurie Ecosse C-Jags leapt into the lead to make a brave showing, but they didn't have enough under the hood to keep up the pace. During the latter stages of the race the 4.5-liter Ferrari of Farina and Maglioli got so far ahead, and the remaining fifteen stragglers so far strung out, that the race might have put many fans to sleep but for a quota of crashes bad enough to satisfy the most blood-thirsty *aficionado*. Forrest Greene, a Buenos Aires auto dealer and a keen Anglo-Argentine enthusiast, died of injuries received when his Aston Martin rolled over and burst into flames. There was no lack of police nearby to offer help, but they were mighty slow about it— almost reluctant, you could say. Neither the cops nor the officials, in fact, had any control over the crowd, which at times got completely out of hand, creating some serious hazards for the drivers. Ian Stewart's C-Jag also went off into the boondocks and crashed when a couple of small-car jockeys forced him off the road, but he was lucky enough to walk away from that one.

Perhaps the funniest part of the whole whacky business was that we Americans won the Kimberly Cup by default, you might say, in spite of our poor showing. This was something like the halt leading the blind. Of the fifteen actual Argentine starters fielding Ferraris, Aston Martins, Porsches, and what-have-you, only one was close enough to Duncan and me at the finish to make it look like a race, and that was a guy named Maiochi, I think, in a 2.5 Ferrari. He was running about a minute and three seconds behind the Allard when the checker signaled the end of the Thousand Kilometers.

There was one other Argentine, Bonomi in a three-liter Ferrari, who seemed to know his way around pretty well. He completed ninety-one laps before his gearbox went on strike, and for a while, there, he had us worried.

The way it turned out, that was the last time I ever drove the Cherryhomes Allard, but I wouldn't be telling it right if I left out the important fact that I had one of the best mechanics in the business—Lucien Harbuck. He proved to be one of the main reasons why I had been able to rack up a hundred per cent score of wins during the season of 1953, and what this guy didn't know about engines you probably could have written on the back of an average-sized postage stamp. But as you know, a driver always has to tell a mechanic what's wrong and why and how he should fix it. You just couldn't say, "Hey, Mac, this baby's acting up today but I'll be darned if I can figure out what the trouble is. Take a look at it, will you?"

If you did that you wouldn't be a smart-aleck hero driver, now would you?

But even now I'm not telling it right. I did lose one in 1953, although that wasn't with the Allard. A Stillwater, Oklahoma, dealer, Tom Grey, asked me to drive an MG for him in a local race, and that time someone skunked me.

-6-

A GENTLEMAN NAMED WYER

FINANCIALLY, BUENOS AIRES did about as much good as a drink to a drowning man, but its possible that some part of my driving in Argentina may have attracted the attention of John Wyer, Aston Martin's team manager. I met several interesting top racing personalities down there—people like Fangio, Hawthorn, Peter Collins, and the rest—in fact, most everybody that was driving a Grand Prix car on the international circuits at that time. And I might add that I got a special kick out of getting to know Fangio, because every driver has his hero and he was mine. I thought his style terrific and his easy stance at the wheel was enough to fill anyone with envy. He had a powerful yet smooth mastery of his car that no one else could imitate or equal. It had to be Fangio.

There was Ascari, too, the only guy who in my opinion could compare with Fangio for three or four years; and of course Farina. He wasn't really so far behind—a fearless guy, enormously determined and aggressive as they come. But it was Peter Collins who did me the most good. Peter and John Wyer and I all happened to be staying at the same hotel, and Peter arranged an informal meeting for the three of us in a bar, where he introduced me to Wyer. Right away, and somewhat to my surprise because of his reputation of a sharp tongue and a sarcastic repartee, the Aston team manager acted pretty nice in paying me a compliment.

"You drove a nice race in that Allard," he said. "Very nice. I was watching you."

"Thanks," I said. "The car ran pretty well, most of the time, except for the bits that fell off."

"Cars don't run well by themselves, old chap," Wyer smiled. "They have to be driven, you know."

"That's right, you know!" Peter agreed with a glint of amusement in his eye. "Absolutely right, by gad."

"Why don't you come to England?" Wyer asked over the rim of his glass. "Plenty of good driving, there."

"I know it," I said, "but there's still one big reason why I can't come to England, or Europe, for that matter."

"What's that?"

"It's spelled m-o-n-e-y," I said. "In America we call it 'cash' for short."

"Oh," said Wyer, "I see." His shrewd dark eyes searched my face for a moment. He was quick to look for hidden meanings, people said, and at times his sarcasm was supposed to be like a rapier thrust. One thing you had better not do with him, I'd been told, was try to act cute. But whatever passed through his mind, his expression didn't change at all. "Well," he said, "you know the old saying: 'nothing venture, nothing have.'"

"I'm afraid it's not as simple as that," I said. "To come to Europe I'd have to have some attractive offer that would make my going into hock worthwhile."

"Come over anyway," Wyer insisted. "We'll try to work out something for you. I don't quite know what, yet, but I like the way you drive."

"Thanks again."

"Mind you, it's not a definite or specific invitation—merely a suggestion."

"Fine," I said. "I'll think it over."

We finished our drinks, chatting of this and that, and ordered another round, and about then Wyer suddenly asked, "I say, have you got a ride at Sebring this year?"

"Nope," I shook my head. "Not that I know of."

"Then perhaps you could drive for us?" Again Wyer studied my expression to see how I'd react. "We're fielding some DBR3's and we need good American drivers. Obviously a financial tie-in with racing, you know. Can't think of a better way to give the DB3's a good send-off in the States."

"I get the point," I agreed. "If you have a ride, count me in."

"Then it' s settled." He held out his hand, looking me straight in the eye, and I got the impression that here was a guy who if he promised something would move heaven and earth to deliver. I don't mean to imply that John Wyer's ever been out to take Dale Carnegie's place, but if the world had more people on whom you could depend to do exactly what they said, we'd be better off. "We'll discuss the matter of your co-driver later."

"Suits me," I nodded.

What I did not know then was the hassle this matter of my co-driver was going to stir up. Naturally, since Aston Martin was making its first serious bid for the American market, John Wyer was interested in having an all-American team drive for him; but the story got out before the race, and as soon as I arrived at Sebring I was deluged by people who told me who my co-driver should be, why this particular guy was the one for the job, and just how the whole thing was going to work out. There must have been at least eight or ten of these experts giving me the benefit of their advice, and pretty soon even the organizers got into it too. But perhaps the most comical character was this guy Irwin Goldschmidt. He was down to drive an Allard and, in addition, was sponsoring or entering a couple of Kiefts, or something like that. But it wasn't enough. He had already made up his mind that a photographer from Long Island, New York, was going to be my co-driver in the Aston. This photographer, Glebb Derujinsky, I think his name was, apparently was well thought of as a driver, although I'd never heard of him, but Goldschmidt sure put on the pressure until he saw that I didn't have any particular opinion, one way or the other, and wasn't planning to back his candidate. This was something for John Wyer to decide. Still, I was reminded that I was lucky to be getting this ride at all, and so many guys apparently had made up their minds they were going to drive with me that I could see myself getting nudged out of this ride altogether.

For some reason that I never found out, the organizers wanted Charlie Wallace in the car and they made no bones about it, so that started another hassle for a couple of days until John Wyer got in. By that time, I don't mind telling you, I was mighty glad to see him and let him carry the ball. Well, he got it all straightened out pretty quickly and the organizers won and Charlie Wallace and I drove the car, which, by the way, carried No. 25, I remember. So that solved that particular problem. Derujinsky, seems to me, ended up by getting teamed with Lake Underwood in a Kieft, so nobody got left out, except maybe Goldschmidt, whose Allard lasted nine laps before it burned a piston.

Unfortunately, we didn't finish either. We seemed to be going quite well, somewhere in the first six—I'll be doggone if I remember exactly—during the first three hours, when the rear axle broke on the seventy-seventh lap and that was the end of that.

Don't know to this day why the organizers were so hepped up about having Charlie Wallace drive with me, but then I don't understand anything about politics or things like that.

Oddly enough, the first job I was offered in 1954 that looked like it would pay me a real living wage had nothing to do with Aston Martin. The offer came from a West Texas "oillionaire" who had built, in his own garage, a sports car which his son had driven on the Salt Flats at 200 mph the year before. His name was Guy Mabee and his pet ambition was to build an all-American sports car that would blow off the Europeans, but good. What he wanted me to do was to help develop this automobile and make it roadworthy; right then, all it could do was run in a straight line.

Designwise there was nothing you might call revolutionary about this Mabee car. It consisted of a tubular chassis and a big Chrysler engine, but it didn't even have independent suspension up front; just a good old-fashioned beam axle. My job, if I accepted the offer, was to try to make this thing go around corners with the same kind of ease that it would travel in a straight line. As you can imagine, this proposition led to quite a bit of thinking on the part of both Jeanne and myself. We had to decide whether to stay with Guy Mabee after Sebring and take a job that would pay a decent living wage, or whether to take a flyer in Europe on something that I knew ahead of time wasn't going to make me any money—because no race driver goes over to Europe from scratch and starts to make money out of racing sports cars. With Formula 1 it might be a different story, but even there you'd have to have great chunks of luck going for you. However, you might possibly make a living of sorts.

So my wife and I discussed it back and forth after Sebring, and despite the odds we decided to take a chance on the European venture. One thing that helped me decide was the fact that Guy Mabee agreed to buy an Aston Martin, which I would drive for him in the smaller, independent events over there when I wasn't on the factory team. This looked like a mighty good thing, a useful way to plug up the holes while gaining experience during my first season over there.

Well, I got to Europe without ever having driven that 200-mph car. Instead I drove one last race in America for Guy Mabee, and that was at Bergstrom Field, Austin, Texas, one of the SAC bases. This was in April of 1954, after which I took off for Europe alone, that is, without Jeanne, at least for the time being.

When I left for Europe, I hadn't the slightest idea who my co-driver would be, so the first thing I did when I got to London was to make a beeline for Aston Martin at Feltham and Mr. Wyer's office. He greeted me with a smile and simply said, "We have a car that we're preparing for you in case you buy one."

This seemed to me a pretty calm way to take things, as he might have expected me to show up with the money in my hot, sticky little hand. So I said, "Don't worry. I'm sure Mr. Mabee will come through," or something like that.

John Wyer did not pursue the subject. Instead he said with his characteristic abruptness, "What I'd like you to do in the meantime is to go to Aintree and drive one of our factory cars there. We're even having it painted with the American colors."

I sure as heck didn't say no to that, so the next thing I knew it was May and I was on the starting grid at Aintree with a good old DBR3. As it happened, I did very well there and outran all the C-Type Jags except the one driven by Duncan Hamilton, to whom I finished second. And not by much, either. It so happened that was the first race ever run at Aintree, aside from horses, I mean, because that's the traditional site of the Grand National, probably the most grueling steeplechase event in the world. For some reason best known to the organizers, they ran the race backward, I mean counterclockwise, although the new car racing circuit had nothing to do with the horse track. It didn't seem to bother stout, jovial Duncan Hamilton, though. He had an amusing phrase that was often quoted in those days: "Let's have a go, boy. Keep that right clog down!"

Keeping that right clog down at Aintree isn't the easiest thing in the world, because there are at least two deceptive turns that can get you into serious trouble if you take the wrong line, but I managed somehow, and John Wyer seemed very satisfied with me. I doubt that anybody expected me to finish that high at Aintree or anywhere else. After all, Americans couldn't road race. They only played at it. Oh, and there are a couple more things I forgot to mention: the length of the race, which was something like seventy-five miles, if my memory serves me right, and the fact that it rained quite a bit and the surface became very dicey. Although Aintree had pretty good drainage, with the result that the water collected only in spots, there was plenty of it in the places where it was trapped. And in those days, remember, we had no such things as rain tires. So I got to figuring my best bet was to follow along behind Duncan Hamilton, which I did for quite a while until some traffic got in the way. After that I never was able to make up the lost ground, but I still wasn't far behind.

To sum up Aintree, it spelled the words Trophy, Recognition, and John Wyer Happy. Even more important, to me, it also spelled a ride at Le Mans on the factory team. The car built especially for Guy Mabee still had not been purchased by him, but under a new arrangement he would do so at the end of the racing season. Therefore, for the time being, it was still very much a factory car.

Guy Mabee came to Le Mans, presumably to see how his future purchase was going to make out, and found me teamed up with Paul Frère, the well-known Belgian automotive journalist and quite a driver in his own right. There were three David Brown entries, the other two Astons being driven respectively by Peter Collins-Prince Bira, and A. G. Whitehead-James Stewart. The Collins-Bira car, No. 20, was exactly four mph faster (144.25) on Mulsanne Straight than we were; but on the other hand we turned in a best lap one-tenth of a second faster, in 4 minutes, 42.4 seconds. Anyway, our No. 22 was going pretty well until I overcooked it at the end of Mulsanne, trying to follow Briggs Cunningham round that tricky, nasty 120-degree turn, and ended up in the sandbank. It took me about forty-five minutes to dig myself out, then I pulled in at our pit for a quick checkout, but the car appeared to have suffered no damage and continued as happily as ever. This happened in the rain, during the first ninety minutes of the race, and for many hours afterward we were able to make up lost time until 1:50 A.M., when the well-known wheel incident took place. I'd noticed a bad shimmy developing in the front end as I came through Arnage, then down to the White House, so I pulled into the pit and told them about it.

Wyer immediately gave the order to jack up the car and the moment the front end was clear of the ground a wheel fell off. This was caused by a broken spindle, due to the bearing freezing on it. Possibly it might have happened when I ran into the sandbank at Mulsanne, but I sure was lucky to catch it when I did. Of course there was nothing to do but retire the car, since it would have taken far too long to replace the spindle and we had no means of realigning the front end, anyway. But I must say that, although John Wyer was naturally disappointed, he never uttered a word of criticism or complaint. I think he was relieved that we had caught this thing just in time to avoid a serious accident.

Paul Frère, too, is a great guy and that rare combination, a writer who can really drive and a driver who can really write. He drove about half the time and I the other half, in four-hour spells, and for our luck, of course, it had to be a very wet year. There's very seldom a Le Mans without rain, but sometimes it turns into a deluge, seemingly without end, and this, in an open car, buffeted by the wind and soaked to the marrow, can make you feel miserable. On top of this, I must admit I was a little nervous when I first got on that Sarthe circuit of 8.2 very fast miles. Especially so because in my view they pull a rather stupid stunt on the rookie drivers. They have to go out for their first ride on the Wednesday evening preceding the race, just at dusk, and find their way around as best they can. I got to like Le Mans and enjoy it pretty quickly, but a lot of the drivers don't ever really get over that first impression, and as a result don't ever enjoy driving there. I firmly believe that the first time a driver goes out on a race course it should be in broad daylight. Then he should be able to go out a second time in daylight and get in some more practice before having to do any night driving. As for the three and a half-mile Mulsanne Straight, I must say that I'd gone faster in Allards on some of our short courses in America than ever I did on that road. The Aston was good for a little more than a hundred and forty, whereas the Allard would do one-fifty on the kind of circuit where it had to get up there a lot sooner. A good-running Allard could hit 150 mph on a three-quarter mile straight; it didn't need anything like three and a half miles to make that speed. As it was, the C-Jags were a full ten mph faster and the Ferraris were going by at least twenty-five mph faster. Even in those days, the 4.9's had no trouble getting up to 165 mph or a bit more.

Still, the unforgettable thing about the Aston Martin was that it handled so well you could call it a viceless automobile. It was what we call a neutral-steer car, the result of very good suspension and ideal weight distribution, and it was forgiving of mistakes, too. You could predict exactly what it was going to do at any time and at any speed, and the only criticism I can think of is that it had a very hard brake pedal, requiring more pressure than usual. This was because we were running very hard brake linings, highly resistant to wear and with what's called a low coefficient of friction. It got a bit tiring after a while, but you could hardly call it a fault or blame the car. In fact, although Aston didn't go to discs until the following year, we had better brakes than the Ferraris, despite this heavy pedal pressure.

I couldn't sign off on my first Le Mans in June of 1954 without mentioning the fantastic performance turned in by the bull-like Froilan Gonzales in a 4.9 Ferrari. Despite heavy rain and the handicap of fatigue because he did the lion's share of the driving, this was probably the greatest performance in his strange career. The most colorful, too. There was that dramatic moment after his final pit stop when the Ferrari's engine wouldn't re-start and the precious seconds ticked away with the Rolt-Hamilton Jaguar getting dangerously close and the Ferrari pit working up a fever. Then the powerful engine suddenly caught and burst into life again and Gonzales was away like a streak. He and Trintignant, that dependable evergreen, set a new record of 301 laps at an average speed of over 105 mph, despite the teeming rain and some other troubles.

Well, by the time the Vingt-quatre Heures was over, I already had four useful races under my belt that year: Sebring, Bergstrom,

Texas, and Aintree. By then, as you can imagine, I had become fairly well acquainted with the DBR3.

Our next big one was the Thousand Kilometers at Monza on June 27, two weeks later. This Italian race is called locally the Supercortemaggiore because it's named after a well-known brand of gasoline. If you've been over there, you certainly must have seen that zany-looking emblem of a black five-legged dragon on a yellow background. That's it. This time, although I had the same car as at Le Mans, it was not a David Brown team entry but a Carroll Shelby private entry. Our team had suffered too badly at Le Mans to be able to field a full complement of three cars in time, so John Wyer said, in effect, "It's up to you. I can let you have the car, properly prepared, and I can suggest a very good co-driver, Graham Whitehead, Peter's brother. I know he's anxious to have a go at it. Matter of fact he owns a DB3, so he knows the car pretty well."

"But from the time we get there we're on our own, is that it?" I asked.

"Just about," Wyer nodded. "You'll have to freight your own expenses, of course."

Even so, I didn't hesitate a moment. Jeanne had just come over to visit and, as usual, I was pretty well broke. As it turned out, Graham Whitehead wasn't much better off himself, though he certainly made up for it with enthusiasm. As much as an Englishman can show, that is. Anyway, we teamed up and split the expenses and everyone knew it was a factory car, even though the entry was made privately. There's a lot of that goes on in Europe, you know.

One look at the entry list and a couple of laps around the very fast course determined our strategy. We decided, Graham and I, to drive a very conservative race, save the car as much as possible, and bring home some of that sorely needed prize money, of which there seemed to be plenty around. The opposition would have made lesser men, or maybe less ignorant guys, mighty uneasy; that I can tell you. Although the organizers had moved the race from a secluded spot where it had been run the year before—Merano, in the Dolomites—and dumped it on Monza, and had also limited engine size to three liters, we still had to face fourteen Ferraris, five Maseratis, and four Gordinis, driven by some of the fastest road-racing guys in the world. When I say "we," there were actually two Astons, the other being entered by Sir Jeremy Beauman, Baronet, and driven by Donald Beauman and John Riseley-Pritchard, just names to me. Ours carried No. 30, I remember, and theirs was 32, but unfortunately they got lost somewhere in the shuffle and finally retired after 135 laps of a drive that deserved better luck.

Luckily for us, perhaps, it rained and the weather was unseasonably gusty and changeable for that time of year, else the race would have been run much faster and our chances would have dwindled correspondingly. Still, when you're paying your own expenses, even on someone else's car, and you hurt for some prize money, you keep a wary eye on that tach and stay well inside the limit and don't try to corner at ten-tenths.

Boy, it sure paid off. The Shelby-Whitehead Aston finished fifth overall and we picked up the sweetest-sounding two thousand dollars I could remember in a long time. This pleased John Wyer a whole lot, I think—so much that he offered me one more ride before I left England. This was to be an official factory team effort of three cars which were entered in a twenty-five-lap race at Silverstone on July 17. Peter Collins had one car, Roy Salvadori another, and I the third, and that was exactly how we finished—one-two-three, all in the same lap. This was the first year of the D-Jags, remember, and the first time we had clashed with them officially since Le Mans, and we sure gave them a black eye, right on home ground. Reg Parnell was fourth in a big brute of a Lagonda that weighed at least twenty-five hundred pounds, and Archie Scott Brown, that wonderful little driver who overcame some pretty serious physical handicaps to beat the best of them at times, placed fifth in a Lister-Bristol under two liters. The best the D-Jags could do was a sixth place, which went to Desmond Titterington, an amazingly deceptive guy who retired a year later when Mercedes-Benz quit racing. If ever anyone didn't look like a race driver, whatever a race driver is supposed to look like, it was Titterington. He was slimly built, with center-parted hair and a polite, precise, quiet manner more suited to some entirely different kind of pastime, like maybe collecting stamps. But make no mistake, once this guy got behind the wheel of a race car, he became positively brilliant.

While I'm wandering away from the point, might as well throw in a little anecdote about good old Reg Parnell, though it was very much connected with the Silverstone race. He and I were having quite a dice for a while, running along almost side by side until he suddenly lost a plug. Without hesitation he waved me on, knowing that the Jags were fairly close behind. But what was really amusing was his statement, openly made to me after the race in that broad Derbyshire accent which belonged to a farmer.

"Don't worry, my boy," he said, "they never had a chance to get close to you—not with me in that big pig there, going sideways around Silverstone!"

And that was just what he did. He was an Aston man at heart, I guess, because he later took over management of the factory team when John Wyer retired; but that day he pulled a kind of delaying action that seemed to block every attempt of the Jags to get by him. It was quite accidental, of course, old chap, but it locked up the race for the Astons. Old Reg is gone now, but he was a wonderful guy and I thank God to have been able to number him among my friends in the racing world.

Looking back on that year with the Aston Martin team, I must say we had a pretty good time together, all of us. John Wyer always saw to it that we were well paid, taken care of, in bed by nine o'clock, and no bull or malarkey around race time. But he'd always close his eyes to what went on afterward, and believe me there was a lot of devilment. For instance, at Silverstone that year, the team occupied the same quarters as it always did, a place called the Vicarage, about two miles from the circuit. It belonged to a parson who ran some kind of an orphans' home there, but he also had rooms for rent.

Well, on this particular night we were all having dinner when a telephone call came for Reg Parnell. I was rooming with Roy Salvadori and when dinner was over we found it was about time to hit the sack, so we went upstairs. Without even bothering to turn on the light, Roy made as if to sit down on his bed to take off his shoes—but there wasn't any bed. So he switched on the lights, which brought a growl from John Wyer next door, and where Roy's bed had been there was nothing but a deck chair. Parnell had gone up on that fake telephone call and had taken Salvadori's bed completely apart and hidden the pieces. So with this, Roy got into his head for some reason that I was the one responsible—maybe he thought I was trying to get even for some other shenanigans that had gone on at Sebring! Anyway, he promptly got up and got the pitcher off the wash basin and turned it upside down on my bed. The hollering that went on was so loud that Reg and Wyer and everybody came in, and finally Parnell, who was doubled up with laughter, had to admit that he was the culprit. It was forty-five minutes before we finally got things sorted out enough to settle down, because during all that time we were in stitches; but Roy wasn't one to give up so easily. He slipped back outside, found a hose, dropped a string from his window, brought the hose upstairs, and was just about to pull it through into the room and give Parnell a real good squirt, when the door opened and in walked John Wyer. And there was Roy, standing in his shorts with the hose in his hand when he was supposed to be in bed and asleep. This really went over big with Wyer.

Come to think of it, what had happened at Sebring was even funnier, though it wasn't Salvadori who was the fall guy then; it was Peter Collins. We were all sitting in the hotel room that time and Collins got smart with Parnell and Salvadori. Unfortunately for him, Peter happened to be sitting on a foldaway bed, so we all picked up the bed, pushed it back into the wall and left him there, pinned upside down, yelling blue murder so you could hear him for half a block. The other two went down to the bar and had a drink, and if the maid hadn't heard him and let him down, I guess they would have let him smother!

Silverstone wound up my connection with Aston Martin for some time, but once again John Wyer proved himself a true friend. I felt obligated, naturally, to buy the car they had built for Guy Mabee, because in the meantime he had changed his mind and decided he didn't want it after all. I guess he and his son and some other guys had gotten their homemade job going well enough so they didn't really want what they called an "underpowered foreign car." And that kind of left me holding the bag, except that Wyer took it without batting an eyelash.

"Not to worry," he said. "You did very well for us and there are people standing in line for the car, anyway."

It wasn't the first time he had taken my part, either. I remember, after I had been in England awhile, making a statement to the press that didn't exactly endear me to them. "Within the next ten years," I told them, "we Americans will have as many good road-racing drivers as the Europeans. What's more, by 1960 an American driver will probably win the world championship."

This brought a lot of guffaws and those newspaper boys thought me very funny, but not John Wyer. "You know," he said openly, "I think you may be right at that."

Fact was I had been around long enough to see that while these drivers over there were pretty good, they really, most of them, weren't all that brilliant. And, as it turned out, my forecast missed by only a year. In 1961 Phil Hill became World Champion.

Anyway, I got back to the States in August, broke and busted, and this time it was Roy Cherryhomes who gave me a helping hand. He bought a C-Type Jag that had been run over and pretzeled by a Greyhound bus in Illinois, and had it fixed so well that it turned out to be the best C-Type I ever drove. I ran it for him a couple of times over here, including the Eagle Mountain Lake course, where I scored another win. I guess I won more races on this circuit than any other place I ever ran, but that was mainly because it was closer to home and I got to know it better.

Those were the last two races I drove for Cherryhomes and it's as good a place to end this chapter as any, though not the year 1954.

–7–

KILOMETER 175

I HAD SCARCELY returned to the States in August of 1954 when a phone call came through from England. No, it wasn't John Wyer, it was Donald Healey, the one and only Donald Healey, from The Cape, Warwickshire. Across three thousand miles of static I heard him ask me if I would care to join him and Capt. G. E. T. Eyston, along with Mortimer Morris Goodall and Roy Jackson-Moore, in trying to set up a bunch of new records at Bonneville Flats.

"Sure," I said. "What kind of records?"

"We're going to try for everything from twenty-five kilometers to twenty-four hours. Class D National records."

"Sounds good. What are you using?"

"We're shipping over a couple of Austin Healeys," he said. "A 100S and a modified 100S with a blower."

"Okay," I said. "What's the proposition?"

He told me and I agreed to the terms and that was that. Soon after, I got on a plane and flew out. This business of records on the famous Salt Flats in the Utah desert was new to me and I wanted to find out as much as possible about it beforehand. Frankly, I was curious.

Well, on August 23, I believe it was, Donald Healey kicked off the ball by setting a bunch of new records singlehanded, from 200 miles at 133.74 mph to 500 kilometers at 133.96 mph from a standing start, after which Eyston joined him and took over. The car they drove was the unmodified S, quite a hot machine in its day—a lightened, more powerful version of the original 2.4-liter, four-cylinder job, put together to really go. Unfortunately, it cost an arm and a leg and so never gained a real foothold on the American sports car market; it was too rich for the blood of the average enthusiast. Still, out there in the shimmering Utah desert it ran like the proverbial clock, although after a while this kind of driving can get pretty dull, just going around and around a 10.1-mile course at full bore.

The whole bunch of us took it in turns after that, going for the Class D Production records from 3000 to 5000 kilometers. This was still with the unblown car and we racked up new records of 132.18 mph for the 3000 k's and 132.27 mph for the 5000 k's. There was a lot more of this, and although I still have a bunch of AAA certificates to show for it, I don't remember the blow-by-blow story. It doesn't much matter anyway. This is not that kind of book, as I said in a previous chapter. You couldn't talk about more than a dozen different races or speed events in any great detail without starting to repeat yourself. But as it comes back to me, Donald Healey went out alone for three hours at an average of 134.10 mph, then was again joined by Captain Eyston as they went on to capture the six hours at 133.06 mph. Then again the whole gang pitched in, except Roy Jackson-Moore, and raised the Twelve-Hour Standing Start to 132.47 mph. After that, with Roy for reinforcement, we took it on to twenty-four hours at 132.29 mph.

Basically these records that we tried for were achieved both from a standing start and a flying start, using both the unsupercharged and the blown car. Of course we had a bunch of mechanics there and enough spares to sink a sloop, but all went well and the records came toppling down one after another without any serious mishap. It was just a matter of keeping within certain rev limits and keeping a weather eye on the other dials. On August 24, the next day, Donald gave me the modified 100S and I pushed eleven flying start records from twenty-five kilometers to one hour, up a notch or two. All of them were above 157 mph, with the fastest at 75 miles, which was 158.08 mph.

I then had a go at the standing start records from 50 k's to an hour (six of them) and they too fell at speeds between 151.32 for the 50 k's and 156.97 for the hour. Seems to me, also, that I took another eleven records from a standing start with the same car (25 k's to an hour) at speeds between 145.61 and 156.97 mph.

Altogether, as a team effort, we set up some seventy new records from 25 k's to twenty-four hours, using both cars and both kinds of start. For this they gave us this bunch of impressive certificates of performance issued by the AAA Contest Board, signed by various officials, and adorned with handsome gold seals. But, as I said, running alone against the clock is apt to get monotonous, and though Donald Healey and his gang were a wonderful bunch to drive with, and later that year Roy Jackson-Moore and I got to share a Healey in the last real Carrera Pan Americana Mexico, still I wasn't too sorry when the business came to an end and I headed for home. The mechanics, as usual, did an unsung but magnificent job of keeping things tuned and being on hand to change tires, refuel, and such.

Gosh, I nearly forgot. Donald also had a go at the 200-mph run through the traps and made it with the supercharged car, and as far as I know, that one still stands. I ran 186 mph for an hour, but then got a signal to lower the boost because bearing life was getting a bit critical and they didn't want to take any unnecessary chances. This entire venture was good from a prestige standpoint, but you can't buy groceries with prestige; at least not for long, and financially I certainly did not come out any better than I had started.

It's hard to put into words my impressions about the Salt Flats, but there's a kind of grandeur about the place, a vivid lightness and a strange sense of being alone, as if on another planet. A million things must have gone through my mind as I raced around and around, keeping an eye on the oil pressure gauge and the other dials—things that had happened in the past and things I wanted to do, and even silly things like Jeanne telling me one time that I needed a haircut, which I did. Still, I wouldn't have missed that trip to Utah. It taught me a lot about pacing myself, and, as I said, it led to Mexico in November of that year, and to what was then one of the two most grueling true road races in the world, the other being of course the Mille Miglia. I guess the Targa Florio would be in that league, too, but it's not as long, thank heavens.

We took two cars to Tuxtla Gutiérrez, the southernmost starting point on the Guatemalan border. One Jackson-Moore and I drove, and the other was handled by Lance Macklin alone. Lance, by the way, figured in that spectacular crackup at Le Mans the fol-

lowing year, when eighty-two spectators were killed in the worst
motor racing accident, ever. To the best of my recollection, he never
raced again after that, but joined Facel Vega in Paris in a sales capacity and eventually retired to England.

So anyway, Roy Jackson-Moore and I got to the start too late
to put in any practice, going the right way. We did drive the car from
Mexico City to Tuxtla, just the one time, going in effect backward; and
on the road, painted in yellow, were lots of strange signs put there at
the various turns by different crews to indicate what was coming next.
Even so, from what we could figure out, many of those signs were
misleading and inaccurate. I know Lance Macklin wasn't any better
off on the practice bit, but when the race started with me driving the
first half between Tuxtla and Oaxaca, and Roy the second half, things
didn't work out well at all. Neither of us felt happy with the other, and
if you want to know the truth we were both as nervous as cats. So we
decided there and then to quit dicing through the mountains, with the
other guy chewing his fingernails, and make it a solo effort from then
on, with the other one flying to the next stop. I would drive to Puebla
and Roy from Puebla to Mexico City, and so on.

Unfortunately, for both of us, he never got his solo stint at the
wheel. I started racing with those big Lincolns and really giving 'em
hell. In fact I passed all of them except Crawford. I had just gotten
by Vukovitch and Verne Houle and taken off after Crawford when
I came around a corner a little too fast and suddenly there was a
big rock standing in my way. The rock never batted an eyelash, but
I went end over end four or five times like the daring young man on
the flying trapeze. Only it was a lot more painful. Maybe you know
those kilometer marker stones, and more especially the 175th kilometer marker north of Oaxaca? You don't? Well, this one went right
through the metal tonneau cover that we had on and a couple of
wheels were torn off the passenger side, which ceased to exist. The
chances were that had Roy been with me, he, too, would have ceased
to exist, so we undoubtedly made a wise decision. No two drivers
ever have the same style or approach or reaction to a given incident.

To put it briefly, I was a mess when the Indians picked me up and
threw a blanket over me. I had contusions every place, broken bones,
a shattered elbow, and cuts that you couldn't even count. Yet it could

have been much worse, I suppose. I was conscious and I knew I had
to lie there, in the heart of the Indian country, at least six or seven
hours before the road was reopened, but the Indians were very kind.
They kept offering me drinks of some strong beer which they carried
in buckets, and then, by chance, two school girls from Brooklyn had
spotted my crash from half a mile away. They had been driving to
Guatemala but had been stopped from going any farther because of
the race. So they were in no hurry, seeing that they were going to be
there all day, anyway. They came down and sat on the blanket with
me and fed me some good strong drafts from a couple of bottles
of Mexican brandy, and along with that Indian beer it sure did the
trick. Long before the ambulance finally got there, the fact that I had
these contusions and the broken arm and everything else ceased to
be of the slightest importance. It couldn't have mattered less.

There was another guy in the ambulance when they hoisted me
aboard, a German bloke named Franz Hammenich, I think, whose
Borgward hit a stray dog and skidded along the road upside down
for two hundred yards. Hammenich was in much worse shape than
I because he didn't have any hide left on him at all and the pain
must have been pretty bad. Anyway, he and I rode that ambulance
together for about a hundred miles to Puebla, where they took us to
the hospital and we were cared for by the most beautiful nurses you
ever saw. Let me tell you a little something about the nurses in Mexico.
At least in Puebla. Seems they come from wealthy families and only
the most lovely women are allowed to take nurse's training and work
in the hospitals. Anyway, we were in that hospital about three hours
while they got poor Hammenich all bandaged up and took care of
his burns, and also got my arm set properly; yet it seemed more like
three minutes. The doctor told me I should go back to Texas without
delay and get my arm set in a cast, as it was badly broken, with the
elbow knocked off. Said I should find a good orthopedic guy as soon
as possible, but the Mexican authorities thought otherwise. When we
got to Mexico City—and I think the nurses at Puebla were as sorry
to see us go as we were to leave them!—I found I couldn't leave the
country. Why? Because, señor, I had signed in for the car and I must
wait for the car before they would let me out. This foolishness went
on for a whole week, just because some Indians had picked up a

couple of the wheels for souvenirs and you had to take out exactly the same number of wheels (and tires!) you brought in. Nothing that the American or British embassies could do had any effect.

"But Señor Shelby lost two wheels in the crash on the way to Puebla," they explained.

"The car came in with four wheels, señores," they were told, "and it must leave with four wheels."

"You don't understand the problem. Someone made off with those two wheels. Perhaps the Indians took them for souvenirs."

"A wheel, señor? A souvenir?"

"They've vanished, at any rate. We've looked every place."

"Four wheels come in, four must go out, señores. That ees the law."

"Señor Shelby is sick. He must go home at once to have his arm set."

"We have good hospitals in Mexico, señores. In Puebla, especially."

You couldn't argue with the official mind. The cogs of the government machine were pre-set to turn at a certain speed and produce certain results. You couldn't change the results unless you stopped the machine. And the combined American and British embassies were powerless to do that.

So there I stuck, in Mexico City, not even allowed to post a bond for those durned wheels. It was a wonder the officials didn't count the number of pieces of broken glass or the number of rollers in the wheel bearings!

I put up at a Swiss hotel, the name of which escapes me, but it had some beautiful gardens all around, so maybe you'll recognize it by that. During my week in quarantine I happened to run into a couple of nurses from Minneapolis who seemed to know who I was. It turned out that some friendly Mexicans told them about my plight— how I was hurt and needed help, and couldn't even get out of the country. So they came around and helped take care of me. Finally a Mexican friend solved the problem when he appeared with a couple of Austin Healey wheels (and tires, of course) which he claimed were the missing ones. ("We finally found them in some scrub, way down the mountain! Wasn't that lucky?")

The officials agreed that it was indeed lucky, nodded wisely, pushed some rubber stamps on inkpads, and let me out. The Rio Grande, with that nice big steel bridge across—ugly but nice! And Juarez, where you could drink uncontaminated iced water at the airport restaurant and eat all the salad you wanted. And then back to Dallas and home.

Right away my doctor went to work on me, putting my shattered elbow in a cast and setting everything shipshape.

"Elbows are bad things to break," he said. "You could lose the proper use of your arm if you waited too long. Then where would you be as a racing driver?"

"Heck, where am I now, Doc? I've got to drive. That's all."

"We'll see."

We sure did see. It took eight months of operations, back in Dallas, to put my arm into proper working shape again, and it wasn't until August of 1955, when things finally healed, that I got rid of the cast for good. So you could hardly call that Mexican safari a financial success, could you? Or any kind of success. Still, in the meantime I couldn't afford to sit around and let time pass me by, so I got to driving race cars again, long before the arm healed. My first stint, in fact, after the Mexico crash, was early in 1955, when I drove that oddlooking, so-called Mexico Ferrari of Allen Guiberson. It was the one with the tail fin, something like a D-Jag, that Phil Hill had driven to second spot in the Mexican road race behind Maglioli. I drove that same tired car at Fort Pierce, Florida, and then came the big thing at Sebring in March, when Hill and I co-drove a new three-liter Monza Ferrari, a special job that Guiberson had bought for the Twelve Hours. We did all right—so well, in fact, that they announced we had won. But then there was a protest and a recount and we found ourselves in second place. Already, by then, a doctor had worked out a special routine for me which proved very effective. I used to take him along to the races, and, thank God, he was a good sport and interested in this kind of thing. He would take the cast off my arm, just before the race, and put on a tough fiberglass cast. Then I would lay my hand on the steering wheel and have it taped lightly to the rim. Oddly enough, this arrangement worked out fine and didn't seem to bother me much. It couldn't have, because I won about ten races during 1955, each time taking off the regular cast and putting on the fiberglass cast so it would enable my hand to fit the wheel. Then I would go to the nearest hospital and put the plaster cast back on, so as to fool the specialist who was taking care of me back home.

After Sebring I drove a couple more races for Guiberson in Texas and won them both, and then ran the one at Torrey Pines in July, still with the old, tired 4.1 Ferrari that had done so well in Mexico. The cams were not the ones originally designed for the Commendatore. They were a special grind by a California outfit, but they sure enough worked. Torrey Pines was my farewell ride in the old Mexico Ferrari and it was a pretty tough battle. I had to blow Phil Hill off, and then Guiberson slowed me after I'd built up a good lead, just to see if I could outrun Phil again. He got a charge out of seeing us race against each other. The Sebring three-liter Monza, however, I didn't drive again until 1956, when I won the last race at Pebble Beach and a total of some thirty races that year with this baby.

But I'm getting ahead of myself. After the Torrey Pines shindig in July, 1955, I started driving for Tony Paravano, so that ended my relationship with Guiberson for the time being.

-8-
WE BUY UP MODENA

NO ONE EVER accused me of being a philosopher, but I've been quoted from time to time as saying, "If you're going to go around worrying about getting killed, you might as well give up racing." That's exactly my way of thinking and always has been. Having a bad arm made no difference; it just complicated things a bit and made the challenge that much tougher. But if you're given to fretting your guts out before every race, my advice is—forget it. It's quite possible, of course, that some guy washing windows might fall off a building and land on top of you, right there in the street, but at least you wouldn't be sweating it out beforehand. I'll have a bit more to stay about race driving later on, but right now I want to talk a little about Tony Paravano. The way I met him was the way you get to meet most people, I guess, when they really want to meet *you*. They seek you out.

After I won the race at Torrey Pines in July of 1955 for Allen Guiberson with the so-called Mexico Ferrari, I was up in Los Angeles one day with Allen, when I got a telephone call. How the caller found out which hotel I was staying at in a city the size of Los Angeles, I'll never know. I didn't ask him. Anyway, this fellow said he was a mechanic for Paravano and would I like to meet the boss? Naturally I said, yes, I would. Paravano's interest in race cars was already something more than a rumor, and this guy was loaded, so you couldn't tell what might come of it. I went out to this garage in Inglewood and there the meeting took place. Paravano was a short, eager little man, not over five feet tall, with a crew cut and alert eyes.

He weighed around 165 pounds and seemed to be in good shape. I guessed his age to be around thirty-five.

"This garage is getting too small," he said waving casually toward eight or ten close-packed Ferraris of all types, "so I'm building a new place where we'll have more room."

"Sounds like a good idea." I decided to let him do the leading and I didn't have to wait long.

"I'm going to buy another fifteen Ferraris," Paravano said, the way he might have been talking about five-cent cigars, "and I'd like you to drive them for me. Any of them, I don't care. Take your pick."

This, of course, is the exact blueprint of any young race driver's dream, only it may sound a bit exaggerated. It wasn't.

"Come with me," Paravano said. "I'll show you the new place I'm building."

He drove me over to where they were putting up a big new garage with a workshop—the whole bit. Then he waited for me to speak.

"This is more like it," I said, trying to sound casual. "With twenty-five Ferraris—"

But Tony wouldn't let me finish. His mind was already running ahead and he was no fool. "Okay," he said. "You've got a deal. We start with one race only. After that we talk again. Okay?"

"You name the race," I said.

We quickly made the necessary financial arrangements, but at that time Paravano hadn't yet started the violent campaign he launched later, about promoters and sponsors paying drivers some decent money. He was getting his stable together and had other things to think about, I guess. Fortunately, I was the only one driving for him at the time.

You know, I drove a lot of races for Paravano, yet I never could quite make him out. He was a funny little guy in some ways, but he did a lot for the sport; he gave it personality and color and excitement. It couldn't very well have been otherwise with the kind of exotic machinery he bought, and always as casually as though they were ice cream cones.

There's no doubt that he loved cars very much, and for more than just what they brought or gave him. He was in the contracting business, building houses like crazy and making millions, but he had started out as a cement contractor and learned as he went along. Actually Tony was a brilliant man in the construction and building trades, and I guess he already was a millionaire a couple of times over at least, from his contracting business in Inglewood and all over southwestern Los Angeles, when he asked me to drive for him.

We decided that my first ride would be in a brand-new 4.9 Ferrari he had just gotten from the Great Man at Modena. The race happened to be a pretty good one in Seattle, Washington. One of the Seafair races, and they held this one at Bremerton, across the bay at the airfield, there. It was a beautiful abandoned air strip, but it went right through bunches of pine trees that had grown next to the runways. A lovely sight, except that on this August day the weather went haywire. It came down to 40 degrees, chilly and whipped by rain. The 4.9 was a pig to handle; there's no other term for it. With all that power on the wet, you might just as well have been on roller skates. It was a new design but still what we call a pig—a huge, long-wheelbase thing with a twelve-cylinder engine and gobs of power.

Come to think of it, Paravano's 4.9 was about the same model that Gonzales had put up this fantastic performance with at Le Mans the year before, but with a slightly different body. You know, Paravane was great for not having a car like anyone else. He'd go to Scaglietti and slip him five hundred bucks to make the body different and old man Ferrari would have a fit. But Tony didn't care; he knew what he wanted and as a result he never owned any model Ferrari that looked like the others.

This race, which took place in August of 1955, was the best airport course I'd ever driven anywhere. It was four miles long with good straights and a lot of fast turns, and just made to order for a real good dice. I got it all right. Ken Miles was there, I think having his first try at the big stuff, and he was driving that evergreen automobile, the good old Guiberson Mexico Ferrari, once again full of pep. Phil Hill drove George Tilp's three-liter Monza—Ferrari hadn't yet produced the 3.5-liter—and Bill Pollock had Tom Carsten's Chevy-powered BMW, or something like that. I won the race despite all those shenanigans of the 4.9; Hill was second, Miles third, and Pollock fourth, I'm pretty sure.

Paravano was so pleased that he asked me to go to Europe with him, where he was going to buy some more Ferraris and Maseratis. As I was still his only driver I agreed, and we flew over in September and went to Modena, and sure enough Tony started buying cars with both hands. In the beginning it was chiefly Ferraris, which are actually built in the suburb of Maranello, but then one day Ferrari made Tony mad by saying the wrong thing at the wrong time (he's famous for that) and Paravano took off for Modena and the Maserati factory and there bought up everything they had to offer. But everything. Three-liters, the first 4.5, that 3.5 job, the two-liter, and even the 1.5-liter. It took him about a year to get all that machinery shipped over, but he eventually did, though heaven knows what for. I never stopped to figure out what that little buying spree must have cost him, but I figure he must have made up for all the tooling costs of the first Maserati 4.5-liter engine, the famous V8. That alone meant $150,000 as a good guess, but I wouldn't be surprised if Tony, on that one day, didn't spend a quarter of a million dollars at Maserati. You never saw anything like it.

Paravano's basic motivation, I believe, where cars were concerned, really came from the fact that he was a disappointed race driver; but this has never been proven to me and it's purely an assumption on my part. I never did see him drive in competition, but he used to have to test the cars to make sure they were safe for the drivers and you could tell he enjoyed that thoroughly.

I stayed and drove two races for Tony in Europe: one at Oulton Park in England with the 4.4 Ferrari, and the other at the Targa Florio in Sicily, where I co-drove his three-liter car with Muneron. The Oulton Park thing was a thoroughly unsuccessful race because this big six-cylinder machine was geared all wrong for the circuit. It was a replica of the car that Castellotti had driven at Le Mans the previous year, when he had run away from the entire field, Mercedes included, for the first hour; it had the same gearing but a different type of body. I guess Tony paid about twice as much for this 4.4 as it would normally have cost, and that was Mr. Ferrari's way of getting back at him for insisting on a different body. But unfortunately it wasn't all. I suspected they sometimes unloaded on Paravano all the junk at the factory.

So to get back to that first race: I had to drive all the way from Modena to England, towing the 4.4 with a two-liter Alfa. And my crew included Mrs. Paravano, his three children, and his lawyer. We could have saved ourselves the trouble. It was a terrible race and I never could get any higher than eighth. The car just didn't have it on a short, twisty circuit like Oulton Park. That was in September, 1955, and I'd sooner forget it.

In the next one, the Tourist Trophy, things went a whole lot better. Masten Gregory and I were invited to drive on the Porsche factory team, and they gave us what was then the new RS, the spider immediately following the 550 model. This car still had the four-speed gearbox—only Richard von Frankenberg was given a five-speed transmission for that race—but it was powered by the real four-overhead cam engine. I must say I was very impressed with this little 1500cc machine and the way it went, and glad to have been asked to drive by Hushke von Hanstein, the power behind the throne at Stuttgart-Zuffenhausen. The invitation to drive came while I was still in Modena, as a matter of fact, about two weeks before the Tourist Trophy, and Masten and I were to be part of a three-car factory team. As I was not committed to Paravano for more than one race at a time, he said okay.

But even though I had nothing but praise for the way the little RS handled, it was a bad race—a scary one run in the rain on a twisting, demanding, and difficult circuit that left no margin at all for error. Either you made it or you didn't. Those dirt banks piled up on either side of the narrow twisting road didn't give you much chance. Until that time I couldn't remember having driven anything more difficult, and the much higher speed of the big stuff added some more problems. Neubauer of Mercedes-Benz had decided to enter a team of 300SLR's only at the last moment in a bid for the International Manufacturers' Championship, and it turned out to be a wise decision. Thanks to Moss's brilliant driving, Mercedes-Benz snatched a narrow victory from the Jaguars, of which easily the fastest was the one driven by Hawthorn. Right at the end, though, something suddenly quit in Hawthorn's gearbox and caused the whole works to lock up; and although I'm not saying he would have won but for that, there's no question that he gave Moss one heck of a run for his money. Moss always made a great thing of it about loving rain (although he admitted in private that this was just race psychology), but it worked like a charm; and whether he liked rain or not, he sure went like hell when it did rain.

There was some pretty hot iron in the competition, I remember: Behra with the new three-liter Maserati, very potent; Hawthorn and those other D-Jags; and of course the formidable Mercedes-Benzes. But there was also a pretty ghastly crop of accidents. It was so bad, in fact, that they never again ran the TT on the old Ards circuit. Cars had become much too fast for any kind of safety—even the small cars.

There was this particular hill, I recall, which was named Deer's Leap, and a better name they couldn't have found for it. Only it wasn't the deer that were leaping, but the cars. You'd come over the brow of that hill with your foot in the carburetor and suddenly you would take off about three or four feet from the ground and fly seventy-five feet through the air before touching down again; and if when you did land all four wheels were not lined up, you might as well kiss the whole thing good-by. Well, about the second or third lap through Deer's Leap, while I was still in the air, I could see flame licking across the road and black smoke starting to drift up and bits and pieces of cars scattered all over the place. One driver had missed his landing and five or six others had piled up on top of him, caroming off each other like billiard balls. The late Ken Wharton happened to be one of them, in a Frazer Nash, but he got away with slight bums. Two other boys, however, lost their lives; one of them named Mayers, who drove a Cooper Climax; the other Jimmy Smith in a Connaught. This boy was really the find of the day and coming up fast and it was too bad he had to get killed in an accident. A bit later another driver was killed in an Elva—Dick Mainwaring; and this, of course, was the race when Jean Behra tilted his Maserati on its side and lost an ear.

I don't mean to sound gory in recalling these details. Anyone who knows about motor racing knows that anything can happen at any time; but what stuck in my mind was that the Ards circuit demanded much more skill than any course I had ever driven before. For this reason, if for no other, I'm sorry they scrubbed it, though

I can also understand why. Yet, the guys like Moss and Hawthorn, driving much faster than anybody else, stayed on the road and really fought it out for four or five hours.

Masten and I just kept going and minding our own business, and we ended up by winning the class and beating the rest of the factory team. Personally, I had no serious problems, other than a singed face from the tremendous heat given off by the blaze when those seven cars piled up. Aside from not having a five-speed box, our car ran just as well as the factory-driven machines and Masten and I were quite proud of our achievement. After all, this wasn't bad going, first time out in a new machine on a really tough course. Not for two young Americans in Europe, the cradle of motor racing. As to what we got out of the Ulster Tourist Trophy aside from free champagne, it amounted to about eight English pounds each. More than enough for a good dinner!

Since the next race, for me, was the Targa Florio in which I co-drove Tony Paravano's three-liter Monza Ferrari with a guy named Muneron, who had been chosen by the Commendatore himself, it won't do any harm to start out by sketching the dramatic results and what was at stake. The Targa was the last race of the year for the Manufacturers' Championship, and after Mercedes-Benz won the Tourist Trophy they really piled into Sicily for the grand finale. There were enough tires to reach as high as the tallest steeple in Palermo; six transporters, in addition to the famous streamlined one-car carrier with the 300SL fuel-injection sports engine which could tote its load at 105 mph; and fifteen sports and touring cars made up of the official team of three 300SLR's and twelve practice machines. There were enough spares to build a complete automobile; enough machine tools to fabricate any part on the spot, plus forty-two mechanics, umpteen technicians, and a raft of mobile-radio vans.

The score stood at 19 points for Ferrari and 16 for Mercedes, and the battle offered the usual awards: 8 points for a win; 6 for second spot; 4 for third. However, since the points go to the cars, not the drivers, no make can score more than once in the same race. Team manager Alfred Neubauer therefore knew that not only did Mercedes have to win, but Ferrari must also be kept out of second place even though no additional points could be earned for doing so. If they could cold-shoulder the Italians, the Germans would win—by one point! Ferrari, on the other hand, couldn't afford to finish anywhere lower than second, as that would also give Mercedes a one-point victory. So it was all pretty tense, as you can imagine. But since you already know the result, there's no point in working up any suspense. The Germans won the thirty-eighth Targa Florio and scooped the championship, with Moss and Collins taking first place and Fangio-Kling second. Then came Castellotti and Manzon with a 3.5 Ferrari, only twenty-eight seconds ahead of another Mercedes-Benz driven by Titterington and Fitch.

If "only twenty-eight seconds" may seem odd to you, just read on a little bit. In the meantime, Muneron and Shelby, but especially Shelby, applied themselves to learning the tricky Targa course as best they knew how. We got there a couple of weeks ahead of time and I went round and round in Paravano's two-liter Alfa, wearing out two sets of tires and four sets of brake drums, to say nothing of the engine and gearbox. It's about forty-five miles to a lap through the mountains of Sicily and something like nine hundred twists and turns—I don't know because I never counted them. The race was to be run over thirteen laps and you sure had to know what was coming up next or you were a dead duck.

The practice period was interesting enough in itself, because save for one morning session before the race the road is not closed. That meant little burro carts, motorbikes, delivery motorcycles, horse-drawn carts, and a whole bunch of trucks and cyclists kept getting in our way. You couldn't ever be sure of what might be hiding around the next turn, waiting to convert your beautiful machine into a mangled wreck.

Another thing that made it very interesting was that we found ourselves right in the middle of the bandit country, and at this time they had just caught and shot Juliano, probably the kingpin of them all. Peter Collins and I used to stop and have an orange at Juliano's sister's place, right around lunchtime, as it made an adventurous kind of break. Juliano sure was a famous bandit. He had an army of five or six hundred people lurking in some thirty or forty Sicilian caves and going out on forays when the time was ripe. They did a pretty good business in this area inside the Targa Florio course, we learned.

Juliano's boys left us alone, but Muneron didn't do so well in the race. He was a very good driver, but he hadn't put in as much practice as I had. By the end of the first lap, when I was driving, we moved up to fifth place overall and were right in there with Moss, Fangio, Castellotti, and Fitch. And that's the way it remained for the first three circuits, or about 135 miles, when I came in and handed over to Muneron. He promptly ran the car into a ravine and though he smashed it all to hell, he was lucky enough to get out unhurt. Paravano was upset, of course, and a little mad, but what could he do? The car was gone. This was the hardest circuit of all to learn and the most difficult to go fast on, consistently. It got so I used to drive the Targa seven times a day for a week, then rest and assimilate it for a day, then drive it for another week, one full day in the race car. That meant I might take it eighty or ninety times— about 4000 miles—before I felt really confident.

Anyway, that was the end of the Targa Florio for us and after that I came back to the States and again drove a Paravano car, this time at Palm Springs in December, 1955. Tony didn't hold the Targa against me in any way. Far from it, he gave me a pat on the back and offered me the 4.9 Ferrari for Palm Springs—the same dog in which I had won the Seattle race. And boy, this time I sure wished I hadn't made a start.

That big red dog of a 4.9 found itself parked in the back row of the grid at the start, whereas it should, of course, have been up front. It had more power and more speed than at least 70 per cent of the field, and to put a car of this type behind a pack of minnows only showed one thing: the officials didn't have much of a clue as to what they were doing. Anyway, I thought I saw an opening, so I put it in first and tromped on the throttle. Just as I got into second gear, somewhere between 75 and 80 mph, one of those home-built specials pulled over smack in front of me, and as it had a little ramp tail-like affair at the back, I got a perfect start. I flew through the air over about twenty cars—and I'm not exaggerating when I say I must have reached an altitude of about fifteen feet—and then came the crash. When the car landed, the impact knocked the wheels off and the rest of it skidded across the track and that was the end, and I do mean the end, of Mr. Paravano's costly 4.9 Ferrari. To say that he was filled with consternation would be the understatement of the year, but I also think he breathed a sigh when I was helped out of the wreck unhurt, except for a little soreness and not even a bad shaking up. I stayed with the car all the way. I was buckled in and luckily finished right side up—I guess because there are no trees in Palm Springs. I just belly landed and skidded along the track.

And that about ended the season of 1955, except for one amusing incident which was the direct outcome of this crash. Masten Gregory happened to be driving a three-liter Maserati for Paravano when they stopped the race because there were bits and pieces and cars strewn every which way as the result of my flight. Luckily no one got hurt, but the fellow I had hit in his home-built Oldsmobile special—there wasn't anything more to it than that, really—this guy was irate and threatened to push my face in. So little Masten Gregory happened to be standing there—he wears glasses and has beautiful manners and stands about five feet eight inches and weighs I'd say a hundred and thirty pounds, soaking wet—and he jumps up in front of this guy and says he's going to whip him first before he can get to me.

I'll say this for Masten, aside from the fact that he was probably my closest friend in racing for years, he has all the guts in the world. Too much guts for his own good, perhaps. When I looked at this guy who drove the Oldsmobile special—a guy who must have weighed something like three hundred pounds!—I must say I deeply appreciated Masten's way of showing his friendship for me. To this day I haven't forgotten it. As I said, Masten is soft spoken and a very gentlemanly guy, and I think no end of him, but the thing I specially admire in him is his tremendous amount of guts.

–9–
DRIVER OF THE YEAR

A LOT HAPPENED in 1956. It was the year that I started driving for John Edgar, and also the year I opened a sports car agency in Dallas—Carroll Shelby Sports Cars—with the backing of Dick Hall, brother of Jim Hall of Chaparral fame. But we'd better take these things as they come along, although I might note here that we did mighty well with the agency and handled a number of different makes and products. Dick, by the way, had purchased a three-liter Ferrari from Allen Guiberson—it's funny how very often the same cars, many of them good and hardly used, others real pigs—can move around from one owner to another in nothing flat. I remember winning Pebble Beach, Dodge City, Kansas, and Eagle Mountain Air Force Base events, all of which were National SCCA races and, for their day, very important.

Before we go any further, I think I had better ram the years 1956 and 1957 into this chapter, because I got involved in so many races that there was hardly a weekend we were not off to some course or other; also, to try to give a detailed account of all these events would be extremely boring and repetitive, besides requiring a volume about the size of the Encyclopaedia Britannica.

My association with John Edgar did not begin until the Cumberland, Maryland, races in May of 1956. I remember driving a little special there—an Alfa Romeo Veloce—for Max Hoffmann, and I seem to recall Ed Hugus having a similar car. (Those Veloces were pretty hot for their day; special cams and two double-throat Webers and different gearing. They went quite well, except for the gearbox, which was a piece of junk, until they eventually went to the balk-ring-type of synchromesh box designed by Porsche. But one thing I want to do in this story of my life is to stay away from a lot of heavy technical stuff, which you can get from the auto magazines, anyway, or better still from the manufacturers. But it comes back to me that those Veloces had not yet been built in sufficient numbers, or some such thing, and the good old SCCA classified them as "modified" cars, which meant we had to run against Lotuses and the like, a ridiculous situation.)

After that race John Edgar came up and said, "Son, how would you like to drive for me?"

And I, being the mercenary cash-and-carry type, said, "I'd like it fine, but what's in it for me?"

"Well," he says, "what do you want? You name it. I'll buy you any kind of car you want."

Sweet words for any driver to hear, I can tell you. Real heady stuff, like the best of wine. But I tried not to let it go to my head. I did some fast thinking and as a result we had a little set-to with Luigi Chinetti and ordered the 4.9 Ferrari that had been built for that great master, Fangio, but that for some reason he never did drive in Argentina. This was probably the best 4.9 ever built, which is not saying an awful lot—but look who was scheduled to drive it in the first place! As it happened, the car wasn't finished yet, so Chinetti lent us an old two-liter single-seater that we went hillclimbing in. We set records at Mount Washington (the Climb to the Clouds, which is just about what it is); and at Giant's Despair, a short one near Wilkes Barre, Pennsylvania. Another thing I enjoyed no end was my ride in the two-liter on that hairy little course at Brynfan Tyddyn (Welsh for "The House on the Hill"), a private road circuit on Senator Woods's estate and one of the most beautiful I have ever seen. There was no room for mistakes because of the narrow road, ditches, stone walls, and trees: this was a course where you had to put a little thinking into your driving, and although I hate to use that time-worn phrase, it did separate the men from the boys. Drivers used to running around airports, with hundreds of yards of concrete apron to spin out on, suddenly found they had to be a little more careful.

Finally we got the 4.9 Ferrari in time for Seattle and won the race there. Last time I had driven that course, just exactly a year before, the weather had been miserable with rain and cold gusts down to 40 degrees. Well, now it was 100 degrees, very humid, and about the hottest race I've ever driven in, and I'm talking about temperature, not pace. Guess I must have lost several pounds from perspiration. Everything I wore turned into a soaking rag and the perspiration even ran down under my goggles and got into my eyes and made them sting. That just shows you how changeable the weather can be in the state of Washington. Seattle was the opener, but perhaps the most amazing thing was the fact that we drove about twenty races with this car without ever doing a thing to the engine except change the plugs. We'd do one on Saturday and another one on Sunday, in places that might be as far apart as Encino, California, and Seattle, Washington, and the durn thing always cranked up and ran like a charm. It had so much power and was so huskily built you just couldn't break it unless you ran it off the road, the way I had done with Paravano's ill-fated machine.

One of the highlights of those twenty races in 1956, 90 per cent of which I won, was the Cuban Grand Prix. I drove the good old 4.9 of John Edgar and finished second to Fangio in a three-liter Maserati. This was in October on the Malecon circuit in Havana, and it sure was a beautiful spot. Cuba in those days, despite the rumble of revolution which was still about a year off, was a very different place from what it is today, but I guess there's not much point in debating all that political stuff in a book about motor racing.

To get back to John Edgar for a moment, he was quite a character. Pretty sharp and nobody's fool, but he tried to give you a square shake. John sort of came into a lot of money, which is not surprising when you remember that his father was one of the founders of the Hobart Manufacturing Company, which makes all kinds of scales, meat-cutters, and that sort of thing. It's a big Ohio company and that's where the dough came from, but I think John might still have made out okay by himself. He liked to dabble a little in the stock market; he had a shrewd eye for a business venture; and he knew which side his bread was buttered on.

At all events, financially I made out very well with Edgar during our association. It was really the turning point of my racing career as far as money was concerned, and after five years of financial struggling as a poor race driver, often getting rides for no more than kicks or the price of a meal, I found myself for the first time in a position where the pressure began to ease off. It was a mighty nice feeling, I can tell you. I was still married to Jeanne, but she was finding it more and more difficult to accept my kind of life, more so as we were expecting our third child the following year. I seemed to be gone so much of the time that it was like running two homes, only my end of it was no home, just a hotel room and a suitcase. Racing, I found out long ago, is absolutely not the way to get rich; its the short cut to the poorhouse, if anything, and I never considered it as a means of getting rich or even well off. Racing was and will always remain a steppingstone for getting into maybe a worthwhile business and putting something tangible together, and that was the way I considered it. No other way, except, of course, that I just loved to drive in competition and always have.

But John Edgar got a big kick, I think, out of watching me drive his cars and win races for him. So much so that when he again asked me to drive in 1957, I went back to Modena and Maranello with him in January of that year; but I had better not jump the gun—the starter doesn't like it!

That year of 1956 we went to all kinds of places that I can't even remember without consulting books and books of clippings, and when you've read one you've read them all, except when something really interesting happens. We were dashing about to places like Lime Rock, Virginia International Raceway, Eagle Mountain, and so on, just constantly on the move. There was Pebble Beach, Monterey, Laguna Seca, Palm Springs—and the same thing all over again a year later, so I'm going to try to stick with those that really stand out in my mind for one reason or another. It was the season, I know, when *Sports Illustrated* named me Driver of the Year and put my face on the cover of their magazine!

At the start of 1957, as the result of that trip back to Italy, and for reasons which will become apparent, I made a deal for the Edgar stable to run Maseratis, not Ferraris any more. Here's what happened. There was some talk about my joining the Ferrari factory team that year, but when I got over there to talk turkey with the Commendatore, he brushed aside my question, "What are the financial arrangements? What's the deal and how do we work out some settlement?" To which Signor Ferrari replied in so many words, "My dear young man, you're at the beginning of your career and you should feel honored to drive for us. What's this bit about money?"

So I pointed out that since Mr. Edgar was having to pay cash on the barrelhead for everything, and at strictly retail prices, perhaps Maserati might prove a bit more receptive. Sure enough they were. Some of the promises made to us weren't held to over the year, but the Orsi people (who, as you know, took over the whole works from the original Maserati brothers many years ago, while the latter moved to Bologna and started the Osca) did try to be cooperative. We got a new three-liter from them and also a 4.5 which had gobs of power. We also made a deal for me to drive for Maserati at Sebring and we started preparing for all the major SCCA races that coming season. As it turned out, we sure cleaned up. In fact, we won practically everything that came our way.

Going back to Carroll Shelby Sports Cars for a moment, my association with Dick Hall, an oilman from Abilene, Texas, began when I drove a Monza Ferrari for him in a few races in 1956, and during that period we often discussed getting into the sports car business in a small way. These discussions convinced us that Dallas was the place to become involved in such a scheme, and so, early in 1957, we began to discuss the line of cars we should handle. At that time there was no one else in Texas handling sports cars at all, or at least competition cars, so we decided on British Motor Corporation products as our bread-and-butter line. Also, since I was driving Maseratis for John Edgar that year, we began buying Maseratis, which no one in the U.S. had ever done up to that time, and selling and making a good business of competition cars. We operated the business under my name, but just before we opened our doors, Dick's brother, Jim, graduated from Cal Tech and decided that he, too, wanted to come to Dallas and learn something about driving sports cars. He also had an idea that someday he was going to build his own car. So Dick and I agreed for him to come in with us and in that way maybe pick up what I had learned during the past four or five years. And I must say he was a very apt student. From the start he was a conservative driver, not trying to go over his head—a very unusual thing for a young man of twenty-two, anxious to become a race driver.

But before we dive into 1957 I'd be leaving out a lot if I didn't mention Nassau Speed Week in December of 1956 and what happened there during the Governor's Cup. Boy, that was a dilly. You have to start with "Red" Crise, who isn't exactly known for his democratic tendencies, and take it from there to an abandoned airport. Not the course they run on nowadays, but the place where the planes now take off. There was cement dust all over the runways and for some reason Crise decided to start this big event near sundown and run the last twenty laps in the dark. The course wasn't marked, and with all this cement dust flying around and nothing to guide you but the usual oil trail left by the drips of other cars, we really had a party of it. God only knows how many times Portago and I bumped into each other or how many other cars we hit, but finally I beat him across the finish line by about twenty feet in the wildest wingding battle you ever saw and a race I think I was proudest to win of any, outside of Le Mans, which came later. Portago was driving a 3.5 Ferrari, and although he had a world of driving ability and was very aggressive, he had almost as much instability as far as driving cars was concerned. Motor racing seemed to be a kind of obsession with him—something that his Latin blood couldn't really cope with, although he felt compelled to race, no matter what. I don't believe he really loved cars as such, or at least not racing cars. He felt he had to tame them like you tame a wild and savage beast, by taking enormous risks. I think that "Fon" de Portago considered motor racing as the one thing he had to do, and do well, if he was to gain the Spanish throne!

At Sebring the Maserati team consisted of four cars and was quite an impressive turnout. Fangio and Behra in a 4.5; two six-cylinder, three-liter cars with Moss-Schell in one and myself and Salvadori in the other; plus a new 2.5-liter, four-cylinder job shared by Scarlatti and Bonnier. The brakes were tremendously improved as the result of lessons learned in Argentina, and the six-cylinder cars put out 274 brake horsepower. The 4.5 developed about 400 brake horsepower and even the 2.5 could muster 220 brake horsepower. Fangio and Behra won it in the big car, while Moss and Schell were second, but these were the only two of our four cars to figure in the results, and then no thanks to our organization. If you want the straight dope on this one, we were badly handicapped by poor pitwork and what at times developed into a first-class snafu. The car I shared with Salvadori was not as fast as the others, or else I had an off weekend, but I remember that my practice time was only one second faster (3:33) than Phil Hill's Ferrari, which was a much slower machine. We might have had a one-two-three Maserati victory but for the fact that our car got disqualified over some infringement of the refueling rules. Some hasty siphoning saved the Moss car from a similar fate, while even the winning Fangio and Behra team were threatened with a sixty-five-second penalty for having too many mechanics working on their car at one time during a pit stop. The day after the race, I recall, Fangio complained of a sore bottom because he had been obliged to drive for a long time, sitting in a pool of raw gas. During one refueling stop a mechanic had apparently mistaken the driver's seat for the gas tank! But all the same, you had to hand it to Alfieri for his fine engine, and to Colotti for a chassis worthy of it. Man, that was some combination.

Though as I've said before, the seasons 1956 and 1957 seem to run into a great big continuous jumble of races, I can tell you of a couple more in 1957 that for one reason or another stuck in my mind.

There was this inaugural Grand Prix at the new Virginia International Raceway, for example. I seemed to be getting all the power out of John Edgar's beefy 4.5 Maserati, no doubt thanks to the fine condition of this car, which was making its U.S. debut. It was an easy race, which I won at better than 78 mph for the 64-mile grind, despite all the fuss that the press had made about the "many dangerous turns" and the "roller climbs," and all that stuff. The Maser seemed to take them all in its stride, never missing a beat, never giving me a moment's trouble. At the start I found myself in the second row of the grid, and when the flag dropped there were a couple of D-Jags ahead of me, driven by Walt Hansgen and Charlie Wallace. Their practice times had been a little faster than mine, which entitled them to the front row, but that didn't really mean very much. Neither of these boys stayed ahead for long. Wallace applied too much power and lost time through wheelspin, and this gave me a chance to cut to his left and slip by Hansgen as I kicked the throttle hard down. Despite the way it might have looked to the crowd, there was room to spare through the gap and I went through the first turn with a small but clear lead which was enough for me to stay ahead for twenty laps and get the checker. Wallace and Hansgen had quite a hassle, I gathered, as Charlie pushed his way up from sixth to third on that first lap and the two white Jags ran nose to tail for the next twelve laps, with Hansgen just managing to stay ahead. Then Charlie got too eager and tried to pass Walt at the first turn. That ruined his chances. He overcooked it and spun out and this took the heat off Hansgen, although Wallace still managed a third place.

Earlier that day there was a sprint race which I was lucky enough to win also, but the details have faded out of my mind and it didn't amount to much anyway.

Why did this particular race stick in my memory? Several things. First appearance, as I said, of that husky 4.5 Maserati. Opening of an important new circuit in Virginia. And last but not least, the deceptive but widely accepted idea that practice lap times really mean something. They don't. I'll grant you it's as good a way of determining grid positions as any other and it makes a lot more sense than that zany SCCA notion which went on for years—just drawing numbers at random out of a bag. But my point is that while some drivers are real tigers in practice, they don't show up so well under pressure of an actual race, running wheel to wheel with a bunch of other guys, or trying to shake off pursuit, or trying to get by someone. On the other hand, there are other drivers whose practice times may show as much as five or even ten seconds a lap slower than their real potential when they go out to practice. But throw them into a race and the old competitive spirit comes out and they really tiger. Running against a clock is never the same thing as running against other guys. No sir.

The other race that sticks in my mind, never without a trace of pain, is that race meet at Riverside International Raceway in California that I mentioned at the beginning of this book, the one that took place on September 21 and 22, 1957. This, too, was a new raceway, although this was not the inaugural meet. It had opened in June of that year. But before I go on to tell you more of what happened to one Carroll Shelby in that race, let me correct a wrong impression that many people seem to have. It was not John Edgar who was responsible for getting this $800,000 enterprise started. He did contribute to it, but the guy who fathered the idea and put the original deal together was a Los Angeles restaurant operator named Rudy Cleye. There might not be any Riverside today without John Edgar, but Cleye does deserve the credit for bringing that baby into the world.

The event I am talking about—the second one—was to be the first shindig of this kind sponsored by the California Sports Car Club. It was a two-day affair that promised plenty of excitement, because of the type of course, and it was designed to teach a driver that *chic* blue two-piece coveralls with elastic bands and zipper fasteners, and soft leather gloves that have holes punched in the knuckles, do not a champion make. But who am I to talk? This time my luck ran clean out on the very first lap of the opening practice session and I converted John Edgar's beautiful and enormously expensive Maserati—his prized 4.5—into something not far from a pretzel. I was very lucky that there happened to be a really good plastic surgeon on hand in the little town of Riverside that Saturday afternoon. Not long before, he had decided to take his family out of Los Angeles and raise them in a small town and this just happened to be his day in the barrel. My luck held in another way, too. This doctor also still happened to have the needles and thread of his plastic surgery days and he did a wonderful job of patching me up. Also, the broken bones were all in my face—nose and cheekbones— while the rest of my body was okay, except for the most terrific shaking up I can ever remember in all my racing career.

When his job was done, the plastic surgeon sent me back to Dallas and home and I can't say that Jeanne was exactly delirious with joy when she saw me swathed in bandages like an old woman with a shawl wrapped around her head; but even so I was luckier than a couple of other guys, one of whom made it to the cold slab at that same meet. One was John Lawrence of Pasadena and the other Donald Billie of Ontario. Lawrence was killed when his MGA flipped; Billie, a motorbike rider trying his hand at the four-wheel game, was critically injured when his Norton Manx slammed into the guard rail at Turn One. He suffered a fractured skull and was out cold for four days, but recovered.

Meantime, back at the ranch, I had a business trip planned in London and Paris and I wasn't supposed to let any number of stitches spoil my plans. When I promised not to race again until the SCCA shindig at Palm Springs in November, the doctor let me go.

"*You* must be getting careless!" he said, his tone a bantering one.

"You know durn well a driver never makes a mistake," I said. "There I was, going through that turn at a modest fifty miles an hour, when what did I run into? A patch of sand. From then on until that head-on collision with the earth bank I had no steering at all."

As I recall it, what made that Riverside meet a red-letter day was the sensational win of fifteen-year-old Pedro Rodriguez who drove his Porsche RS to a 40-second win through a tough field in the under 1500cc modified class. He did it both days and walked away with all the marbles and a new title.

You want to know whether the Maser finished in a junkyard? Not at all. John Edgar had a mechanic working for him who was also an excellent body man. His name was Joe Landacker and by some magic of his own he put that baby together again and got it ready for the November races at Riverside. This event was not sponsored by the *Times Mirror*, but it was the first of the big races that have since been held annually in the fall.

Gosh darn, I've got to go back six months in 1957 for just a moment, to tell about the opening of Carroll Shelby Sports Cars, Inc. When our doors swung open at 5611 Yale in Dallas, I guess the public found we hadn't exactly been doing things by halves. We even handled Rolls-Royce!

Okay, the Riverside crash didn't cool off my love of racing one little bit. I still hadn't, at this time, achieved what I wanted to do in racing, and when you have this thing in your blood, nothing much is going to cool it off till you draw your last breath. Or until you accomplish what you set out to do.

But don't get the notion that 1957 was just a DNF at Sebring, an easy win at VIR, and a nasty crash at Riverside. Not by a long stretch. As I've already said, we ran so many of them and won so many that this thing could become just a long list of dull results, colder than yesterday's soup. Already in April of that year I not only ran my favorite course, Eagle Mountain Lake, but was also planning my debut in Formula 1 Grand Prix racing at Monte Carlo in a 250F Maserati two-liter single seater. This was scheduled for April 19 and I was to run in at least four of the six remaining races which would count toward the International Manufacturers' Championship. I suppose I should have felt flattered at being the first American driver ever to sign a contract with Maserati to drive Grand Prix cars. The contract was for two years and my teammates were to be Fangio and Moss, about the highest company a guy could wish to keep.

I remember a writer once asking me to define what it takes to win at this kind of racing.

"It's the ability to drive a car as fast as possible without tearing it to pieces," I told him.

"Anything else?" the reporter persisted.

"Yep. You have to *know* a road course as well as have a feel for the machine and the power to concentrate. That's the only way to stay with the leaders who, by the way, ignore this advice nine times out of ten!"

I didn't go Grand Prix that year. Fangio won the Monaco Grand Prix for Maserati, with Moss second, but Shelby wasn't there. The deal fell through as these things often do, but I still had that potent double-overhead-cam V8 Maserati of John Edgar's to drive, completely recovered from its earlier crash, and in November, on the same Riverside course, I set out to make amends. And nearly pulled another spectacular booboo! The main event of the afternoon was a 100-mile race for unlimited sports cars with forty of America's hottest drivers battling for victory. Not the least of them was Masten Gregory in another 4.5, Walt Hansgen in Briggs Cunningham's D-Jag, and Dan Gurney at the wheel of a 4.9 Ferrari—the first time he had the opportunity to drive something worthy of his skill. The car belonged to Frank Arciero and Dan gave it the ride of its life. As to what happened, I jockeyed my way through the pack till I got the lead with No. 98—and then made another mistake. Trying to broadside through that tricky downhill bend they call Turn Seven, I spun out and off the course. I wasn't hurt and the car didn't have a scratch, but the Marshals sidelined me for twenty-three seconds while the entire field went by, and I got hotter and hotter under the collar! Then I started a frantic chase to catch the other thirty-nine starters—especially people like Hansgen, the then National SCCA champion, and Masten Gregory, fresh from Europe. Masten had actually finished higher on points for the world's championship than any other American before him. And, boy, Dan Gurney might be a newcomer, but he sure as heck knew how to drive a race car!

Well, to cut a long story short, I whittled away, lap by lap, at the margin that separated me from the leaders, while I prayed the race might last just long enough to get me back up front. Luckily that spin-out had been on the first lap, and as the hour-long race passed the halfway mark, I found I had overtaken more than thirty guys, not counting those who had dropped out. Then I caught sight of Gurney and started pressing him. The crowd got pretty excited, I was told, but I couldn't hear a thing except the roar of the exhaust. Oddly enough, as we again neared Turn Seven, many laps after my spin-out, I again pulled a broadside and shot by Gurney without going off the course. Then I put her in a drift and took a rather startled Masten Gregory, who couldn't figure out where the heck I had come from. At the end of the long back straight I caught Hansgen and outbraked him into the turn and so regained the lead. And this time I didn't make any more mistakes.

There were about 45,000 fans at Riverside that day, and they went wild when I brought the smoking Maser back into the pit after getting the checker. A bunch of photogs and reporters and well-wishers crowded around and all wanted to know the same thing: "How did you spot three of America's finest drivers the best part of half a minute and then come back and beat them?"

One guy was very insistent about this. He wanted a straight answer—something to do with motivation, I think—and I gave it to him.

"Well, sir," I said, "after making a durn fool of myself on that Turn Seven, I reckon I just got *mad!*"

This was widely quoted in the papers afterward, and in cold print it sounded funny, but it didn't really contradict or disprove that famous moral: "*Don't* drive when you're mad!"

* * *

My third child was born in 1947—a boy named Patrick Burke; so that made two boys and a girl, but I still had no home life, just moving from town to town and hotel to hotel, and after a while this became pretty tiring. There was nothing stable about it, nothing you could really count on or call worthwhile except my main objective, which I was determined to achieve, whatever the cost.

I'll talk about that in the next chapter, but meantime, as all good things do, my association with John Edgar came to an end at the close of the year. John Wyer had offered me a chance to come back to Europe in 1958 and I felt I wanted another year or two in Europe before I retired from racing. So John and I had a very amicable parting and back I went to work for John Wyer.

Although the Aston Martin Formula 1 Grand Prix car had been more or less shelved dining the previous year, there had, in fact, been an enormous amount of experimental work going on in the shops at Feltham, and some information on this might not be amiss where the racing buffs and performance bugs are concerned. Looking back, I can't do much better than quote from an article in a well-known British monthly magazine called *Motor Racing*.

"Racing," this article said, "is considered by Mr. David Brown to be an essential part of the development of his cars and to have a definite bearing on production and sales." (What was that—GM?) "It is the company's firm belief that it would be more difficult to see cars of a thoroughbred type if they did not take part in competition."

"Aston Martin reputation stands high," the article went on, "and moreover racing keeps a development team *alert and interested*" (the italics are mine), "whereas if production and costs are the only incentives, stagnation is apt to set in. The David Brown group as a whole, including Lagonda cars and even tractors, derive benefit from racing cars." (Wow!) "Reg Parnell, who has been works driver for the Aston Martin team since its inception, is now team manager, and his nephew, Roy Parnell, is chief tester and in charge of racing experimental work."

It's a tried-and-true philosophy. You can look back through history at the names which have launched automobile empires by introducing their products to the public through racing. It's an impressive list: Henry Ford, Chevrolet, MG, Rolls-Royce, Will Durrant, Fiat, Bugatti, Ferrari, and Mercedes-Benz, to name a few.

I know how much it's meant to me to have people at Ford who appreciated this fact. And, at Ford my debt runs deeper than to just the people in racing and technical positions. There are guys like Ed Dayton, Bill Ennis, Frank Martin, and Sev Vass, who have helped shape and guide my own company, Shelby American, and who have offered invaluable advice. Without their help there would be no Shelby American.

-10-

CASTRO WINS A GRAND PRIX

BEFORE WE START on the year 1958 and begin another search through the clippings, I'd like to let up on the racing for a bit and talk about something which to me, then as now, was of the greatest importance: my ultimate objectives. Except at the very beginning, I never considered motor racing as an end in itself, but only as a means to something bigger, more important, and more permanent. Racing is a terrific lot of fun, and as I've said and will never get tired of saying, once this virus, or whatever it is, gets into your blood, then, brother, you have had it. There is no cure known to man, no drug or injection, no therapy, that can get you to give it up willingly. There is always the chance you may get killed, of course, or so badly hurt you'll not be able to race again, but I've already expressed my views about that.

Always, at the back of my mind, perhaps not even consciously, was the thought, "If Carroll Shelby can get famous enough in this motor racing game—if he can get known to enough of the right people, then it might lead to something more important." Just what, I wasn't sure. You can't just yank an able-bodied and somewhat suc-cessful race driver out from behind the wheel and shove him behind a desk instead. It doesn't work that way. Yet the longer I went on racing and was around the limited-production factories in Europe, the more I realized that America was missing a big bet, a winning bet, and that it was time someone responsible got their eyes open. To put it briefly, that winning bet I'm talking about was the design and production of an all-purpose, all-American sports or grand touring car that you could drive to market and also race during the weekend, without having to spend $15,000 or $17,000 or go into hock for the rest of your life, only to own an automobile which, next year, might be out of date technically.

Sure thing, it was a nothing life, this business of living out of suitcases and spending so little time at home, yet I felt that it was the only way to make the necessary contacts, enough of them, and build myself a big enough name to do what I wanted. After all, my father hadn't left me a million dollars that might have put me in a nice position to build my own car just the way I wanted it, so these sacrifices, I told myself, were really worth it in the long run because I knew where I wanted to go and felt sure I also knew how it had to be done.

Designwise, to sketch the thing out briefly without going into a mass of technicalities (I want to sell this book!), my idea was to build something around a big-bore American engine, something that would sell at a reasonable price and service at a reasonable price. Nothing very sophisticated so far as the chassis was concerned, because when you get away from parts that are already in production and start to manufacture your own stuff and get too "smart," then up goes the price at once. It goes up so high that you practically eliminate all your chances, right there, of turning the venture into a commercial success. At that time I was faced with an additional problem that was pretty serious, insofar as competing with American iron was concerned. The CSI (International Sportive Commission) had a decree out that three liters, or approximately 183 cubic inches, was the limit of piston displacement for an engine in sports car competition.

Oddly enough, or perhaps logically enough, I had never tried to interest either Tony Paravano or John Edgar in producing the kind of car that was beginning to take shape in my mind, because, let's face it, I think I must have been about the only person on earth who seriously thought such a thing could happen. Every time I talked to anyone about this pet idea, even casually, they'd laugh a big belly laugh. "Ha, ha! Yeh, yeh. Look what happened to Briggs Cunningham who put this big 4000-pound monster into production in that nice little multi-million dollar factory of his in Palm Beach. Sending those chassis to Italy to have the body built, and then bringing them back! Know what they lost on each car? Why, heck, if Briggs hadn't had the good sense to quit, even he would have gone broke."

"That's not the way I'd do it," I would argue.

"Okay, then. Take Reventlow. He went a lot further for a lot less money with that Scarab. It *really* had the stuff in the sports car races. But look at what it cost to build! As for buying one—you're just kidding, pal. Seventeen thousand bucks?"

"The kind of car I have in mind doesn't have to cost that kind of dough."

"It doesn't, eh? What are you going to use for raw materials? Old bedsteads, melted down?"

I had to agree that there sure as hell was no mass market at fifteen grand, and that the people who had that kind of money to spend just didn't believe we, in America, could ever hope to match the Europeans. As for its being commercially feasible—why that was the biggest laugh of all. There was nobody, but nobody, willing to listen to me with a straight face, except maybe Harley Earl and Ed Cole of General Motors. At least, during 1956 and 1957, they were willing to discuss the idea in its preliminary stages. If these two farseeing men—a vice-president and a chief engineer—had been allowed to have their say, my idea would probably have been a Chevy-based car; but as luck would have it, the people who were running the Corvette and sports car end of GM's vast automotive empire didn't even want to listen to anything that wasn't their idea, or allow anything to be done that wasn't their baby. This, I suppose, was understandable, since their minds were cast along regular or orthodox patterns of thinking. And besides, the Corvette wasn't exactly standing the world, or even America, on its ear. The first Corvette was a pretty miserable machine with that outdated six-cylinder Blue Flame, or whatever they called it, engine and a lot of other timorous features that turned it into an apology of a sports car. It was a very different product from today's fast and handsome Sting Ray, but for this Zora Duntov deserves a whole lot of credit. He absolutely does. Without him, the Corvette would have been written off as just one of those things—a blunder that cost a few million. Even today, if Duntov had any notions about building a sports car with something Ford in it, I'm not so sure that I wouldn't say, "Come on in and work with me."

That, as a matter of fact, was his attitude at the time I was talking to Mr. Cole and Mr. Earl. Duntov is a genuine enthusiast who has had one objective in view for years—to create and market and sell a mass-production American sports car that could hold its own against the European invasion. But he wasn't allowed to do what he really had in mind, and he never will be so long as he's in the hire of a big Detroit automobile company. Going forward a bit now, that's the reason why I think Don Frey and people like him at Ford have been exceptionally well oriented and have shown a lot of forward vision in permitting us to run our own company with a minimum of interference. Mr. Frey is an academic, college professor type of man who wears glasses and talks softly, but he never says anything for the sake of hearing his own voice. He represents one of the most progressive elements at Ford today. And he's not alone, not by any means. I could name more people at Ford who have stood behind my project: people like Dave Evans, Jacque Passino, Ray Geddes, Leo Beebe, Lee Iacocca—it's a really impressive list.

But to get back to what you call the bureaucratic mind, there's a brief story worth the telling, although I'm not sure whether it came from General Motors or Ford or Chrysler. But there was this executive making a speech at a banquet and he said, "You know, we're not too afraid of a steel strike, but if they ever had a paper strike that would shut down our companies completely!"

Now that I'm standing on the soap box, I'd like to ramble on a bit more, if it's all the same to you. I'm not talking about the Cobra project at all. That came much later. What I'm trying to do is put into words the thoughts that were going through my mind in those days, around 1957 and 1958. Well, it just seemed to make sense to me that if a Porsche, as beautifully finished as it is in every detail, could fetch $5000 on the American market, and a Corvette could fetch $4000 just the way it was, tilting the scales at 3300 pounds or so, then all it would take would be a simple American engine, a V8 pushrod type with an output of, say, 300 brake horsepower, and gobs of torque, plus a slightly more sophisticated chassis than the Corvette then had, to turn the trick. What kind of chassis? Maybe something like an Austin Healey type of automobile that you could then market for $3500 or $3700 and that would weigh at most 2600 pounds. It seemed to me there was a market for a car like this and that the American market was starving for lack of such a product.

As I've said before, of course, nobody would go along with the idea. Even when you talked about it to a European who didn't really have much of an ax to grind, he'd tell you, "No, boy. It takes a good 1500cc or two-liter engine and a small chassis to do the trick. And if you want proof, don't take my word for it. Just look at the way that type of car goes around your bloody Corvette!"

But Texans are hardheaded people, and I just couldn't get it out of my mind that there was a definite market for a car like this; and there was also a market for a car that would be even lighter than this—say, a 2000-pound car of very limited production that would compete with Ferraris selling for around $15,000. Something that you could sell with all the options for no more than $6000 or $7000. But another thing that stuck in my craw was this idea that since Europeans were building an awful lot of automobiles beamed at the American market—especially the U.S. sports car market—and since they were depriving themselves of cars to sell them to us, why in heck didn't they do what seemed to me the obvious thing? The obvious thing would have been for them to take advantage of their much lower labor rates to build some rather more sophisticated, lighter chassis and drop American-type engines into them and sell them *here*. It seemed to me they were missing a sure bet—something that was staring them in the face, because American engines cost so little and put out so much more power per dollar and could be serviced so much more easily, without all this waste of time waiting for parts that were three thousand miles away.

A five- or six-liter engine obviously didn't make sense in Europe, but for export to the dollar-and-"sense" market, that was another story. They could have shipped over the complete car or installed the engines over here. And still they would have had something that could also be sold at home, because this type of a chassis would lend itself equally well to European needs and European engines of two liters or so—V6's and V8's then in the making—which were so designed that as time went on and the home economy improved, there would be little trouble in opening them up to three liters.

Well, you can't ignore that bit about hindsight, I guess, but the fact remains that I did see it clearly, and that everybody I turned to said, "Nope, it can't be done. It just can't." They didn't stop to think that even if Europe did buy our engines, it would be selling them back to us in complete cars.

If you want me to be a bit more specific yet, what I had lurking in the back of my mind was something to compete against, say, the Austin Healey that brought around $3500 and sold as many as 7000 or 8000 cars a year in this country and still used an engine that surely must have been descended directly from a 1918-model London bus. It would have been so easy to get an American Chevrolet V8 or something like that and come up with the same thing at the same price but with a vastly different performance: a car that would have been fifty mph faster with almost double the acceleration.

This was the type of thinking that was going on in my mind. I wasn't particularly interested in the idea of building some kind of a "special" or an out-and-out racing car. In fact, despite the present General Motors policy which pretends to condemn racing as useless in improving the breed, and "dangerous" to boot, the only reason why I'm racing today is because from an advertising standpoint it's cheaper for me to race than take ads in *Time* and *Life* or anything of that sort. Racing, aside from the fact that I enjoy it, costs far less—an awful lot less—than a two-page spread in a big national magazine, say. And I get more mileage out of racing, or in other words more advertising and sales rub-off for a given outlay.

Looking back now, it's a strange thing how an idea can stare people right in the face and they don't even see it. Besides GM I went to other companies, trying to peddle this idea. I went to Jensen in England (and what do they have today but a whopping big Chrysler V8 mill that makes this car, heavy as it is, one of the fastest production machines in the world, at any price!). I talked with John Wyer of Aston Martin; I talked to Maserati and to de Tomaso; I argued the point with people in all walks of life and at all levels of the automobile industry—in fact with anyone who would listen, and they all thought it was a pipe dream. Everybody seemed to think I was smoking marijuana! Finally, this thing became a standing joke. "Ha, ha! Shelby's gonna build a car. He's gonna build the car to end them all. Only thing is, he doesn't have any money! Ever heard that before?"

No, my faster, easily serviced, cheap-to-buy automobile, one which would combine the virtues I already mentioned—the ability to go to market or race at weekends—this, people said, was not "practical." Let's stick with Austin Healey and Triumph and the others, but let's not take any chances.

I will say this for General Motors, they did have some cause to feel sensitive because of the big egg that the Corvette had laid. This project at about that time was so groggy that they were uncertain whether to go on with it or write it off. Saleswise, the Corvette had practically no success at that time, and, in fact, it didn't really catch on until they began to race it. Racing was the thing that actually saved the Corvette and proved its turning point. Lessons were learned in racing, even club racing, that could never have been learned in a hundred years of proving-ground tests. And so the car was improved and in turn the improvements began to sell it until it really hit the jackpot. Don't let anyone kid you. That was exactly how it happened.

At the time I was waging this struggle—this absurd losing battle you might call it—no American automobile had won anything of any importance in racing since Ralph Mulford won the Seventh Vanderbilt Cup at Savannah in 1911 with a Lozier. Perhaps I should correct that to read, "No American production-based automobile had won a major international road race"; otherwise I'll have all the Brickyard fans on my back! Okay, there was one exception to this: Jimmy Murphy in a Duesenberg won the very first Le Mans road race, but it wasn't the Twenty-four-Hour grind, for sure! And not enough can be said about Briggs Cunningham's efforts with his cars, which did notch a victory at Sebring, you'll recall.

I have great respect for those historical purists who keep records to the third decimal place of everything that ever happened to American automobiles since we began to build them; but no one is going to argue with the spirit of what I am trying to say. The American car, so far as international road competition was concerned, was the Cinderella. And I don't think I'm too far wrong in saying it was the Cobra that saved the act!

Okay. Now that I've done for a while with thinking aloud, let's get back to the action part of the Carroll Shelby story. Nobody likes to listen too long to an I-told-you-so guy, even if he did prove right.

Let's see, now. We're at the beginning of 1958, and my good friend John Wyer said he thought he could use my services on the Aston Martin team, and so that decided my course of action for a couple of years. But first there was Cuba in February of that year. My second Cuba, and also the last Cuban road race ever run before that bearded guy took over. When I think back on the Gillette safety razor ads I was soon to endorse, it seems to me that Castro should have been the one to use a good razor blade and take that bird's nest off his face. But right then, you'll remember, dictator Batista was the bad man while Castro, fighting up there in the hills, was the "good guy," the hero of the piece. So Castro, who maybe thought motor racing was not the proper thing to do at this time, decided to kidnap Fangio. He didn't waste any time on ordinary mortals in the racing game; he went straight to the top. Fangio happened to be staying at the Lincoln Hotel, a much less pretentious and plush kind of place than the big Havana hotels like the National, the Riviera, or the Hilton, but Castro's boys found him there when they discovered this was the headquarters for the factory Maserati team. Right in the lobby, just before dinner on the night before the race, with Maserati people like Ugolini and Bertocchi standing there, and Moss, Trintignant, and Behra on their way to the dining room, who walks in but this kook *Fideliste* in a soiled checkered shirt and pants that were just as dirty, wearing a Colt. And that was all. Quick as the bat of an eyelash, this character disarmed the private detective assigned to Fangio by the Batista people and said something like, "Get up and follow me!"

Fangio didn't really believe it at first, I don't think. He suspected maybe some kind of a leg pull, another of those shenanigans that race drivers are always dreaming up. But he soon found out this was for real when a car whisked him off into the darkness.

Fangio, of course, had a special value at that moment because he had put up fastest practice time that day, and also, I guess, because he had taken Batista's General Miranda around for a lap of honor in his Maserati. It's possible some of the guys in that hotel lobby might have made a fight of it, but what can you do against a gun toted by a screwball? This thing might have turned into another St. Valentine's Day massacre, because those Castro boys weren't kidding, let me tell you.

The race itself didn't count toward world championship points, but it was laid out on a very nice course, which took in the long Malecon Boulevard, the same as the year before, and there was lots of prize money and starting money—the whole bit. Also you could fly across from Miami in about an hour, which was very convenient for the drivers.

John Edgar had lent me his 4.5 Maserati for this shindig, and as far as I can remember it was the only other one besides that driven by Fangio. However, ours was a private entry. Nothing to do with the factory team as such.

Well, everybody was there; the twenty-four starters and an expected crowd of about 150,000 fans, and a whole bunch of decorations and stuff, with I don't know how many hundreds of smartly dressed cops to keep order; so the show just had to go on, even without the world's champion. Batista's bloodhounds were turning practically the whole of Cuba inside out all during the night, trying to locate Fangio, and the dictator was being made to look pretty silly, which seems to have been exactly what Castro had in mind.

The race was scheduled for ninety laps of this 3.1-mile circuit, and when at the last moment before the start there was still no Fangio, they gave his car to that going Frenchman, Trintignant, whose name I never have been able to pronounce properly. Trintignant gave up a ride in a D-Jag to take over the Maserati, and Stirling Moss drove a 4.1 Ferrari, which was pretty unusual for him. Following some kind of an argument with the Commendatore, long before this time, Stirling had vowed never to drive a Ferrari, at least not for the works team. But Ferrari was well represented apart from Moss, who drove for the North American Racing Team. There was my old buddy, Masten Gregory, with John Edgar's 4.9 Ferrari, and von Trips and Phil Hill also fielding the products of Maranelo.

By two o'clock a huge crowd had assembled to watch the fun, and by 3:45 P.M., when the starter finally dropped his flag, our nerves were getting a bit ragged. There had been a couple of false starts that brought engines to boiling point, and tempers, too; but none of this affected Masten's determination. He was first off the line and made a very good start, but couldn't hold off Moss for long. Stirling soon got by him to build up a slender lead of about three hundred yards, while I held the third slot without sweating it out too much.

Because of the Maserati's thirst for gas, Joe Landacker (my mechanic) and I had decided we would try to run this thing nonstop and so get the jump on many of the others. Boy, did we ever cram on the gas. We had piled in enough tanks in every corner of the car to hold approximately eighty gallons. There was gas just about everywhere and we were going nonstop, provided nothing else broke.

Well, nothing much happened for about five laps. It was still Moss by a narrow margin, then Gregory and I, not far behind. But suddenly on the fifth lap all hell broke loose. Gregory got by Moss into the lead by some pretty daring driving, and moments later red flags popped out all over the place, stopping the cars, and the Cuban Grand Prix was over. A Cuban driver named Cifuentes, I think, had lost control of his two-liter Ferrari and missed a turn and plunged into the densely packed crowd, killing six people and injuring thirty more. It was bad, I can tell you; another thing like Le Mans in 1955, but on a much smaller scale, thank God. I wasn't in any way involved in that crackup; in fact I didn't even see it happen except from a distance. But it was an odd thing, all the same, seeing all those red flags pop out. It was kind of prophetic as to what was going to happen to poor old Cuba before very long.

Anyway, the race was stopped and ambulances rushed to the scene to carry away the dead and wounded, and they announced over the public address system, I believe, that there was going to be a restart later on. But meantime a bunch of the drivers got together and decided by a majority vote not to continue. The whole thing was too dangerous because the course had become covered with oil slicks dropped along the way by leaking and badly prepared cars; also we felt there were too many drivers around, men with almost no experience at all, trying to compete with cars they couldn't handle and going in over their heads. Likely as not we'd be faced with another pile-up long before those remaining eighty-five laps came to an end. Although it wasn't really up to the drivers to make this decision, we did make it and we felt justified in doing so. Just as an example of what I mean about oil being all over the course, Miere's Porsche had already stopped through losing all of its oil, Perdisa's

Maserati was in the pits taking on more oil, and Bob Said's Ferrari could be seen clearly leaving a trail of oil through the corners. Some of this stuff I didn't see myself, but I saw the oil slicks all right, and some of our automotive magazines wrote a pretty good account of what took place on that circuit.

So we never did get to find out whether that little smarty we were planning to pull—the nonstop run—would have worked or not. But financially I made out pretty well in Cuba. The money there was awfully good, cash money, starting money, expenses, and everything.

But the guy who made out best of all was Stirling Moss. When the red flags came out, Masten slowed down but Moss kept his foot down and regained the lead before he was stopped. So that made him the winner after only five laps, and he went home with most of the marbles.

Still, if you really want to know who won that Cuban Grand Prix, I don't think it was Stirling Moss; I believe it was Fidel Castro! He sure loused things up.

-11-

ASTON—BY TWO POINTS

BELIEVE IT OR not, my reasons for going back to Europe to race during the next two seasons, 1958 and 1959, had nothing to do with any ambitions in trying to become a world champion or any such thing. Of course I wanted to race and this was going to put me back right in the middle of the Big Time—the international merry-go-round; but what I had in mind above all else was to educate myself some more about building a sports car along the lines I've already indicated. By keeping in constant contact with the people who ran the various small factories in Europe, and associating myself with their thinking, I figured I would end up in a better position to build the car that I had been working on with GM during the previous two years, or at least talking about with them.

John Wyer and I had built up a very close and friendly association over the years and I don't recall for sure whether it was I who called him or whether he got in touch with me; but the outcome was the same. I made ready to pack and go back over to England. Of course there was good old Sebring in March that year, which we had no intention of missing, and in this twelve-hour grind I drove a DBR1 for the factory team, which that year consisted of two cars only: Stirling Moss and Tony Brooks in one car; Roy Salvadori (my old partner!) and I in the other. Moss took an early lead in the Aston, closely followed by Hawthorn's new three-liter Ferrari Testa Rossa, then Salvadori with our car and Phil Hill (also in a Testa Rossa) running about five seconds apart and twenty-eight seconds behind the leader. Moss sure made that Aston go, but we also had an ace up our sleeve—the new disc brakes which could stop us much sooner, while Ferrari still relied on drum brakes.

Stirling really seemed to have the bit between his teeth that year and consistently lapped at speeds which brought his times well below the previous years fastest. The three D-Type Jags and the two Lister-Jags were having their quota of problems, especially poor Archie Scott Brown, whose Lister got stepped on by Gendebien's Ferrari at the last turn before the pits. It was the darnedest thing you ever saw. Archie braked pretty hard when his engine blew up just as Gendebien was getting ready to pass him. Gendebien did pass him but not at all as he had planned. The sharp nose of the Ferrari first shunted the Lister, then climbed up its back as though trying to make it a piggyback ride. The Lister was just about demolished and the Ferrari sustained quite a bit of damage to the left side and nose, but luckily both drivers escaped unhurt. In fact, Gendebien was able to continue after losing a lap in his pit to make the necessary repairs.

When the race was less than two hours old, Stirling had pushed the DBR1 at such a rate that he held a clear two-minute lead over the entire field, and I think at that point John Wyer began to get nervous. No machinery could stand that pace, even if the driver could, but a sudden flat tire relieved him of the need to make any decision. Moss had to come in right away, and then Brooks took over after a slow pit stop that took nearly four minutes for refueling and a tire change. Then it was my turn to take over from Roy, and I'll be darned if after a few laps the gearshift didn't break off! The weld broke and there was nothing we could do about it. At the time I was pretty mad, but I made a lot more out of it than I really felt. It was a great chance to act up and chase John Wyer all over the pit and make like I wanted to start a brawl, although of course it wasn't in any way his fault. Still, a driver is never wrong, you know. He has to have a scapegoat!

Scratch one perfectly good Aston Martin DBR1, but that still left us the other car and the lead was still in our hands. Tony Brooks, despite that slow pit stop, did a great job of hanging on to first place and beating off a full-strength Ferrari attack which gave him no breathing space at all. Then at 2:15 P.M. he came in to let Moss take over again. This time the car was in the pit three minutes and thirty-two seconds while more tires were changed and new brake pads were put on.

Moss took off as usual like a scalded cat, determined to close the gap that now separated him from the lead Ferrari driven by Peter Collins. Soon afterward luck seemed to play into our hands, when Collins had to come in for gas and Hill took over, but the Ferrari crew moved along pretty fast and got their car out again in one minute, forty-five seconds. During that time, Moss gobbled up so much scenery that he actually came to within fifteen seconds of Hill and everyone started to get really excited. But that was about the end of it. Soon after, the transmission broke and that was the finish of our Sebring effort.

For some reason, Sebring seemed to be particularly hard on transmissions that year, especially among the big cars. With only two hours to go, Hawthorn's Ferrari suddenly dropped out when the transmission quit; then the von Neumann-Ginther Testa Rossa was sidelined for the same reason. Fitch's Ferrari had gone out earlier for the same reason; so with three cars knocked out by similar trouble, Ferrari's team manager started to get as nervous as a cat and a pit signal went out right away, telling the Collins-Hill and Musso-Gendebien cars to slow down. And that was the way they finished. Third spot went to an outstanding two-liter car, the Schell-Seidel Porsche Spyder.

But one thing I don't intend to do is get bogged down in a lot of detail of this kind. The reason why I went into this particular race in some detail was that with only two factory cars against five new Ferrari Testa Rossas, we gave them a real rough time and, in fact, ran them ragged until our team was wiped out. And being a spectator a lot of the time, I had an opportunity to watch what the others were doing.

I don't know just what my plans would have been for the next race—I mean whether I would have taken off for Europe right away to try my hand at Grand Prix racing—but about then an offer came through from Jack Ensley which put a different complexion on things.

"How would you like to try your hand at Indy?" he asked.

"Hadn't thought about it."

"Well, I've got a Kurtis roadster that I'm going to use to take my driver's test. If you want to try to qualify as a rookie, you're welcome to use it."

"How is it going?" I asked.

"We've had it all apart," Jack said. "It's the one Pat O'Connor drove last year."

I made a sudden decision. I'd tried about everything else, so why not have a go at the oval? "Okay," I said. "Think I'll give it a try. And thanks for the break."

"You won't have too much trouble," Jack said in his usual breezy way. "I'm sure of it."

He proved right—up to a certain point. I got up there and passed my physical and they said I could go ahead and take my driver's test. So out I went in the Kurtis and after a few careful warm-up laps I finished my 110, 115, and 120 mph runs without any trouble, when they flagged me in.

"Oops!" said chief steward Harlan Fengler. "Is this your car?"

I shook my head, wondering what was coming next

"It's the car Jack Ensley took his test in, isn't it?"

"Sure. Anything wrong with that?"

"Afraid there is," Fengler said. "We have a rule around here that two men can't take their drivers' tests in the same car.

"Why the heck not?" I began to get mad because this didn't seem to make any sense.

"I'm sorry." Fengler shrugged. "But that's the rule."

"No one told me about it."

"We can't tell everybody about everything," he said. "It's in the rules and that's all there is to it."

"Guess you're right," I said. "And my answer to that is the hell with it. I have plenty of jobs that I can drive in Europe."

"It's nothing personal," Fengler insisted.

"The heck it isn't!" I snapped. "If you want my opinion, you people are just trying to give a rookie a hard time. Well, I don't believe that I care to sit around and argue with this kind of reasoning."

I got out of the car and walked away and that was the end of the Indy business. That same night I caught a plane to New York and on to Europe so I could drive at Spa in Belgium the following weekend.

I had been giving up races every weekend during April and part of May for these durned rookie tests and it wasn't worth it anymore. Not when I had a good ride waiting for me over there any time I wanted it.

This happened on a Thursday, and by Saturday morning I was with the Aston Martin team and John Wyer at Spa, ready to co-drive a DBR3. Paul Frère had a similar car and we were entered for the Belgian Sports Car Grand Prix on May 18. I remember that Masten Gregory drove a Lister-Jaguar and Ivor Bueb a 3.8-liter Jag. Jim Clark, the future world champion, was there and so were the evergreen Jack Fairman and Peter Whitehead. It was a real fun race, I remember, over a circuit that I got to like very much because it demanded an equal combination of the ability to drive fast and corner like scat. You need a few laps to get used to Spa, but it sure is a beautiful spot in the Ardennes Mountains and probably the fastest circuit in Europe. The DBR3 was a pretty heavy machine, yet it handled very well for such a large car. Unfortunately it was way underpowered, and for this reason John Wyer gave up racing it after a while. Too much heft and not enough horses.

Well, to get to the point, Masten won this event of 220 miles in his Lister-Jag; Frère was second and I finished third, ahead of Bueb. I think we all had a ball, but it's the easiest thing to get sucked into corners like Stavelot, at the end of the long back straight, and that nasty La Source hairpin, just before the start, where Dick Seaman was killed in a Mercedes before the war. You just have to watch it all the time and pace yourself. A lap is 8.82 miles, or 14.2 kilometers as they say over there, which is a little bit longer than Le Mans.

Talking of fatalities, I was shocked to learn, two weeks later, that Pat O'Connor had almost been killed on the opening lap of the 500-Mile Memorial Day Classic.

Okay. My next one with the Aston Martin works team was the Nürburgring Thousand Kilometers, run early in June. As usual, Ferrari showed up in force with some of the best troops at the wheel—guys like Hawthorn and Collins; Musso and Hill; Gendebien and von Trips; Seidel and Muneron. These four cars were basically the same three-liter, twelve-cylinder jobs that had swept Sebring earlier in the year. Against them we had three Astons, each a brand new DBR1 with an engine that had a much more efficient cylinder head putting out some 260 brake horsepower. Each also had a five-speed gearbox and the Girling disc brakes introduced that year—altogether a far more potent combination.

I should mention, by the way, that a week earlier John Wyer had entered one of those new cars in the Targa Florio, in what you might call a trial balloon. The drivers then were Moss and Brooks; and Stirling went out and set a race lap record of 43 minutes, 7 seconds. Moss, that time, first hit one of those big roadside stones, damaging his rear wheel, and had to spend thirty minutes in the pits. Then he took off again, going like a wild man in an effort to make up lost time, but his crankshaft damper fell apart. Finally his transmission gave out—a not unfamiliar complaint, you'll remember!

In the 1000 k's of Niirburgring our team consisted of Moss and Brabham; Brooks and Lewis-Evans; and Salvadori and myself. Ecurie Ecosse had three D-Jags, which were nothing new, except that the piston displacement had been reduced from 3.4 to 3 liters to conform with the new CSI edict. Practice went on for two and a half days in exceptionally good weather for the usually rainy Black Forest and right away you could tell that the battle was going to be between the Testa Rossas and ourselves. Unfortunately, the car I shared with Salvadori was sidelined early in the race, due to that now typical Aston Martin complaint—gearbox trouble. Brooks had dropped back after spinning out and having to extinguish a small fire, but Moss, as usual, was going like all the witches in hell were after him. It took him only three laps to build up a 21-second lead over Hawthorn and a 54-second advantage over third man, von Trips. On lap ten, Moss pulled in just long enough to hand over to Brabham. This was a mistake, because Brabham didn't have that same mastery of the Nürburgring and pretty soon he lost a minute's lead to Hawthorn, who then got by him.

Because of the rules which limited any one driver's spell at the wheel, I guess, Moss and Brabham played this game of seesaw with Ferrari once more, and once again Stirling saw the lead he had built up whittled down to nothing. But this time the gearbox held and Moss got the checker with a lead of three minutes and fifty-five seconds over Hawthorn, winning the tricky Nürburgring 1000 k's for Aston two years in a row.

Winning is always a lot of fun and, as a rule, the guy who gets that checker deserves it. Moss certainly did for a brilliant drive, but as far as Roy Salvadori and I were concerned, it was a fairly uninteresting race. One thing I've often been asked is how in the world a driver can memorize all the twists and turns, the corners and bends, in each fourteen-mile lap of the ring? Seems you would need a memory like a computer, but the fact is that you don't. Sure, some drivers are much quicker to learn a circuit than others. That's really what governs the number of practice laps you should drive and the time you need to become familiar with the course. At the ring, I feel you should drive around it until you've put in 200 or 300 miles at varying speeds and then think about it; study the points that still bother you, make a special note of them, and go out and do it all over again for another 200 or 300 miles. Then you'll know exactly where the road goes and just where and how the camber changes and what grade to expect next and how to position your car so you can go full bore through a "blind" turn and come out facing the right way.

This time I went to the top of that old castle overlooking the course and watched from up there and enjoyed a truly beautiful view, more so because the weather was unseasonably good. Those pine-clad Eifel Mountains are really something to behold and even if Hitler did have that circuit built as a kind of a boondoggle, you have to hand him the credit for one of the few useful and constructive things he ever did. I sometimes wonder what kind of an enthusiast dreamed up the countless snakeline twists of this extraordinary circuit, because many of its 176 corners per lap are "blind."

As to how you feel while you're actually driving the Ring in a race, you're never really isolated despite all those strange writhings of the road. During the 1000 k's you can nearly always see someone, either ahead of you or in your mirror, but it's very seldom you get crowded and can't take the proper time to set up your lines.

The German people I never quite understood. They're a bit cold and not too many things happen around you to make much of an impression. Or maybe they appear cold to Americans who can't speak the language. I guess that because of this I must have missed some very amusing things that went on; but one thing does stick in my mind. That year we stayed in the little town of Adenauer and what went on after practice was quite an eyeopener. I'm talking about Saturday nights when everybody got skunked on beer, even the seven- and eight-year-old kids! Mothers and fathers and whole families staggered happily all over the streets while Salvadori and I moved about from one place to another, getting an eyeful of this. I guess it was the first time I'd ever seen an entire city loaded! I've seen a lot of people high at one party, but never a whole town wandering up and down the street inebriated. Well, there's always something new to learn, no matter where you go.

After the Nürburgring came Le Mans—that wonderful twenty-four-hour race to destruction! Salvadori and I were again teamed in a factory DBR1 Aston, along with Moss and Brabham, Brooks and Trintignant. In addition there was the two-year-old DBR1 of the Whitehead brothers. Rain! Boy, you never saw anything like it. For twenty-four hours it just seemed to come down in buckets without any letup. Roy and I both had dysentery, yet I couldn't make up my mind who was the more to be pitied—ourselves or those poor guys huddled up there in that open press stand, compelled to watch cars dash by in a haze of spume for twenty-four hours! Our team seemed to be the favorite among the enormous crowd of 150,000 who gathered there at the start despite the rain. Moss's customary fastest lap time naturally had something to do with this. Moss went around (during practice and on dry roads, of course) at 121.7 mph for a time of 4 minutes, 7 seconds, with Tony Brooks only a little slower and the rest of our team still faster than all the other entries, including the D-Jags and the Ferraris.

However, after a few hours I got so desperately sick that I had to be relieved as co-driver to Salvadori and Stewart Lewis-Evans took my place. At this point, to be honest, I couldn't have cared less. All I wanted to do was he down and die. For the first couple of hours the same relentless battle took place between Moss and Hawthorn, both pushing to the limit and both taking too much out of their cars. Very spectacular, but not always the most profitable race strategy. Anyway, after about three hours of this, Hawthorn's Testa Rossa began to suffer from a slipping clutch, but not even Moss's lead of 1 minute, 35 seconds could save him when his crankshaft broke. Brooks and Trintignant went out during the night with gearbox trouble, while our car also met with disaster when Stewart Lewis-Evans dumped into a sandbank at nine o'clock that evening in an effort to dodge some other car which should have known better. Ironically enough, it was a privately entered, older Aston that finished second behind the Hill-Gendebien Ferrari and saved the day for us.

After Le Mans I got an invitation to drive Formula 1 cars for Scuderia Centro Sud, a racing stable of GP cars then sponsored by a Barcelona auto dealer. It was Mimo Dei, the guy behind Centro Sud, who invited me, and despite the fact that his GP equipment was getting pretty much out of date and noncompetitive, I accepted the offer in order to gain the necessary "open wheel" experience. The cars were mainly old six-cylinder 250F, 2.5-liter Maseratis, which had no chance at all against the kind of opposition that was then beginning to appear—rear-engined stuff like the 2.5-liter Cooper Climax twin cam and such; but at least I learned. I hadn't had a go with a Formula 1 car since 1955 at Syracuse (forgot to mention this earlier), so the experience was doubly welcome. Now I was driving exactly the same kind of Maser as I had done three years earlier, but with a lot more confidence. However, you can't put something in there under the hood when the car doesn't have it and you can't put roadability into an obsolete chassis. I believe I ran three GP races for Centro Sud but only finished in two of them and never did better than sixth. Nothing much worth talking about, really, but it set me up pretty well for Formula 1 racing with Aston Martin the following year.

My most enjoyable Grand Prix, that year, and probably the one in which I had the most fun, although I didn't even finish, was the Portuguese GP (*Grande Epreuve* No. 9) run at Oporto on August 24, over fifty laps. For this one, Temple Buell had lent me the 250F Maserati that had been driven by Fangio at Rheims, where he had experienced a lot of trouble with the front suspension wishbones fouling the chassis. This was now cured and the car had plenty of power for a minimal weight, even though it was already an antiquated design. But somehow that power wasn't converted into anything useful and basic—like speed—and I was forced to lay back and await developments.

The Oporto circuit, for my dough, is one of the nicest in Europe; it's fast yet easy on the car and all its bends and turns are predictable. Finally my chance came after about eleven laps when von Trips had to bring in his Ferrari to secure the hood. I moved up into his slipstream and got a real nice tow and we traded fifth and sixth places several times before I suddenly had a brake lock at the end of the main straight, the Avenida da Boavista, on that right curve heading toward the grandstands. The Maser spun off unpredictably and clouted the sidewalk and that was the end of my drive, but I still had a ball, even though there was nothing in the result to justify talking about it. But some circuits just hit you right, and that one in Portugal with its 4.6-mile laps suited me just fine. I would have liked to go back there.

Meantime, there's another question I've often been asked that I can answer right here: How does it really feel driving an "open-wheel" car, seeing your tire treads spinning around at high speed only a few feet from your head, up front, and much less than that in back? All I can say is that it didn't feel much different to me and after a while I paid no attention to it at all. What I was looking to do was not to learn to accustom myself to a GP car but to find out if it handled any differently from a sports car. It didn't. Either you can drive, or you can't. If you have that driving sense, much like a guy has or does not have a musical ear, then you can handle anything at all. It doesn't matter whether it's an open-wheel car or a sports job, an 1100cc machine or a 4500cc job with slingshot pickup. Your car oversteers or understeers or neutral-steers. Your car goes and stops and if it doesn't do the things it's supposed to do, you find out what the trouble is and try to cure it. If it's handling, it may be the shocks or the springs, or even a simple thing like tire pressures. You'd be surprised, by the way, how effective the right tire pressures can be in curing things like oversteer and understeer. The broad rule is that in an understeering car you put more air in your *front* tires, while with one that oversteers you increase your *rear*-tire pressures. Don't ask me why. I could explain it, I guess, but it can get very confusing and this is not the place.

All in all, though, I don't believe there's all that much difference between good cars. Pigs are something else again. I'm not thinking about them. But I've never heard a person who was an outstandingly good sports car driver say that an openwheeled car bothered him.

Mimo Dei, by the way, was a real enthusiast who ran a driver's school in Europe—a very good one which he operated from Modena and with all kinds of fast cars using the aerodrome there. He even had Taruffi running it for him, but later they moved the whole outfit to the Monza track. I believe that at one time Dei was trying to get financed by a man who was an auto dealer in Brazil, but that deal never did go through and something else opened up.

For me, 1959 was not only my most interesting year in Europe, but it might also be considered as the peak of my racing career. It was the year Salvadori and I won the Le Mans Twenty-four Hours, and it was also a year when I started to drive Aston Martin Formula 1 cars in earnest. I'll tell more about Le Mans in the next chapter; in fact, because so many interesting things happened during and before that race, it became the subject of a book by Stirling Moss—a very good book, well worth reading. But I want to tell that story from my own point of view, so we'll come back to that.

The 2.5-liter Aston Martin GP cars of 1959-60 were really great machines, but they came too late. It was almost at the end of the international formula limiting engines to 2500cc's unsupercharged and they were a bit too heavy. Another thing was that Ferrari and Lotus were already coming out with completely new rear-engine cars which improved handling beyond belief and reduced weight at the same time—especially what is called unsprung weight.

Still, the GP Aston Martin was a fine-handling car, a beautiful design, and in 1959 when I test drove it around Silverstone and Goodwood airfield circuits, our times, compared with those of many other GP machines, showed up pretty well. Of course, Aston and John Wyer were far from happy at the thought that a project on which the David Brown company had lavished a lot of time and a mint of money was about to become obsolete. It kind of put them off the whole business of Grand Prix racing. But the cars were built and tested, the performance came up to expectations, and the races were there. So there was nothing for it but to go ahead.

The first major race we ran, I remember, was at Silverstone, and both Salvadori and I in those new 2.5-liter Astons were right up there with Jack Brabham in his 2.5-liter Cooper Climax. He couldn't get away from either of us. Unfortunately I dropped a valve on the last lap, but Salvadori still finished a close second. But after that, every effort to get more power out of the engine seemed to produce just the opposite effect. They tried this and that; different timing, different cam configurations, modifications to the cylinder head—you name it. All that happened was that the engine seemed to *lose* power on the dyno, while the rear-engined Coopers and Lotuses seemed to improve race by race. It was a very ill-fated Formula 1 effort but a beautiful-handling car. If the rear-engine situation hadn't come up I'm sure we would have at least finished second in the world championship behind Ferrari. We might even have possibly won, but I guess that's hindsight of the worst kind. No one really knows what *might* have happened. What counted was that it *didn't* work out the way we had hoped. Nor did the success of Vanwall and BRM help us much either, come to think of it. The competition was pretty fierce, although the new GP Formula 1 limit of 1500cc's was not scheduled to come into effect until 1961.

For those who like facts and figures and dates, even in limited quantities, a search through the records reveals the following. Work first began on the Aston Martin prototype Formula 1 car in 1957, but was shelved for various reasons in 1958 and not resumed in earnest until in 1959. That was when Salvadori and I agreed to drive more or less regularly for the works team. During 1958, as far as Formula 1 was concerned, the absence of any works racing program caused some of our best regular sports car team drivers to look elsewhere for rides. Moss and Brooks, for example, both went over to Vanwall, then moving toward a crest of success. Roy Salvadori took to a Cooper Climax and our old friend Masten Gregory went that route a year later.

The Aston Martin Formula 1 was such a fine effort and so close to what was needed to make the big time that it deserves a bit more of a technical description than I have given it. I've said it was heavy for that day and it was, tilting the scales at fourteen hundred pounds. Why the power didn't come on as it should, I never did figure out. The engine was a six-cylinder, all aluminum, twin-cam job with valves inclined at 95 degrees, two plugs per cylinder, and three double-choke Weber carburetors. It was mounted vertically, in front, but offset from the longitudinal axis of the car, and drove a combined five-speed gearbox and ZF limited slip differential mounted at the rear. The rear suspension was of the de Dion type with torsion bars, while in front independent coil spring and damper assemblies were used. The car looked very handsome and purposeful and was well finished in every detail. It had a good rigid space frame and I'm not kidding when I say it would outhandle just about any of the other Formula 1 competition of the time. But the engine, for some reason, seemed to develop most of its power at the top end and this led to relatively poor acceleration unless you were prepared to push those revs up constantly to a critical limit and punish the clutch. Also, what power we did get was apparently not in the same league as the 265 to 270 brake horsepower or more of some of the hotter contenders with engines of similar displacement.

I mentioned a while back that our test drive times around Goodwood and Silverstone were way up there with the best of them; well, here's a sample of what I meant. At Goodwood the prototype Aston Martin GP machine came to within two seconds of the absolute record jointly held by Moss (Cooper) and Hawthorn (Ferrari).

But that was in 1959 and I'll come back to it in a moment. Right now, so as not to confuse things, we re talking about 1958; and with the Aston Formula 1 program temporarily on the shelf and not too many sports car entries, we were no more than mildly active in that field. I recall one race at the beginning of May when Roy Salvadori and Tony Brooks finished fourth and fifth with DBR1's in the over-1500cc sports car class of the Daily Express Trophy at Silverstone, but this was not much to brag about. The RAC Tourist Trophy on September 13 at Goodwood was a horse of another color. Here we scored an outstanding win with three factory DBR1's, driven by Moss and Brooks, Salvadori and Brabham, and myself with Lewis-Evans, when we finished one-two-three in that order, all in the same lap. Salvadori had one bad moment when he spun at the Fordwater turn and clobbered a stray Lotus, knocking it out of the race, fortunately without injury to the driver. Ivor Bueb in a Lister-Jaguar, who happened to be close at hand—a bit too close for his own good!—took what the British press called "violent evasive action" to get out of the way. Unfortunately for him, he was so successful that he ended up in a ditch and stayed there. Roy was able to carry on, though he spent twenty-four seconds chewing his nails in the pit while Reg Parnell made sure the car was okay and safe for him to drive. He didn't lose his finishing spot, after all, and the fourth place Behra-Barth Porsche was four laps behind while the nearest D-Jag of Gregory and Ireland (fifth) was five laps behind.

In December, as a makeweight, I drove John Edgar's 4.5 Maserati at Nassau in the Tourist Trophy, and for a time things looked very good. I took the lead at the end of the first lap, closely followed by Pedro Rodriguez in a three-liter Ferrari and Chuck Daigh's Scarab. Bruce Kessler was driving another John Edgar entry, a 4.9 Ferrari, and Jim Rathman still another, a Maserati-Pontiac! Rathman, a great Indy guy, went out almost right away as did Daigh, but Rodriguez stuck to me like glue and by the fifth lap he was still there and a few yards closer, with Reventlow's Scarab now third, thirty-six seconds behind and no great threat. On lap eleven, however, Reventlow took Rodriguez and moved into second spot, and a lap later Kessler was out with a flat tire.

So was I, at just about the time I had begun to think that this race and a nice jackpot might be in my pocket if I played it canny. I got back to my pit as quickly as I could with a tire that was torn to shreds, and the Edgar crew put on two new tires (rear ones) for me in a smart twenty-eight seconds. Nice work, except that when I pressed the starter it wouldn't work. And that was the end of the race for me, and also of a pretty spotty 1958 season, in which few of my European hopes seemed to have materialized.

But if, as that famous British automotive writer and former race driver—S. C. H. "Sammy" Davis—so aptly put it, "Motor racing is a mixture of exhilaration with absolute despair," luckily for the race driver he recovers quickly from the knocks and is ever ready for another "go."

The following year, 1959, we were quite active at Aston, both with sports and GP cars. In June, Salvadori and I won the Le Mans Twenty-four Hours in a DBR1/300 which ran like a charm and never missed a beat, but I want to come back to that in the next chapter. Too many interesting things happened for us to pass that one up in a few paragraphs; in fact it proved to be the high point not only of the European trip but also of my entire racing career. That year, too, Aston Martin won the International Manufacturers' Championship for sports cars by winning three major international races out of four, one of which was, of course, Le Mans.

As a side comment, Aston Martin came out with a very handsome GT coupe in 1959, called the DB4, but this was not raced and was intended primarily for export and for enthusiasts in the home market. Only a limited production was intended.

But to get back to the racing, I think it would help keep the record straight if we kept the sports car races and the Formula 1 Grand Prix which we ran entirely separate. We did extremely well with the D BR1/300 and extremely poorly with the GP car. So we might as well start with the happier experiences first.

At Sebring, in March, we had one factory car entered which was driven by Salvadori and me. The result was a DNF—a flop, but for a real oddball reason. The car was the same as the 1958 model, but after a meteoric start it dropped out with clutch trouble. The thing that skunked us was *too much* oil pressure! The oil blew past the seal into the clutch housing and by the time this excessive oil pressure was detected and put right, it was too late. The damage had been done.

Roy was first away at the Le Mans start, going like a cat on a hot tin roof. But the race was less than an hour old when he made his first pit stop with a slipping clutch. This dropped us way back, and after a restart that proved nothing, the car was retired. A privately entered Aston Martin GT, driven by Sheppard and Furlong, also quit in the first hour with a blown cylinder head gasket. Not our day. Ferrari romped home in the first three places.

The next big one on the sports car calendar was the Targa Florio on May 24, but we skipped that one for various reasons. Barth and Seidel scored an unexpected win with a Porsche.

Then came the Nürburgring 1000 k's, June 7, and this marked the start of our winning streak. We ran only one factory entry in that rough grind and that was a DBR1/300 driven by Moss and Fairman. The second car was a private GT entry of Whitehead and Naylor; a supporting cast, you might call it. But as it turned out, Moss and Fairman needed no help. They won the race against huge odds and the toughest opposition, and so cut the first notch in our sports car belt. Carroll Shelby didn't do too badly, either. I drove a Porsche for Wolfgang Seidel of Germany and for at least the first three laps made out like a bandit. The car ran extremely well and I was leading all the works entries without having to push too hard, when we dropped a valve. Just one of those things, and I can't help feeling that but for this engine trouble the result would have been very different.

Le Mans, which took place two weeks later (June 21-22), I intend to talk about in some detail a bit later and tell how Roy and I took home the marbles, although (as in the previous year) we both suffered from dysentery and ran the race on Coca-Colas!

The wind-up of the sports car season, and our third straight win, was the Tourist Trophy at Goodwood, September 5. While it cinched the International Manufacturers' Championship for us, it was nothing like the snap that it had been the year before. This time, Reg Parnell had shuffled things around a bit, so that Roy drove with Stirling while I shared a car with Jack Fairman. Trintignant, however, stayed with Frère, perhaps because of the language problem! We also had two private Aston Martin entries, one of them driven by Whitehead; but that wasn't all. Next, we had a fire which consumed our lead car, bathed the entire pit in flames, gave Salvadori some minor but painful burns, and consumed Parnell's briefcase with a lot of the firm's money in it!

At the start, we knew this was going to be a keen one. Ferrari had 18 points to our 16 for that season, while Porsche's score was 15 points. Anything could happen and both the Italians and Germans came loaded for bear. There were three 12-cylinder, Le Mans type three-liter Testa Rossa Ferraris to be driven by Brooks-Gurney, Hill-Allison, and Gendebien-Cabianca, and Porsche also had three cars. These were the latest 1700cc jobs with von Trips-Bonnier, Maglioli-Barth, and Herrmann-Bristow. There was a lot of other stuff, too, but these were the principal contenders and no one was kidding. The score was much too close for that.

However, we did have what the press called a "secret weapon," and that was a new type of compressed-air jacking system with one built-in jack at each corner of the car. Just to help the psychological warfare along, we gave a little demonstration and were able to change four tires and refuel in a maximum of thirty seconds, while the fastest Ferrari could do was a whole minute!

Goodwood is a nice course, but I'd say a lap of under two miles was a bit short for an event of this sort, when you have to keep going around and around for six hours! Anyway, off we went. Moss pulled out in front right away and I followed him, with Whitehead, one of our private entries, hanging on to my coattails!

The first casualty, soon after the race started, was Phil Hill, whose Ferrari was sidelined with a broken rocker arm. Not a thing that happens very often. But the field quickly changed positions, and although when Moss opened the taps wide I was able to stay with him without sweating it out, poor Whitehead quickly fell back and was gobbled up by Dan Gurney (Ferrari), who drove with the dash and skill and determination of an old pro. Things stayed that way for the next hour, with me thoroughly enjoying myself around that Goodwood circuit and Dan trying every trick he knew to close the gap on me.

An hour and twenty minutes after the start, Parnell flagged Moss in, had the car refueled and the tires changed (Goodwood is murder on tires!), put Salvadori in the driving seat, and got the car away again in twenty-eight seconds, still in first place. Next, Fairman took over from me and also kept second, while Edgar Barth's 1700 Porsche now held third and Frère, spelling for Trintignant, fourth spot.

Well, there was some more of this merry-go-round, and pretty soon it was time for Salvadori to hand back our lead car to Moss—and that's when the fireworks really started. Seems like the high-pressure hose was thrust toward the gas filler and someone squeezed the grip before it was properly home. Gas spilled on one of the disc brakes that was almost red hot and the next thing that happened the car was enveloped in a mass of leaping flames. Roy jumped out with his coveralls burning but managed to put the fire out by rolling on the ground. Still he had to be treated for bums on his arms and face which were luckily more painful than serious.

Considering that the pits were made of wood, it was a miracle that the fire didn't spread and engulf the whole works, but the British fire brigade did its stuff with typical coolness and got matters under control soon enough. They weren't able to save the car, of course, but I learned that our timers and scorers kept right on with their job while the pit was blazing away merrily around them!

Scratch one, so Parnell called in Fairman, put Moss into our car, and let the three of us share it—Moss, Fairman, and myself. Of course this little caper had cost us the lead; in fact it had dropped us back to third place. Bonnier's Porsche was now leading with Gendebien's Ferrari chasing him the way a dog chases a cat. But Stirling didn't take long to reshuffle things and get back into the lead. By 3:30 P.M., a little past the halfway mark, he was once more at the head of the pack with the Porsche and Ferrari snapping at his heels and Trintignant's Aston nicely holding off Maglioli's Porsche and the Brooks-Gurney Ferrari. So that put Aston in first and fourth places and everyone in our pits breathed a sigh of relief. But the fat was far from being out of the fire! With the score as it stood, in order to win the championship we not only had to win the race but also had to keep Ferrari out of the second slot. Otherwise it would be a tie—24-24. Remember, it was 8 points for a win, 6 for second, and 4 for third.

Parnell scratched that wise old head of his, but even he couldn't get around this simple arithmetic or figure out how to prevent a Ferrari from finishing second, always assuming nothing more happened to Moss!

During the last hour of the race, seeing that the situation was desperate, Ferrari had an emergency bull session and decided on an immediate change of strategy. They called in their two fastest drivers, Brooks and Gurney, and put them in the Gendebien-Allison Ferrari, which was closest to the Porsche, in a last-ditch endeavor to catch the Germans.

It didn't work.

Bonnier and von Trips, whose Porsche was going great guns, weren't about to give up their hard-earned second place, so they did the trick for us. They kept Ferrari out of that slot and so ensured that we got the championship. Full credit was also due to Moss, though, for the way he pushed that Aston around during the closing stages. No one could get near him. He set a new Goodwood lap record of 1 minute, 32 seconds, and got the checker a full lap ahead of the

Porsche! Some guys react brilliantly under pressure and Moss was certainly one of those. The more pressure on him, the faster he went.

So, anyway, we ended the season with a score of 24 points; Ferrari had 22 (18 plus 4 for a third place); and Porsche 21 (15 plus 6 for a second place.) It was close enough.

So much for the sugar-coating, and now for the pill, which was the Grand Prix side of our season's racing. We ran four races in all: the Dutch GP at Zandvoort, May 31; the British GP at Aintree, July 18; the Portuguese PG at Oporto, August 23; the Italian GP at Monza, September 13; and that was it. We skipped the German GP at the Avus which took place two weeks later, because that happened to be the fastest track in the world and one thing we did *not* have was speed.

I think a brief review of these four unhappy races is worthwhile, because it serves to show how consistently we were bugged by the same combination of troubles, even though we had one of the best handling GP cars then available—if not the best.

At Zandvoort, although my practice times were only 2.5 seconds slower than those of poleman Joe Bonnier (BRM), I landed in the fourth row of the grid. That's how close the times were. I went out with a seized engine in that one, but not before I had a hairy moment that scared me plenty. It happened on a fast sweep at about 150 mph and I headed for the nearest sandbank, completely out of control, so I went for the bottom of the car to get as much protection as possible. But suddenly it decided to come back to the middle of the road in a big puddle of oil, with cars whizzing by on both sides of me, only inches away! Zandvoort is what you might call a cold circuit, with lots of sand and very few trees. This is not surprising since it was built in the Dutch dunes, only a few miles from The Hague. It's as though you were to build a circuit say in Amarillo, Texas—a circuit that really has nothing of an airport course yet somehow reminds you of one. The roads are narrow and not too smooth and I think that of all the circuits I ever drove on, Zandvoort did the least for me. The way the place got built is interesting enough, though. The Mayor of Zandvoort got the labor together and was given permission to build the course right under the noses of the occupying Germans. In those days they didn't seem to have much doubt as to who was going to win the war.

By the way, right through this unhappy four-race program with GP Aston Martins, Roy and I were the regular works drivers. At Zandvoort, so far as I recall, he didn't finish either. He started in the row behind me, less than one second slower, but somewhere along the way his engine, too, quit.

In the next one, the British Grand Prix at Aintree in Lancashire, I must say that Salvadori's practice times filled us with great hopes. This was the twelfth British GP, run on a course of 2.98 miles, just outside Liverpool, and we lost very little sleep at the prospect of the works Ferraris not showing up. There had been some kind of a strike in Modena. Roy's car, fitted with a new body carrying No. 2, and a four-speed transmission in place of the usual five speeds, put up fastest practice time of 1:58, along with Brabham's Cooper. So that put them both in the front row of the grid. I was in the third row, I recall, with a time of 1:59.6, and once again couldn't find any of that much-needed power low down. It rained to beat hell, then eased off, then drizzled, but Roy and I managed to finish sixth and seventh, although Salvadori kept getting sprayed by an oil leak and I lost one magneto and a lot of power I could ill spare. There's no doubt that but for the excellent roadability of our cars we would have finished much lower down.

Then came the Oporto GP, which, as I've said, happens to be my favorite course for that kind of racing. The year before, driving the outdated Maserati, I'd locked a brake. "What," I wondered, "is going to happen *this* year?"

Salvadori and I both found ourselves in the fifth row of the grid, with only three-tenths of a second difference in our times! He clocked 2:13.28 and I clocked 2:13.58. Well, our cars looked great on the turns and handled about as well as they looked, but speed— we hadn't any. Acceleration? What's that? Roy finished sixth and I was eighth, I think, though still ahead of Tony Brooks's Ferrari, which must surely have been running on half its cylinders! End of round three. Very little fun, this time, and even less money!

Then came Monza and the Italian GP and the end of our sorry efforts in Formula 1. Monza isn't the fastest course in Europe—the

Avus is (which was why we skipped the German GP that followed two weeks later)—but we shouldn't even have gone to Monza. For the last time in Aston Martin GP racing, Salvadori and I represented the factory team, but they had now given Roy back his five-speed box. Otherwise he had the same car as the one they'd offered him for the British GP, redesigned body and all, but no more horses. Salvadori's practice times put him in the seventh row with 1:44.7, while I was in the eighth with a slightly slower time. Moss did fastest in a Cooper, clocking 1:39.7, and he won it going away. We were completely outpaced and I did well, I reckon, to finish at all, which I did—in tenth spot out of fifteen finishers and twenty starters. Roy went out before the end when something broke, but I no longer remember what it was. You try to put the bad ones out of your mind and I had no difficulty forgetting all about those GP outings with a machine that was out of date even before it could be fully developed.

And that about wraps up the 1959 season I had in Europe with Aston Martin; a season wonderful in some ways and miserable in others, but surely one that I'll never forget as long as I five. After David Brown won the championship that year, he retired his cars and that ended my direct association with the company, so far as racing was concerned. Needless to say, we've remained on the best of terms ever since, and if there's a finer bunch of people around than the Aston Martin group, I'd like to meet them.

–12–
WORLD'S TOUGHEST RACE

SOME DRIVERS THINK Le Mans is boring, and for that matter so do many spectators. Other drivers feel strongly about the danger element which results from having very fast cars and relatively slow cars all going around the same circuit together at the same time. I think they have their point, too, but a poor driver is going to get in your way, no matter what kind of a car he's in. Not much can be done about that except to try to reduce the speed differential a little by not permitting cars below at least 1000cc to run, which is what the FIA has done anyway.

Now if you want my honest opinion about the Le Mans Twenty-four Hours, I think it's much too long. It knocks the hell out of a driver and it knocks the hell out of a car, and I don't know how much it really proves. You can learn an awful lot about a car in a twelve-hour race. Still, I guess there's nothing quite like the prestige and publicity you get from winning at Le Mans, certainly not in the sports car racing game, though for myself I'd sooner go Grand Prix racing. Two or three hours is about as much as I like to drive in any one race.

Yet, looking back on Le Mans of 1959, despite that durned dysentery that seemed to hit Roy and me every time we went back there, I wouldn't have missed that race for the world. So many things about it stick in my mind that I don't really know just where to begin.

First it was something that David Brown and the team from Feltham, Middlesex, had dreamed of for years and never quite made. In the nine years, 1950 through 1958, Aston Martin had finished second three times and won the three-liter class five times. On five different occasions (1952, 1953, 1954, 1957, and 1958) the entire team was wiped off the slate, either with mechanical trouble or by accidents, but never before one or more of the Astons ran the opposition ragged while they ran and put up an outstanding performance.

The year that I won it with Salvadori was actually the factory team's tenth consecutive try, and no matter who might have been the winner among our three entries, David Brown sure as heck deserved that success. But don't imagine for a moment he just took things as they came and left anything to chance. On the contrary, Mr. Brown was more determined than ever to have one of his cars "show the way home" to the opposition, and on his orders an enormous amount of care and time was lavished in preparing the cars for the race. This was one of the reasons why only one works Aston ran at the Nürburgring two weeks before Le Mans, and the fact that Moss and Fairman won with it was not interpreted as having any special meaning in regard to the Twenty-four-Hour race.

Another thing that left me open-mouthed was the fantastic organization engineered into the team's schedule by that bluff but tremendously efficient Derbyshire farmer, Reg Parnell. In what he termed the "Aston Martin Movement Schedule" from Sunday, June 14, through Tuesday, June 23, he didn't miss a trick. Every mechanic and every driver was accounted for at all times; each of us knew exactly when he would leave, when he would get to Le Mans, and when he would start back for Feltham. Also what he would be doing during every working moment in between. It was even decided beforehand just what plane back to England Alan Dakers, the Aston Martin public relations guy, would take in case we *did* win the race and just how the publicity would be handled! Reservations, tires, gas, spare parts, transportation—you name it—every last detail was worked out beforehand about as efficiently as the Germans at their best. For some of these logistics, like room reservations and trying to cram fifty people into forty rooms and seeing they were all fed at the proper times, full credit must go to a gal named Jill Harris, who was secretary to the Racing Department at Aston Martin. How she did it, I'll never know, but I'm pretty sure the average male would never have held up under the terrific pressure that was put on her. If anything went wrong that didn't directly involve the cars, the first thing you did, without even thinking, was holler, "Jill!" And she was always there to set things straight.

Let me give you just one small example. I'd brought my son Pat with me to Le Mans that year and the lad was anxious to go fishing. Pat was twelve, then, and the River Loire held a kind of irresistible lure for him as a fisherman. So I called out, "Jill!" and she said, "Yes, Carroll?" And I said, "What's the French for worms'?" And she told me but I couldn't pronounce it properly, so she said, "Leave that to me." And in a very short time Pat had enough worms to catch all the fish in the Loire!

That was about the way it went.

As to the team of drivers, our three cars were allocated as follows: Moss and Fairman, No. 4; Salvadori and I, No. 5; Trintignant and Frère, No. 6. All three cars were the latest DBRI/300 Astons, and for those buffs who like technical stuff I can refresh your memory with a few details. The engines were six-cylinder, twin overhead-cam units of 2,992cc with a compression ratio of 9 to 1 and an output of 260 brake horsepower at 6000 rpm. There wasn't much sense in going above that limit, especially in a long and grueling race like Le Mans, though peak torque of I forget how many pounds/ft came in at a high 5500 rpm. There were three Weber 50-DCO sidedraft carburetors, fed from a forty-gallon (Imperial) gas tank, and the oil tank held 4.5 gallons. The gearbox had five speeds, but what amazed me was the very small capacity of the 12-volt battery, which was only 10 amps. It's true that once the generator is working you're taking nothing out of your battery, but every time you make a start it's a dead short. And if the engine happens to get balky—! Well, it's taking a lot on trust.

There was a small weight difference of about ten pounds between each of the three cars, although in every detail they were identical. The Trintignant-Frère machine was the heaviest at 1900 pounds, we were ten pounds lighter, and the Moss-Fairman car scaled the least at 1880 pounds. All three cars had right-hand drive, of course, but on a clockwise circuit that's an advantage definitely helpful on corners or when passing another car on the inside.

The cockpit was nicely laid out with a big tach smack in front of you, complete with telltale hand! The oil and water temperature gauges were either side of this, also plainly in view, as was the oil pressure gauge at upper left. Seating was comfortable, but after a very short time the heat in the cockpit became absolutely unbearable. It was like being in a Turkish bath! One of the reasons was that on this model they carried the twin outgoing-exhaust pipes directly under the drivers brake and clutch pedals, and as if to make things even worse, the ample air ducts used in previous years had been dropped in favor of hood louvers that let absolutely no fresh air into the cockpit. Each of us drivers, I think, suffered more from heat prostration than actual fatigue or tension or anything else.

If we're going to talk about the drivers, then the mechanics and many other useful guys behind the scenes also deserve mention. Bearded chief mechanic Eric Hind, and his boys, Jack Sopp, Hones, Creswick, Murray Litt, and Smith really did a great job in preparing and maintaining the cars; the Avon tire fellows, "Tommy" Thomas and C. Herbert, worked like Trojans keeping us shod; while K. Suckhy and John Dalton of the Aston Martin "Catering Department" kept that chow wagon going great guns throughout the twenty-four hours, so no one ever had to go short of something to eat. In fact, we caught Innes Ireland red-handed, enjoying an Aston Martin meal after his Jaguar quit!

La Chartre, a picturesque and lost little village a few kilometers outside Le Mans, was the place where our team stayed and where we worked on the cars, practiced pit stops, and went swimming in the Loire. Aston had been coming here for several years and the pleasant isolation of the place was very restful, off duty. To preserve my sanity and avoid blowing my top, I had a minimum to do with Le Mans scrutineering, which is about the biggest bunch of hokum you ever saw and is designed for one purpose only—to infuriate entrants and drivers and raise their blood pressure! Instead, Roy Salvadori and I played endless games of gin rummy and Masten Gregory (who came visiting) taught Roy some fancy new card game and promptly lost seventy-five dollars to the beginner!

There was a fourth Aston in the race, as a matter of fact—a DB4 coupe which was to be driven in the GT class by Aston Martin's Swiss distributor, Patthey, but he kept apart from the factory team, although our mechanics gave him all the help he needed. The

Hotel de France, however, at La Chartre, was our clubhouse by tradition since John Wyer had discovered the place years before.

Naturally, when you win a long race like Le Mans—an endurance event—people always ask what your "strategy" was; what kind of plans you formulated beforehand which in some mysterious way enabled you to put the hex on the other competitors! Well, that one's easily answered. So far as Roy and I were concerned, we *had* no strategy except for one thing—we planned to be the two most relaxed drivers in that twenty-four-hour grind. Roy had been to Le Mans so many times and always had some kind of trouble with his car that we couldn't see planning a dam thing. In fact, I guess we did less actual practicing on the Sarthe circuit than any other drivers. We just quit worrying about the whole business. Reg Parnell had given us a maximum lap time, so we decided to just go out there and keep a little bit inside that and forget the rest. If we finished fifth, we finished fifth. If we won it, we won it. I guess it wasn't too corny a philosophy at that. We just avoided getting under any pressure at all. Also there was a very friendly team spirit with no jealousy or rivalry, where everyone was anxious to work together. You can't beat that. So many teams min their chances because every two-bit driver acts like a prima donna and wants to steal the show. All I was interested in was trying to make a worthwhile living out of motor racing, and I guess Roy felt exactly the same.

Of course we had certain basic orders from Reg, and he wasn't kidding when he told each of us what he expected, but none of this was designed to put pressure on anyone. I doubt, in fact, if I can do any better than quote pretty much word for word what Parnell told us at our briefing.

"Now Roy and Carroll. Roy will start and do thirty-four laps with a fuel load of thirty-two gallons. Your plan time will be 4 minutes, 20 seconds, providing conditions are the same as now—hot and dry. This plan time is the same for both of you. Remember the signals. Hand on your helmet if you have to go on reserve. Point to the signaling pit at Mulsanne if you have to come in. That's all, except one thing: remember, both of you, to save your brakes. Don't use them as hard as you did in practice or you'll be in trouble. You had the highest brake wear of the three cars. This year it's a bit harder to change those pads, so we want to reduce that kind of work to a minimum. The pads will be checked during tire changes, but as you won't need new tires until your third pit stop, it might be too late to warn you about that then. Anyway, I should think that with a 4:20 average you'd be able to keep off 'em quite a bit. Any questions, Roy?"

"None that I can think of, right now."

"You, Carroll?"

"I guess we can use the same rev limit as Stirling?"

"You can, but you shouldn't have to. With our present torque curve, there's nothing to be gained by going through the gears higher than 5700 rpm. If Stirling can get a tow, his limit is 6100 rpm. Otherwise a strict 6000. That goes for all of you. Remember that Stirling's job is to extend the opposition as much as he can without breaking the car."

We knew that using the 3.24 rear-axle ratio installed in the car, along with 7.00 × 16 tires, 6000 rpm in fifth gear would mean about 165 mph, and that wasn't bad. It was much better than ever before, in fact. We also knew through the grapevine that the new three-liter Ferraris had an 8000 rpm limit, but if they kept this up the oil pressure started to go down. Also, none of the drivers seemed very happy about the way these cars handled, although no one could tell exactly why.

"Watch out for the Ecurie Ecosse D-Jags," was Parnell's parting shot. "They may turn out to be our greatest threat."

We also had the use of a beautifully prepared map that showed the exact shift points for every turn and bend, along with what rpm to use and which gear. I'd thought we probably might not be able to use fifth much beyond the long Mulsanne Straight, but as it turned out we were able to use it in two other important places: accelerating out of Mulsanne Corner between kilometers 8 and 9; and again out of that nasty right-angled turn out of Arnage, close to kilometer 11. In fact, you could stay in fifth right through the White House, easing off to about 4500 rpm and then on past the pits and under the Dunlop Bridge, right down to the Esses just beyond kilometer 1. On Mulsanne you could shift into fifth gear shortly after kilometer 3 and then hold 6000 rpm all the way down to about 350 yards with a full tank or 300 yards with a partly empty one, before you stood on the binders. Instructions were so precise that we were told not to exceed 5700 rpm in third going through the Esses, and so on.

This was what you might call driving to a blueprint, but it worked just fine. In fact I'd say it won the day for us. All we had to do as a team was to follow Reg Parnell's simple instructions, given in that broad Derbyshire brogue of his (boy—I'll bet my Texan "drawl" sounded just as odd to him!), and provided the car stayed together we couldn't very well go wrong. I don't mean by this that we held the winning number in our pockets. Hell, no. Le Mans is the biggest motor racing gamble of them all, and luck I would say plays an 80 per cent part in whether you finish at all; but at least by careful preparation, good pitwork, and sensible discipline you reduce the pitfalls to the level of calculated risks. And that's saying plenty, believe me.

Stirling Moss's problem was a little different. He was supposed to set the pace for the team and fill a minimum requirement. "If you find you can't keep in contact with the Ferraris," Reg Parnell told him, "you have just got to maintain the gap between yourself and them. Ferrari will probably have to change their brakes as often as we will, so if there's anything you can save, save the brakes."

"Okay," Moss nodded.

"On the other hand," Parnell went on, "I don't mean you to come back and say I saved the brakes and I'm ten seconds a lap slower, wasn't I marvelous!"

"What tire pressures are we running?" Fairman wanted to know.

"Fifty-five pounds," Parnell said, "but you don't have to bother yourselves with tires. They'll be looked after."

His words turned out to be more prophetic than he imagined, because as it happened a tire problem was one of the major Aston Martin dramas of the race. But I'm getting a bit ahead of myself.

When it came to Trintignant and Frère, the team manager was equally explicit. "Maurice will start," he said. "We want you to do thirty-two laps each—*trente-deux*, Maurice! Translate that for him, will you, Paul? We might bring you in at thirty laps, but I'm not sure. We'll just wait and see what happens. Now your plan time. My original idea was to run you at 4:24, and I still think it would be a wise move. At that speed there's a good chance you might be able to make your brakes last the entire race. At the faster times you did in practice, they'll only last sixteen and a half hours. Anyhow, be that as it may, I've decided to run you at 4:22. Okay?"

Both drivers nodded that they understood, but Parnell added an interesting side thought. "I'm *convinced*," he said, "that this race will not be won at a greater speed than 4:24."

There was a good bit more of this kind of meticulous briefing that I don't remember, but Stirling Moss sure sums it up well in his book on the 1959 Le Mans race by saying, "As you'll appreciate, there's a lot more running in the Twenty-four Hours than just jumping in a car at four o'clock on Saturday and putting your foot down!"

There sure is.

Because of the job they had to do, Moss and Fairman were not set any actual lap times; instead, as you'll remember, Parnell gave them a rev limit—which also held good for the rest of us. When the briefing was over, I asked Stirling casually a question which I had put to him before and about which I knew he had been thinking.

"You still think Ferrari's going to win this thing? I mean after all that display of temperament Tavoni [the team manager] has had to cope with?"

"Figure it out for yourself, old boy," Moss said. "Those three works cars are very fast indeed. Gendebien and Phil Hill [who won it last year] and the Behra-Gurney combination are going to take a lot of beating. Even their junior members—Allison, Da Silva Ramos, and Gurney—have all been lapping in practice around 4 minutes, 5 seconds. It's obvious, therefore, that all three cars are capable of being run at the same speed, and that's faster than we can go. But a lot of things can go wrong, of course."

"One of them may push that fast, but I doubt if they all will," I said.

"That's why I think they'll last," Moss said. "And if one of them gets through, that's enough. They'll win."

"You're just a natural optimist." Salvadori laughed. "Besides those three, I'd say the Ferrari competition doesn't have to keep us awake thinking about it. The other seven are all privately entered GT machines, and nothing too much to worry about if we keep going."

"Don't discount them, either," Moss said. "Their drivers are going to keep chugging on at a nice, easy pace and one of them could easily win on reliability alone."

"How about a little hand of gin rummy?" Salvadori said.

Moss was too impatient to spend much time playing cards, but Roy and I got into those interminable games and found them soothing and a lot of fun. They passed the time, anyway, when we might have been standing first on one foot, then on the other, asking ourselves and anyone else who'd listen: "Whaddaya think of the Jags?" Or "What's the Ferrari strategy going to be?" Or "Can we hack the kind of lap times that are even going to make those Ferrari boys look at us?"

What the average driver forgets is that while he's fretting his guts out with all kinds of frightening mental pictures about the opposition, the opposition isn't any better off, psychologically. Its drivers are doing exactly the same thing.

I don't intend to give you here a blow-by-blow, or even an hour-by-hour, description of what turned out to be the greatest and most important race of my life, because to try to do this would take a book and at least one very good book has been written by Stirling Moss about Le Mans, 1959. So what I'll try to do instead is give you the highlights as I saw them, both from the sidelines and the cockpit.

Moss got off to his usual flying start, although he wasn't actually the first guy to get into his car; but he made a real smooth getaway and led the pack and came around at the end of the first lap leading the whole field, hotly pursued by the Innes Ireland Ecurie Ecosse Jag, Trintignant in our No. 6 Aston, Flockhart with another Ecosse Jag, Bueb's Lister-Jag, and Graham Hill. Behra, whose Testa Rossa was feared about equally with the Gendebien-Hill Ferrari, made a very poor start and came around twelfth on the second lap. But then he really started to fly. He was tenth on the third lap, ninth on the fourth, and by the seventh lap he'd moved up to fourth spot. Moss, meantime, wasn't exactly sitting around chewing on straw, either. He'd opened the gap on himself and the two Ferraris of Gendebien and Da Silva Ramos, which by then were in second and third positions, and we'd clocked him on one lap at 4 minutes, 7.9

seconds—well inside whatever maximum lap time Reg Parnell might have had in mind. That's for sure! And of course Stirling couldn't take advantage of any "tow," since there was no one ahead of him. Next time around, Behra answered with a 4-minute, 4.1-second lap, getting by Ramos into third. There was no holding the Frenchman with the plastic ear, and, boy, when that guy got the bit between his teeth he was a hard man to stay up with, let alone beat. Besides, he and Moss had become sort of traditional rivals and Behra made it clear he liked driving sports cars a whole lot better than he did GP jobs. Just the opposite from me.

Behra wasn't finished yet and there was nothing we could do to help Stirling. He was getting the last ounce out of the car without running over the edge, but he couldn't hold off the Frenchman much more. On the seventeenth lap we got a call from our Mulsanne pit and a rather tense voice said, "Behra came around first. He took Stirling on the long straight."

"Not to worry," Parnell said mildly. "This is just the beginning. And what did you expect, anyway? We can't match those bloody Ferraris in speed to within twenty miles an hour!"

"Thought you'd like to know so you wouldn't be surprised when the Ferrari comes by the pit straight in the lead."

"Make yourself a cup of tea," Parnell said and signed off.

We had the watches on Behra, of course, as well as Stirling and we'd known for several laps what was going to happen—especially when Jean put in a lap at a sizzling 4 minutes, 3 seconds.

But things weren't so bad as they seemed and Reg was right, as he nearly always was. Behra had to come in and hand over to Gurney, which put us back in the lead; then Moss came in and Fairman took over and was away in no time, thanks to the marvelous Aston Martin pitwork. Fairman, however, while an excellent driver, was of a different temperament from Moss. It took him a few laps to warm up, as might be expected, and Dan took full advantage of this to gain ten seconds a lap on us. Phil Hill was in third place with the second Testa Rossa, followed by Allison, who had relieved Ramos in the third Ferrari. Masten Gregory, now spelling Ireland in the Ecosse Jaguar, was going great guns and all four cars were in the same lap. A lap behind came Lawrence in the Ecosse Tojeiro-Jag, followed by our own Paul Frère, running strictly according to Parnells orders and saving those brake pads and the engine.

Soon after, we learned that the Allison Ferrari had been wheeled into the dead-car park, and that good old American expression, "Scratch one!" was the first thing that came to my mind. Via the grapevine, we also learned that all was not well with the Ferrari works team, despite their much higher speed. They were undergeared and to get 180 mph in fifth, which they could only use in one place, and then only for a short time, they had to wind up to 8000 rpm. "Were not far from flat out all the way down Mulsanne," Allison confided, "although Tavoni set us a 7500 rpm limit which was unrealistic. No one's bothered to observe it!"

On the forty-sixth lap, Gurney got by Fairman into the lead, and three laps later Hill also took him; yet we could see from the lap times that Jack was getting the swing of things nicely and that it wasn't his fault. He just didn't have the speed.

At about the third hour, Roy came in and handed over to me, and he had nothing to complain about except the appalling heat in the cockpit. "Wish we could strap some icebags to our feet!" he quipped, but he was obviously in some pain from the vicious cooking of those searing-hot exhaust pipes passing just under the floorboards. Two laps earlier, Trintignant had already pulled in and handed over to Frère while the car took in twenty-seven gallons of fuel. Maurice, too, said "Ouch!" when you asked him about his feet.

When my turn came, I'd just gotten over an attack of cramps from that durned green-apple quickstep, politely called dysentery, although it was nothing like as bad as it had been the previous year. Neither was Roy's similar complaint, although I think his cooked feet turned his mind to other things. How many ailments can you worry about at once!

Our pit stop took only fifty-three seconds, and dining that time they pumped in thirty gallons—Parnell had figured it right on the button—checked the tires and oil and water and asked if anything was wrong, which it wasn't.

Moss, meantime, had taken No. 4 back from Fairman and again had it through the gate, driving to the absolute limit without getting off the road. When he pulled in again, thirty-eight laps later, we were back in the lead and Moss had opened up a ninety-second gap on the closest Ferrari—enough for a free pit stop. That pit stop took only sixty-five seconds, so Jack got off without having lost the lead. Moss has that great knack of cutting a fifth of a second here and a tenth of a second there and maybe half a second some other place, and it all adds up on any one lap. Multiply that by thirty or more laps and you've got the reason why he could outpace much faster cars whose drivers, good as they were, just didn't quite have the Moss touch.

Meantime, back at the ranch, a guy named Carroll Shelby, sitting in a pool of his own sweat—pardon me, perspiration!—was tooling around as relaxed as Perry Como in a car that ran real sweet. There wasn't a thing I could put my finger on, apart from that ghastly heat, that wasn't right on the button. I was pretty much used to the handling of Astons by then, and I could only feel sorry for the Testa Rossa boys, all of whom claimed during practice that their cars didn't really handle well. When you asked what it was, they didn't know. But either you can predict exactly what your car is going to do, or you're trying to walk across a darkened room on a floor strewn with marbles! And that's nobody's idea of a picnic.

We were in fourth place at this time (about 8 P.M.), with the Behra-Gurney Testa Rossa leading (Dan at the wheel), Jack Fairman in second, and the Ireland-Gregory Ecosse Jag holding third. Jack was doing a very nice job, consistently lapping around 4:12 to 4:13 on a wet track, but, as I said, he didn't have the speed and there was no sense in wrecking the car. The cars behind me weren't pushing me especially hard, so I kept a wary eye on that rev limit and Parnell seemed perfectly happy. Back of his mind, he may not have counted too much on No. 4 going the distance, but cars 5 and 6 were his reserve troops and he wasn't going to ask us to do anything that might jeopardize our chances of finishing—because everyone who knows the first thing about Le Mans knows that if you finish you can't help finishing "in the money." It's what the boys with the vocabularies call a "war of attrition." With one of the three Testa Rossas already out of the race this soon and because the Ecosse Jags didn't have that much on us, our chances went up correspondingly, no matter how you sliced it.

Another thing that was going for us was that the Gendebien-Hill Ferrari had already made a couple of longish pit stops, and that was why they were running eighth, behind No. 6 Aston of Trintignant and Frère. Another notable retirement at this time was the Lister-Jaguar of Hansgen and Blond. And long ago, our DB4 Aston driven by Whitehead had been pretty badly shunted at the White House by Naylor's and was put out of the race.

Around dusk, as I sped past the lighted pits, I happened to notice No. 12, the Behra Ferrari, in the pits, with mechanics tinkering under the hood. This was good news, though I'd no means of telling what kind of good news. Then, I learned later, Fairman came by in second spot, but instead of taking the lead, he too pulled into the pit. This was the routine scheduled refueling and driver-change stop, but Jack had already been in a little earlier, complaining that his oil gauge was jumping about all over the place and not registering properly. Moss took over, anyway, and blasted off, but came back one lap later with zero oil pressure and that was the end of his ride.

It was about the worst thing that hit our team, so I'm going to divide the 1959 Le Mans shindig into two parts—the pre-Moss and post-Moss phases, you might call them.

-13-
"YA'ALL USE GILLETTE!"

A COUPLE OF times during part of my night spell I had to take to the grass suddenly to avoid some of those poop-poppers who never seem to look in their rear-view mirrors, and one of those departures was a little bit hairy. Going through the second kink in the "straight" road down to Mulsanne, about kilometer 6, when your foot's well in the carburetor, I had to get on the outside and run along the grass to avoid a shunt that could have been disastrous, and someone got a picture of this. But there was no other way to solve the problem. Even at, say, 145 to 150 mph, you have to think fast. No time to say, "Er . . ."

Sometime after 1:30 A.M. the Behra-Gurney Ferrari handed in its chips after some sizzling laps with only one headlight working! There was some malarkey, I learned later, about a broken gearshift lever, but I always thought it was Shelby who had the monopoly on this particular ailment! Fact was that the cockpit was swimming in oil and how much oil can you get into a shift lever knob!

So now our real opposition was the Hill-Gendebien Testa Rossa, very much back in the running and sounding as healthy as any Ferrari could, considering the fuel system problems that had been bugging it earlier. At around five minutes after two I came in, three minutes or more ahead of our planned schedule, and handed over to Roy. The car was refueled and had the rear tires and brake pads changed in five minutes, twenty-seven seconds. This meant that the pit stop actually cost us two minutes, twenty-seven seconds, then away again, everything as smooth as silk. Still, the delay gave the Testa Rossa a chance to build up a 3-minute, 52-second lead on us, although Parnell wasn't biting his nails. He knew this margin could be made up when the Ferrari came in for tires and brakes, as it was certain to do, sooner or later, probably sooner. So we just kept the wheels turning according to plan. No sweat. Or rather, plenty of sweat but no panic. That cockpit was a bit cooler at night, but not so you could forget about it.

Our third place Aston, No. 6, also came in for a routine pit stop and driver change and Trintignant handed over to Frère with the machine going like a Pullman car. This dropped them to about four laps behind the leader, but No. 6 was our reserve car anyway, and its drivers didn't have a thing in this world to worry them. Fourth position was held by Bonnier and von Trips, who were about seven laps behind the lead Ferrari.

Driving conditions were very good for most of the time that year, and apart from a little rain, earlier on, we were able to get around as fast as Reg would allow us to go. Even the fog that usually bunches up at the White House turn was mostly absent. Still, there were many things that impressed me or stuck in my mind for one reason or another. One thing I won't ever forget was the wonderful pit organization masterminded by Parnell. We always knew exactly where we were, and from the maintenance standpoint the way our mechanics had their jobs coordinated was absolutely superb. I think "fantastic" would be an even better word.

Another thing that was a great boon, although ironically enough neither Roy nor I got much benefit from it, was the excellent chow tent set up by Joe Waldron of our Catering Department. All kinds of hungry people drifted in there, and Innes Ireland and quite a few other scroungers from the various teams had a field day in the Aston Martin tent.

I also want to comment here about the so-called trickiness of the White House turn. The general feeling is that no matter how well you may do elsewhere on the 8.2-mile Sarthe circuit, if you goof at the White House or lose time there for any reason, it's going to show up on the stopwatch. This is taken as gospel by many drivers and team managers and timers and armchair critics who can talk a good race, but I don't know how true it really is because the White

House never seems to have bothered me. It's true there's always oil on the course at that point, and there's often fog, too; but you'll notice that it's the tiddlers that seem to come to grief there—the small stuff and not nearly so much the big cars. You see them laying against the fence, or burned out, or pulled off the road, or just plain wrecked. And I think I know the explanation for this. In a big car you *must* slow down to go through the White House; or at least you did when I drove there. (Suspensions have improved so much since that in 1964 Richie Ginther was taking the Ford GT almost flat out through the White House!) But going back a little while, the fast cars and drivers had to slow down if they wanted to stay on the road. You come over the crest of that hill between the two steep banks, going maybe 120 mph and all four wheels come off the ground. Then you're headed downhill for a short stretch, and then there's that right sharp bend followed by another very short stretch, and finally the nasty left on a diminishing radius and into a narrower road for a bit. So, with anything that really moves you have to slow down or end up in somebody's orchard or through a bam on the inside. But with a smaller car there's very little slowing down. You try to take it at 115 mph, say, and it gets hairier than hell. One minor mistake and you've had it. Almost no slowing down. That's the point I'm trying to make. The small-car driver is going through on the fine edge of danger, like some kind of a tightrope walker balancing a billiard ball on his nose. With a big car you slow down so much that it somehow seems a lot easier.

For my dough, going under that Dunlop Bridge and down toward the Esses at full bore is much more difficult than the White House. I'd say it was probably the most difficult turn to take at Le Mans. You try to keep your foot hard down, but it seems like someone's got a rope on it and pulls it back halfway through; and if you have any water around there, then I guess it won't do you any harm to say your prayers! Taking that turn at full bore in a properly controlled drift in *dry* weather is about as much of a thrill as I ever want to get out of motor racing.

On sheer speed, Mulsanne starts getting a little bit twitchy at between 165 and 170 mph. The only safe way, if you can call it that, to take that nasty little jog in the road near kilometer 6 is to use *all* the width. You come in from the left, chop through the apex, and gradually drift back toward the left again.

But we'd better get on with the race, I think.

Our positions at the halfway mark were Ferrari, Aston, Aston, with Porsche a long way back in fourth. But suddenly, at about 4 A.M., with most of Salvaduri's stint over, we were faced with the biggest crisis of the race. Our Mulsanne pit had already phoned us to say Roy was coming in and to get ready for him, but they didn't know what the trouble was. Outwardly the car looked fine.

We soon found out. The moment Salvadori cut the engine and hopped out and got his breath, he shouted, "The whole car's vibrating! Bloody thing feels as though it's shaking itself to pieces!"

"Front or rear end?"

"Rear!"

"You're seven laps short of your driving spell," Parnell told him. "Get back in there and come in at the proper time. Thirty laps. We'll signal you."

"But—"

"Off you go," Reg insisted, and Salvadori did.

He ran 6-minute laps which further increased the Ferrari's lead, but he finished his stint. Parnell didn't waste a minute. He got in the car, selected a gear, and popped the clutch in. That was all he needed to know.

"Change that left rear wheel!" he told the mechanics.

They got it off in a few seconds and there, embedded in the tire tread, was a hunk of metal Roy had picked up somewhere along the course. No wonder the wheel was vibrating. It was completely out of balance, to say nothing of the danger of a blowout.

"You've got me, chum!" Salvadori shook his head in relief and wonderment. "I could have sworn it was a broken de Dion tube or something wrong with the propellor shaft!" Part of the tread—for a length of maybe eighteen inches—was chewed almost down to the canvas, and it spoke well for the tire that nothing worse had happened. But I can tell you one guy who breathed a big sigh of relief, and that was Carroll Shelby, Esquire.

They refueled the car and got me off in jig-time, but by then things didn't look so good anymore for us. The lead Ferrari had stretched the gap between us to at least two laps and was four laps ahead of our No. 6, the Trintignant-Frère car which we held in reserve. I started to go again and the good old DBR1 ran as sweet as a nut. No problems at all. The only thing was that I knew I was losing a few seconds a lap to them and there was nothing could be done about it without bursting the engine.

Soon after I got back in, something happened that was both dramatic and funny, and it helped take my mind off the unpleasant fact that once again Le Mans looked like it was slipping through our fingers. As I pulled away from Mulsanne Corner, I noticed this Frenchman that had gotten off the road in his Lotus Elite, obviously with some kind of trouble. Helmet in hand, he was walking away from the abandoned car, looking pretty dejected. He was about a hundred yards away when I passed him, but the next time I came around the corner the car was on fire and the Frenchman was running back toward it as fast as his legs would carry him. The thing was consumed by flames and obviously beyond help, and eventually, in some mysterious way, it burned down to a hulk. What had started the fire, no one seemed to know. Not a soul had been near the car. So you might call it spontaneous combustion of some kind, but I can imagine how the poor guy felt.

Shortly after 5 A.M., as I raced up the straight past the pits toward the Dunlop Bridge curve, I spotted the lead Ferrari, No. 14, parked in its pit with mechanics working on it. Routine driver and tire change, I thought, and at once opened the tap as wide as I dared in the hope that we might unlap ourselves before they got going again. We did cut nearly a lap out of their four lap lead, but I also knew that at the present rate our hope of winning Le Mans was getting thinner by the hour. Still there was nothing to do but press on, and press on we did.

Probably about the two worst times for a driver at Le Mans are dawn, when the sun starts to come up at you and you know you've had a sleepless night, and again around eleven o'clock in the morning, when you feel as though the darned race is never gong to end. True, our two remaining Astons—Salvadori and I, and Trintignant and Frère—were so securely in second and third spots that it would take the worst kind of luck to dislodge us; but neither was this situation going to win us the grueling Twenty-four-Hour classic. The sixty-four-dollar question in the minds of the huge crowd was whether the Ferrari would stay glued together for another five hours. Everyone loves the underdog and I'll bet many were hoping something would happen to give us a break.

It did. About that time several things happened in a hurry. First the Hugus-Erickson Porsche dropped out and, soon after, the Kerguen-La Caze Porsche took the same route. But this was nothing compared with the fact that the Hill-Gendebien Ferrari was beginning to sound rough. Gone was the snarling beat of twelve cylinders going great guns. The car was plainly losing speed and it didn't take many stopwatch readings to find out that the elastic band was beginning to unstretch and we were regaining several seconds a lap on the leader. About then Gendebien pulled into his pit for a consultation and you could imagine what was going on in Italian! Phil Hill's Italian was not so dusty and he was having plenty to say, too.

Anyway, after a longish pow-wow with Tavoni and much waving of arms, Gendebien went back into the race at a much reduced speed, sounding rougher than ever. It didn't take us long to bring the gap down to two laps, then to one, and finally to start unlapping ourselves. Some time later I got the Ferrari in my sights as it limped down toward Arnage and passed him without any trouble. Now we were in the lead and it looked as though David Brown would fulfill his lifelong dream and we guys would get to drink champagne after all. Next time around Mulsanne I got an extra signal that said something like, "Good show!" and just for the heck of it I poured on the coal just a bit. Always within the rev limits imposed by Parnell, of course. Just before I came in and handed the car back to Roy for his last stint, I had put two minutes between myself and the Ferrari.

There isn't a heck of a lot more to tell about that race. Salvadori started it and I got the checker. That was the way we had planned it, I guess, although he drove a bit longer than I did—maybe about ninety minutes in all.

What did it feel like, winning Le Mans? Well it felt pretty good, that's for sure. You get a bit numbed there toward the end and do things automatically, like shifting and braking and taking the right line through a turn. Your reflexes aren't as sharp anymore—don't let anyone kid you—but they're probably a bit sharper than those of the guys who didn't win! And of course you're already spending all that money they haven't paid you, yet—"millions of francs," as Roy later put it. The fact was, taking everything into account—the second-place money of our No. 6 car and the Index of Performance, which apparently we won as well—the team took home about $28,000. This wasn't exactly peanuts, but it was certainly chicken feed compared with what David Brown had spent to get this result.

Anyway, there were no complaints. The ad endorsements started to come in and side money from accessories and all that stuff, so we made out all right. Most of the cups, with the exception of "The Motor" Challenge Trophy, were pretty crummy, though. Cut glass and that cheap gilded stuff and so on.

But I couldn't end this Le Mans episode without telling at least one funny story that happened right at the end. When we got the checker and started toward "Victory Lane," which is more of a technical inspection than anything else, to make sure you don't finish with more pieces than you had at the start, Miss Europe was supposed to ride along, too, as well as David Brown, who was proud as a peacock and had changed into his latest tweed suit for the occasion and looked like a fashion model. So Mr. Brown gets in and—whammy!—along comes some enthusiastic Frenchman and dumps Miss Europe right in his lap! Just that one contact was enough to transfer twenty-four hours of oil and grease and dirt all over Mr. Brown's beautiful clothes, and was he mad before they got Miss Europe out!

Then the next thing that happened was just about as zany. I hadn't eaten a thing in twenty-four hours but had kept going on Cokes, and before I know it some joker tilts an open magnum of champagne into my mouth. It took at least three big swallows before I could get it away, and you can imagine what three swallows would do to an empty stomach under those conditions. It wasn't but fifteen minutes before I was running around drunker than a billygoat, but luckily John Bolster came through, deerstalker cap, handlebar mustache and all. He wanted me to go up to the BBC stand and say a few words, and then he helped me back to the Aston

Martin shooting brake (station wagon to you) so I could get a well-earned rest.

Come to think of it, soberly, winning the Twenty-four Hours was probably the greatest thrill I ever got out of racing. I can think of plenty of other races that carry their quota of thrills for the winner, but when you win this one it kind of gives you license to go out and tell people you're good, and that often helps get some other deals together. So it's not just the money, by any means. Also I don't think it would be out of place to add that Roy and I set a new record for Le Mans that year. We covered 2720 miles at an average speed of 112.5 mph, while Trintignant and Frère covered 2684.5 miles at an average of 112 mph. After us came four Ferraris, all GT jobs, the fastest of which averaged a bit over 103 mph. Two other American drivers finished high. George Arents, who co-drove another GT Ferrari with Billet, was fourth; and Bob Grossman in yet another GT, which he shared with Tavano, finished fifth.

But in this motor racing game, more perhaps than any other, you're here today and forgotten tomorrow unless you can think up something new to keep the ball rolling. Naturally it crossed my mind many times during the race and afterward that I would like to see an American car succeed where Briggs Cunningham so gallantly failed; more so because of this idea that had been bugging me for years—to build something really fast and practical and not too expensive, powered by an American engine.

But the moment wasn't quite ripe, yet. No one came along and handed me a check for a hundred grand and said, "Here. Go right ahead and make your dream come true. Use this money as you think fit, to build the kind of American sports car you have in mind!"

No one did that. But the endorsements and commercials started coming along thicker than fleas, and they paid good money and brought a lot of laughs, too. Maybe the funniest were from such people as Gillette razors and the hair oil companies. Can you imagine it—I'd do all these commercials and then they would dub in an English accent! We really had a time making those commercials. "Ya'all use Gillette!" They even offered me that Lukozade soft drink stuff, but I figured I'd better leave that one for Stirling Moss.

He was an old customer.

All in all, though, Le Mans was a lucrative venture. John Wyer (who had moved up in the company from being a team manager) paid us the same way as we pay our drivers in the States. We give them 90 per cent of whatever they earn and the mechanics get 10 per cent. The manufacturer gets nothing, because the prize money is really inconsequential as far as the amounts you invest in putting the car together are concerned. We had a prior arrangement in the Aston team that whoever won what, it would be split evenly among all six drivers. That gave everyone a fair shake and prevented any of this nonsense of drivers of the same team battling against each other, because when that happens it usually ends up with nobody getting anything at all but a burst engine or a wrecked car. This way, I think the six of us ended up with about $8000 each, which wasn't too bad at all. I use the same system with my drivers today and it works just fine. No one has any gripes about being left out and no one tries to race another guy on the same team, which is absurd!

However, when you stack up the most that a European sports car race can offer by way of prize money against the Indianapolis pot of gold, and when you compare the amount of effort involved, road racing does leave a little to be desired, doesn't it?

And there's another thing. At this writing we hear that the Commendatore has decided to pull out of sports car entries because he can't get his Prototypes homologated and it "ain't fair!" Well, maybe there won't be any more direct Ferrari factory entries, but don't think for a moment that the dear old Commendatore is going to give up the struggle as easily as that. He can find a dozen teams and as many drivers as he wants, all eager to race his products under their own name. If they win, Ferrari gets the publicity; if they lose, it's this private entry or private team that looks bad. Not the factory. So it's heads I win and tails you lose. Not a bad kind of deal.

I'd heard that for years Signor Ferrari had been running races all over the world to suit himself, merely by putting the right amount of pressure at the right moment on governing bodies like the FIA (International Automobile Federation) and CSI (International Sportive Committee). Think back a little. Just about the time that Lance Reventlow got that Scarab really in high gear and started beating

Ferraris all over the United States, what happens? They lower the piston displacement to three liters (183 cubic inches), knowing full well we don't have an engine that small.

Then, more recently, Ferrari got us all hoodwinked with that silly Prototype weight limit. It doesn't make any sense, any way you look at the thing. It's just a gimmick to get everybody tied up so Ferrari can catch their breath.

I just don't go for that stuff, and one of these days I'm going back to Europe and Le Mans with one of my own cars and win it. No ifs or ands; no buts or becauses. The best car wins. The fastest car wins. That's it.

When everything was over at Le Mans, bar the shouting, the telegrams started to come in like an avalanche. There were dozens so I won't quote more than two or three here, but I'll bet the French and British postal clerks really fell for this Salvadori-Shelby crew. Some of the cables arrived at Le Mans, but many more were waiting for us at Feltham.

Here are some samples, all from good friends:

"Congratulations to you, Salvadori, Trintignant, and Frère. All very happy at the Round Table. Maurice and Rene [Dreyfus]."

The Round Table was the special luncheon table at Rene's restaurant in New York, the famous Chanteclair, where the real motor racing buffs used to sit around and shoot the bull.

A couple of cables that I especially liked came directly to the Aston Martin factory. One, from John Zink of the hot Indy cars bearing his name, was a lulu: "Good men, like good whiskey, improve with age."

Another one that was terse and to the point, as always like its sender, came from Lance Reventlow. "Congratulations on Le Mans win," it said, but it meant a lot more.

We all know, of course, that nothing succeeds like success, and even the French paper waxed sort of lyrical, if that's what you call it. Translated, one headline read: "Salvadori and Shelby bring to Aston Martin the victory of wise ones!" (Wise drivers, they meant— not wise guys!)

Carroll Shelby, driving a 250F Maserati, failed to finish when the car's brakes locked at the Grand Prix of Portugal, Oporto, 1958. (Bernard Cahier / The Cahier Archive)

Shelby racing in Sicily's Targa Florio, 1955, in a 3-liter Ferrari.

(Bernard Cahier / The Cahier Archive)

The 1959 Portuguese Grand Prix in Monsanto, driving an
F1 Aston Martin DBR4. (Bernard Cahier / The Cahier Archive)

Winning the Tourist Trophy in Goodwood, England, 1959,
in an Aston Martin DBR1. (Bernard Cahier / The Cahier Archive)

In the laurels—Shelby and Moss clinch the world championship for Aston Martin by winning the Tourist Trophy in Goodwood, England, 1959. From left to right: Roy Salvadori, Carroll Shelby, Jack Fairman, and Stirling Moss. (Bernard Cahier / The Cahier Archive)

The exciting starting minute of the 1959 24 Hours of Le Mans. Maurice Trintignant (No. 6), in an Aston Martin leads the field. (Bernard Cahier / The Cahier Archive)

Nearing the end of the 1959 24 Hours of Le Mans, Carroll Shelby is in the lead. Moss's car had broken down and had to be retired from the race. (Bernard Cahier / The Cahier Archive)

Moments of victory after Shelby wins the 1959 24 Hours of Le Mans, with Reg Parnell (left), Aston Martin team manager; David Brown (center), head of Aston Martin; and Shelby (right). (Bernard Cahier / The Cahier Archive)

Carroll Shelby brings the Aston Martin DBR1 under the checker as Jacques Loste gives his traditional salute at the 1959 24 Hours of Le Mans. (Klemantaski Collection / Getty Images)

After giving up racing due to his heart condition, Shelby began producing the Shelby Cobra, pictured here in 1962, with a V8 engine to compete against the best European cars and "blow the Corvettes into the weeds." (Bernard Cahier / The Cahier Archive)

Shelby cooks chili at home for his wife, Jeanne, circa 1966. (Martin Mills / Getty Images)

Actor Steve McQueen (left) and Shelby stand by McQueen's
Shelby Cobra in Los Angeles, 1963. (AP Photo / Dick Stroebel)

Ken Miles (left) and Shelby with the trophy for winning the overall
GT class of the 1964 Bridgehampton 500 Race. (Dave Friedman)

Shelby at Sebring, 1964. (Bernard Cahier / The Cahier Archive)

Bob Bondurant (left) and Masten Gregory at Le Mans, 1966. (Bernard Cahier / The Cahier Archive)

Ken Miles (left) and Shelby before the race at the 1966 24 Hours of Daytona. (Herb Scharfman / Sports Illustrated / Getty Images)

Ken Miles in the Ford GT40 Mark II at the 1966 24 Hours of Daytona, which he won driving with Lloyd Ruby. (Dave Friedman)

In the pits at the 1965 24 Hours of Le Mans, defeated by Ferrari. Not a single GT40 Mark II finished the race. (Bernard Cahier / The Cahier Archive)

Dan Gurney (left) and Phil Remington at the 1966 24 Hours of Le Mans. (Bernard Cahier / The Cahier Archive)

Enzo Ferrari, during testing in Modena in 1964. Ferrari won every 24 Hours of Le Mans from 1960–1965. (Bernard Cahier / The Cahier Archive)

The 1966 24 Hours of Le Mans is about to start. (Bernard Cahier / The Cahier Archive)

Ferrari takes an early lead at the 1966 24 Hours of Le Mans. The Ferrari 330 P3 is driven by Lorenzo Bandini/Jean Guichet. Following right behind it is the Ford GT40 Mark II driven by Ken Miles/Denis Hulme. (Klemantaski Collection / Getty Images)

Shelby (right) strategizing with Ken Miles during the 1966
24 Hours of Le Mans. (Bernard Cahier / The Cahier Archive)

Henry Ford II at the 1966 24 Hours
of Le Mans. (Roger Viollet via Getty Images)

Leo Beebe, Ford's public relations man,
at the 1966 24 Hours of Le Mans. (Bernard
Cahier / The Cahier Archive)

Shelby talking to Chris Amon (left) and Bruce McLaren (right) who drove the victorious No. 2 Ford GT40 Mark II at the 1966 24 Hours of Le Mans. (Bernard Cahier / The Cahier Archive)

Ken Miles, driving the No. 1 car, broke the lap record at the 1966 24 Hours of Le Mans. Miles was leading the No. 2 car by four laps, but Ford's decision to get a photo finish ultimately cost him the win. (Bernard Cahier / The Cahier Archive)

Ford gets the checkered flag and takes all the podium places at the 1966 24 Hours of Le Mans. McLaren/Amon finishes first in the No. 2 car, followed by Miles/Hulme in the No. 1 car, and then Bucknum/Hutcherson in the No. 5 car at left edge of frame. (AFP via Getty Images)

Shelby at the 1964 24 Hours of Le Mans. Leslie Kendall, curator of the Petersen Automotive Museum in Los Angeles, would later say of Shelby, "He was the only individual to influence the designs of all three major American automakers. Everything he touched became legendary." (Bernard Cahier / The Cahier Archive)

–14–
AIMEZ-VOUS *JADE?*

DESPITE MY BUSY European safari with Aston Martin, and the fact that we bade each other a friendly farewell after David Brown won the championship for sports car manufacturers when we scooped the Goodwood TT for him, my racing year was not yet quite over. There were still the Nassau races in December of 1959, and my old friend and partner Jim Hall had prepared for me a 5.7-liter Maserati, specially for the main event—the Nassau Trophy. We had every hope that with his powerful brute I might be able to bring home the bacon, but it wasn't even fated to start. During practice the car developed one of those sudden and violent oil leaks that smother everything in sight, including the driver, and after a consultation it was decided that we would not be able to repair the car in time for me to drive it.

However, all was not lost yet, so far as I was concerned. I was offered a ride in a three-liter Birdcage Maserati instead, and of course accepted this. The car was part of the Camoradi (Cassner Motor Racing Division) team and had originally been assigned to Dan Gurney. But Dan was in a bind. He had injured his foot quite badly in a Go-Kart accident, no less and, on top of that, Ferrari would not release him from his contract to drive exclusively for them. So he lost the Camoradi ride on account of this rather than his injured foot, though I frankly doubt whether he could have made it at all, even if the Commendatore had given him the green light.

Well, there was quite a bunch of us in there: Moss, I remember, drove a DBR3 Aston, and so did George Constantine, the ultimate winner, who was fielding Elisha Walker's car. Though the second

DBR3 was a private entry, Reg Parnell managed both cars with his usual skill and calm organizing ability. Then there was Jim Hall, with a 4.5-liter V8 Maserati which he was driving for Frank Harrison of Chattanooga, Tennessee, and there were Pedro Rodriguez and Joe Bonnier. Rodriguez was fielding one of those "secret weapons," the new Dino V6 Ferrari, while Bonnier had a Camoradi USA Porsche RS60.

Stirling Moss led for about half the race, but I kept him in sight until he broke a brake disc. That put me in the lead with a 90-second advantage over George Constantine's DBR2, and with only about fourteen laps to go I could see a nice $13,000 jackpot falling into my pocket. Then a de Dion tube broke on the Birdcage and that was the end of the ride. I was pretty sick, I can tell you. I'd already begun spending some of that money!

Constantine was the boy who picked up the marbles when he got the checker 30.47 seconds ahead of second-place man Phil Hill in the von Neumann three-liter Ferrari. Holbert was third with an RSK and world champion Jack Brabham fourth, driving a two-liter Cooper Maserati. The race was shortened because of the onset of darkness (they don't believe in lighting up the course at night in Nassau), but in any event that was the finish for the DBR2. This model was not raced again.

The year 1960, which was to be my last racing season, started with a big rush, as we were scheduled to take part in the New Zealand Grand Prix near Auckland on January 9. When I say "we," I'm talking more particularly of Joe Bonnier, Harry Schell, and myself. Temple Buell had offered me the lightweight, special 250F Maserati Formula 1 GP machine that Fangio had driven at Rheims in 1958—his last race. Who was I to refuse? Bonnier had his own BRM and Harry Schell was given a Maserti similar to mine, with a five-speed box and disc brakes, an older car, and not connected with Temple Buell, who had even sent along Guerrino Bertocchi, chief Maserati test driver, along with us. There were many others besides us three, all drawn by the excellent starting and prize money and other side benefits, and chief among them was Moss, who, like Brabham, had a 2.2-liter Cooper. Flockhart was there with a BRM, Jim Clark drove a Ferrari, and MacLaren was in another Cooper.

In all, twenty-one cars started, and Bonnier, Schell, and I decided to split any of the loot that might come our way. There were some preliminary heats, but for the Grand Prix Bonnier landed in the front row and Schell and I in the second row. Schell ran second to Moss (who had started from the back), but quit after twenty-five laps when he lost all his oil. Three laps later Bonnier dropped out of third spot when his steering went bad, so that left only Shelby in our group, and I was having one hell of a time of it, fighting off both MacLaren and a bad cramp in my leg, for third place. So I pulled in and handed my car to Schell, whose day this seemed to be, and finished fourth overall. This meant a nice chunk of dough, but the organizers were slow in paying, and then they sprang it on us that we couldn't take the money out of the country. It was against the law. Well, you had to know Harry Schell to guess how he would react. He blasted them with a shrill fury, and Joe and I, taking our cue from him, joined in the chorus. At least this got us the money, but after we'd stuffed all those five-pound notes in our shoes and shirt pockets, we got to wondering how the heck we were going to get them out of New Zealand. If we tried to fly to any country outside this currency bloc, they were bound to search us and take the dough away. But Harry came up with an immediate solution.

"Let's get the hell out of here," he said, in that flawless English of his with the faint tinge of a Parisian accent. "We can go over to Australia."

"Why Australia?" Joe and I wanted to know.

"I've an idea," Harry said. "A roundabout one but it might work."

So we flew across Australia and then on to the Philippines, and from there on to Hong Kong, where we decided to stay a week. And what a week it was! Harry, unbeknown to Joe or me—or, for that matter, to anyone else in the racing game—was quite a collector of jade.

"It's not only beautiful," he said, "but you can carry it around. Got the idea?"

We got the idea. Here was all this New Zealand money for which they'd give us only 50 cents for a dollar, even in the open city of Hong Kong, so we started a real buying spree: jade, suits, lamps, and God knows what all we bought. At the end of about three or four days we had the three-room hotel suite completely filled, but apparently even that wasn't enough for Harry. One day, while Joe and I were playing gin rummy, Schell came bursting in with this silver fish! You know the kind. One of these fish that has silver scales and actually moves.

"Just look what I bought for thirty-five dollars!" Harry says.

So I looked at it and I said, "Boy, that's beautiful, Harry! What do you do with it?"

"Do with it?" he says. "I don't think you get the point, Carroll. That's silver!"

"I doubt it," I said. "Take a closer look. Seems to me like it's flaking off."

"Why—that can't be!" Harry says.

"That's the way it looks to me, too," Joe agreed.

For a moment Harry just stood there, his jaw slack with dismay, but then I came up with a suggestion.

"Why don't you take the darn thing down to American Express and have them evaluate it?"

"That's a good idea," he agreed, and started off at once.

Sure enough, the fish was brass, not silver. All it had on the scales was a thin coating of silver.

"Why that sonovabitch!" Harry fumed. "I spent five or six grand with that lousy shopkeeper and he pulls a stunt like that on me! I'll get even with him. Just you wait!"

He took off again, without waiting to tell us what his plan was, but whatever it was it sure worked. About forty-five minutes later Harry returned with three little boys following him, and each was loaded down with packages, almost to the ceiling. It looked as though Harry had lost his mind and bought out the entire store.

"What in the world have you done this time?" I asked him.

"I did all right," he grinned. "I gave the guy a check on my Swiss bank."

"So?"

"So, I'm going right down, now, and send a telegram and stop payment on that check."

"You can't do that!"

"Can't I? Who's to stop me? We're leaving tomorrow morning, anyway."

And stop it he did.

"You mean you don't plan to pay him for that stuff?" Joe asked.

"I plan to make him sweat," Harry said. "And sweat, and sweat."

"What did you do with the silver fish?"

"That piece of junk? Hell, that was easy. I traded it back for some other stuff. And now that bandit's going to have to wait for his money!"

We left Hong Kong the next morning and headed for the airport a lot richer in goods if not in cash. I sent home a houseful of furniture that I had bought, plus a lot of clothes and stuff—shipped everything across the Pacific to Los Angeles. All I had with me was my regular clothing. We were headed for Bangkok and from there on to Rome and back to London. Harry and Joe weren't so smart. They had between them at least two hundred pounds of baggage, which would have cost them a fortune to take along on the plane. Harry alone had bought a bunch of fifteen to twenty lampshades, but this gave us an idea to avoid paying excess-baggage charges. We checked the lampshades through to Rome, telling the airline clerk that we thought we would carry them with us. But meantime we left the bulk of our excess hand baggage outside.

The rest was easy. We took the tags off the lampshades and put them on those bulky bags that would have cost a fortune in excess weight; then we carried the bags in and just dumped them at the spot where they were loading the baggage. That little bit of freight that we got away with would have cost us $1000 in excess all the way to Rome. So with that, of course, we were stuck with carrying those lampshades to Bangkok, Rome, and elsewhere.

What happened to us in Bangkok is another story, but I just wanted to bring up this little anecdote for a special reason. Poor Harry lost his life motor racing in a kind of silly accident that shouldn't happen to anybody, but it was perhaps only after he had gone that we realized how much one of us he had been and how greatly we missed him. Though Schell will never go down to posterity as a great race driver, he did have his moments and there isn't a man of our era who hasn't a warm place in his heart for the memory of a guy of his very special caliber.

There are many other stories about Harry Schell that are worth the telling; things that were done to him and things that he did to other people, and all of them were good for some unforgettable laughs. One of my favorites about Harry goes back to the previous December (1959) at the time of the GP of the United States at Sebring. If you've already heard how Schell ended up in pole position on the starting grid, just let me tell it again for those who haven't. This one was a lulu. Harry was driving this two-liter Cooper (he told everyone it was a 2.2, but we all knew it was a two-liter) which was actually about five seconds a lap slower than the fast Ferraris of Gurney, Tony Brooks, and von Trips—to say nothing of Jack Brabham and Stirling Moss in their rear-engine Coopers. But that didn't faze Harry for long. He decided to do a little readjustment on his own. If he couldn't get his car to go any faster, the next best thing was to speed up the stopwatches!

Well, where the Esses are at Sebring, there's a turn about that point that brings you back on the road circuit, on the other side, and connects up with the Warehouse Straight. It's quite a short cut and it gave Harry an idea. He stood at that turn, just where the Esses begin, to see how long the cars took to get from that point, down around the Hairpin, and then along the Warehouse Straight to the Webster Turn. He timed a number of cars very carefully and checked everything out to be sure, then he got in his own car and took off, but instead of going the regular route he made that short circuit and chopped about a couple of miles off the course. He rejoined the course near the Webster Turn at exactly the right moment so he would be about a couple of seconds faster than anybody else.

It was all done very smoothly and quietly and when Schell roared past the timing stand around that turn at the end of the back straight, and Joe Lane's electrical timing equipment registered his time, Joe couldn't believe it. The timing crew felt convinced they had made a mistake, so they just conveniently forgot about that lap and decided not to make any announcement. It *had* to be an error. Harry Schell two seconds faster than anyone else? Impossible.

And that's where Harry got his big laugh. Next morning, as they were lining the cars up on the grid for the start of the Grand Prix, Schell set up an awful squawk when he found himself in the fifth row.

"What's the big idea?" he asked indignantly. "I made the fastest lap yesterday and you stick me back here? What gives?"

"We don't know anything about that," the course officials said, and they didn't. No one had told them. "That's the spot you're supposed to be in."

"Well, that's not the place I'm starting from!" Harry fumed. "Why don't you guys check your times? I had fastest time yesterday!"

"But—"

"But nothing. Check your times, that's all."

And believe me, when Harry set his mind to it, he could really raise the roof.

"What kind of a deal is this?" he kept shouting. "Check your times. Go on. Check them."

They had to do as he asked and finally, feeling sheepish, Lane had to admit that the records upheld Harry's claim. He *had* clocked the fastest time! Well you can imagine how Tony Brooks and Jack Brabham felt, to say nothing of Stirling Moss, with the brannigan going on between them. Brooks looked a pretty safe bet to become the next world champion, but if he didn't place in the first three it might be a different story. Anyway, Schell created such a scene that they put him in the front row with Moss and Brabham, while mechanics reluctantly wheeled Brooks's Ferrari back into the second row!

Of course it didn't make any difference. Moss shot out in front anyway, followed by Brabham, but Tony was so mad that he got in a shunt at the Webster Turn, and this probably cost him the world championship. Brooks was leading von Trips in another Ferrari by a hair's breadth, but when he got to the corner he couldn't stop, either from anger or from skidding on some gas that had been spilled on the track. Whatever the reason, he went straight on and von Trips hit him in the back, damaging the nose of the German's Ferrari. Brooks restarted his stalled engine and made it back to the pits for a quick check, but the mechanics could find nothing wrong, so he went off again. The stop, however, set him back so far that he could never make up all the lost time, although he did finish fourth. Brabham ran out of gas on the last lap, about a quarter of a mile from the finish and had to push his car the rest of the way, but even though Brooks finished third, just ahead of him, Jack had enough points on hand to keep his championship of the world secure. It was Bruce MacLaren who won the race and the funny part of it was that Bruce and Jack had traded cars because Brabham didn't like the suspension on his own car! Had he kept that original Cooper, he probably would not have had to push his way over the finish line and would have won the race as well.

As for Schell, who had stirred up all the trouble, he disappeared from the race early with a burned-out clutch! I know Harry got a big charge out of the whole mess and the way it stirred Brooks into such a state of fury that he very likely lost the chance of becoming world champion. In a way, I suppose, Brabham had Harry to thank for keeping his title, or rather for not having it snatched from him in the last Grand Prix of the season; but that day nobody felt like thanking Schell for anything, and if he hadn't volunteered the information, no one would ever have figured out how he managed to lap Sebring two seconds faster than a driver who was already champion of the world in everything but name!

And when you look back and think of the many stunts we pulled on poor old Harry Schell—like that time in 1958, at Reims, when we carried his Vespa minicar all the way up to his hotel bedroom and left it there!—I guess he was entitled to a little caper on his own. He sure made the most of it, too.

To get back to 1960, we were back from that crazy round-the-world trip following the New Zealand GP, and I was visiting in Dallas when I woke up one morning with a sharp pain in my chest. I happened to be staying at the apartment of a friend of mine, Bob Schroeder, who had worked with us at Carroll Shelby Sports Cars and is now the Goodyear distributor for that area, and I didn't rightly know what to do. There were various problems on my mind just then, not the least of which was that Jeanne and I had gradually grown apart over the years with my being absent so often, and things were just no longer the same any more.

Well, I put that pain out of my mind, but it kept coming back every morning for a week or so. It would go away as the day wore on, but first thing in the morning it was like a knife being stuck in my chest. So happened that Red Byron was around, too, and I knew he had previously had one or two heart attacks, so I told him about it one morning when it got to be really bad.

"Red," I said, "my chest hurts terribly. The pain's awful. I can't stand it."

"I think I know what your trouble may be," he said without hesitation. Then he handed me a pill and said, "Take one of these. Just stick it under your tongue." I put the pill under my tongue and it dissolved and the pain went away. It was then that he told me they were nitroglycerin pills and he used them regularly. He gave me a couple more of these pills and said, "You'd better go and see your doctor. I mean now. Right away."

So I did just that. I went to see Doctor Val Scroggie, an old friend of mine, a big, jovial three-hundred-pound guy who was the area governor for the Texas region of the SCCA and also the best-liked figure in our region. Sad to relate, he has since passed away of a heart attack.

"Well," he said, beaming, "what seems to be the trouble with you, young man?"

I told him about the pain and the nitroglycerin pills and he shook his head almost disbelievingly. "I don't honestly see how you could have heart trouble," he says, "because I've checked you out enough times since you started racing and you've always been the picture of health and as active as all get out!"

"Still, Doc, there's that pain. It hurts like hell and I can't think of any other reason for it."

"Take off your shirt and let's listen to your ticker."

He listened for a while, moving the stethoscope around my chest, then he took my blood pressure and let the air out of the gadget and shrugged.

"Nothing there that leads me to suspect you have heart trouble," he said. "All kinds of things can happen to give you a pain in the chest, you know."

"I guess so, Doc, but—"

"Okay. You have a nasty pain in your chest. I don't doubt that." He made a little gesture like he wasn't especially worried. "But my guess is that it's more likely to be a scalene muscle."

"Scalene?" I stared at him. "What in heck's that?"

"It's just the medical name for one of the muscles that helps you turn your head." Doc Scroggie smiled at my astonishment. "But sometimes an odd thing can happen. This muscle can wrap itself around the subclavian artery and shut off the blood supply to your arm. Then you get a nasty pain and numbness."

"But the pain's in my chest, Doc."

"There's such a thing as referred pain," Doc Scroggie explained. "The trouble's in one spot and the pain's in another. It travels along certain nerves. . . ."

"Well, if you say so, Doc." I didn't know whether to feel relieved or confused. All this talk about a scalene muscle and a—what was it? subclavian artery—why, heck, I didn't even know I had such a thing. "That's okay with me."

"Just to set your mind at ease," Doc said, "we'll take an EKG— that's an electrocardiogram—of your heart action. And I'm betting we don't find anything."

He proved right, at that. The cardiogram didn't show any wiggles on the chart that looked other than normal, and that was the end of it. At least so far as he was concerned. But unfortunately the pain didn't go away. It kept coming back all that season—every time I exerted myself or the weather got a little cold, that awful stabbing pain came back. The only way I knew how to get rid of it was to keep taking those nitroglycerin pills that Red Byron had first given me. I don't know how many races I ran that year with a nitro pill under my tongue, but it sure did the trick. I'd get rid of the pain in no time, at least for a while.

Well, in February of 1960 I moved to California and decided to make a fresh start. The reason I decided to come to California was because it seemed there were more people there involved with the hot-rod movement—which was getting started big then—who would also be capable of putting together a limited production sports car. I needed talent and that's where the talent was. I stayed in a little town called La Mirada, which is down near Disneyland, in southeast Los Angeles, and Jeanne and I decided to make a clean break of it. She didn't feel she wanted to move, especially with the kids growing up and going to school in Dallas, and I couldn't see any real future for my plans but in California. So we decided to go our separate ways and stay friends, which we have done ever since.

Meantime, too, something else had come up. The late "Lucky" Cassner was trying to recruit what he called the top drivers for that fantastic Camoradi stable of his—I never did understand where the money came from to pay for all those expensive race cars—so Stirling Moss, Dan Gurney, Masten Gregory, and I decided to string along with Camoradi USA. And my first race for this outfit was in Havana, Cuba, February 24 through 27, 1960. Castro was firmly in power by then, of course, and it was interesting, though sad, to note the way everything had changed for the worse since the Fangio kidnapping business two years before. Buildings looked kind of neglected; some of the plush hotels had closed down; and there was nothing like the same amount of goods in the stores. Everyone looked glum and you couldn't walk a yard without bumping into a uniform or a beard!

But still, it was the new Grand Prix of Cuba and it paid money and we were supplied with cars by Camoradi and all the freight and expenses were paid. Stirling drove a new Birdcage Type 61 Maserati; Dan had an old three-liter Maserati, not a Birdcage—it was a rather tired dawg that someone had palmed off on Lucky; and I had this two-year-old Porsche. Masten Gregory also got a Porsche but did better. His was much newer than mine.

The Gran Premio Libertad, as Castro liked to call it, was run on a military-airport circuit with an added road section near the beautiful Havana golf course. It was 3.2 miles to a lap and nice going for all the drivers. Camoradi USA won the GT class in the sports car race when Moss and Gregory shared the checker for first place overall and in the two-liter class. The rest of us Camoradi boys, Dan and I, didn't even finish, but we had an interesting bunch of pro drivers from the USAC circuit—men like Rodger Ward and Eddie Sachs and Jim Rathmann; all seemingly having themselves a ball. But the interesting part of the Gran Premio Libertad (notice the name) was that we drivers had special limousines furnished us so we could get to the course. This would have been swell, except that our car stalled and we backed up the traffic for a couple of blocks. Almost immediately about eight or ten helicopters showed up overhead, hovering low while soldiers sat out of the sides with submachine guns pointed in our general direction. So then we waved to them and pointed down and held up our racing helmets for their inspection. They seemed to get the message and some of the helicopters landed and picked up a number of stalled drivers and took them out to the circuit. Included among them were Joe Bonnier and I, and we had a lot of fun, riding over the traffic that way.

I don't think the pressure was on Castro then to the extent that it is today, and even though things had already begun to look shoddy, the place didn't seem to be the armed camp that we know today. But all the same, we didn't enjoy the race nearly as much as we had done in former years. The old spirit was gone.

-15-
THE LAST LAP

AFTER CUBA IT was soon time for Sebring again, where I accepted another offer to drive for Camoradi USA. I'm not going to waste much time on this one because it turned out to be a dead loss. One twelve-hour race is pretty much like another, especially on the same course, even when you drive a different car; but you do like to finish, just the same. If you remember, 1960 was the year of the big hassle over the fact that American Oil held the exclusive right to supply gas to *all* competitors at Sebring, and this was against official regulations. But Amoco saw it one way—they were putting up $20,000 in prize money for the privilege of having that exclusive right. The European manufacturers saw it another way: especially Ferrari and Porsche, who happened to be under contract to another brand of fuel. So, as a protest, both teams withdrew their official factory entries and let the "private" guys go ahead on their own instead.

The late "Lucky" Cassner was not embarrassed by little things like that. We had three 2.9-liter Birdcage Maseratis entered, one driven by Moss and Gurney; another by Masten Gregory and me, and so on. There was a fourth 2.9 Birdcage belonging to Briggs Cunningham and prepared by Momo, and that also failed to finish. Ed Crawford and Walt Hansgen were the drivers. Out of the four Birdcage starters, three went out with rear end trouble and ours had to blow a gasket, just to be different. Crawford, by the way, spent a long time digging himself out of the sandbank at the Warehouse Hairpin, which didn't help any. An Osca and a Porsche on the Camoradi team also failed to finish, as did a couple of Corvettes that Cassner had managed to scam out of Chevrolet. One of them, it seems to me, was driven by Fred Gamble. It was to Moss's credit, however, that the Camoradi *Tipo 61* set a new lap record of 3:17.5, beating his own previous best (in 1958) by 2.5 seconds. As a matter of fact, we were all a bit surprised that the temperamental Birdcage not only set the pace at an average of over 90 mph, but also lasted eight of the twelve hours before Moss had to call it quits.

But something else came out of Sebring, as one thing nearly always leads to another. While we were down there, I asked Lucky if I could borrow one of the Birdcage Masers to drive in the "Examiner" Grand Prix at Riverside the following month. He said it would be okay, so we went on to Miami, prepared the car there, then flew it to California. I had my old mechanic, Joe Landacker, back with me and that brought back some of the good racing flavor of the John Edgar days. It was almost like old times again, with the car running fine. In fact I won the race and that gave my morale a much-needed boost after the fiascos at Havana, New Zealand, and Sebring. Not all financial flops by any means, but unsatisfactory from the standpoint of actually winning a race.

The newspapers billed this event as "the battle of champions," but I would hardly call it that, although there were some good chauffeurs present, with machinery of top caliber in some cases and tired automobiles in others. Brabham, for instance, had a weary Cooper Monaco; Ward burned out four specials, none in top shape, in two days of qualifying runs; the Scarabs were there, but Reventlow had oil pressure trouble; and so on. But there were some good ones, too: another Birdcage, like mine, driven by Bob Drake, who put up the fastest qualifying lap; Gurney giving Max Balchowsky's 5.5-liter Buick "Old Yaller II" the ride of its life; and Billy Krause with potent Chevy-powered D-Jag.

Anyway I started in fourth slot, worked up to second place behind Gurney, then took over the lead when he gave up, and won easily. I had plenty in hand all the time and never drove a better-running Birdcage. The race went twenty-two laps and I crossed the line seven thousand bucks better off than I had been at the start. My average for the 203 miles was, I think, a bit over 87 mph. Ken Miles finished second in a Porsche RS60. Pete Lovely in Jack Nethercut's three-liter Ferrari was third. The chest pains bothered me before the start, but the nitroglycerin did its job and I very soon forgot about my trouble, although even then California doctors were shaking their heads and saying I should quit racing. They didn't agree with Doc Scroggie's diagnosis but couldn't come up with one of their own. They only suspected something else.

Guess what helped me win, too, was an extra jerrycan which we connected up in the tail of the Maser, as the fuel problem was fairly critical and I would probably have run out of gas since I didn't make a pit stop.

But Riverside did more for me than win me some money and polish up my prestige a bit. It was the beginning of my association with Goodyear racing tires—the same make as I had used at Nassau in December of the previous year—which turned out to be a very successful and profitable venture for both of us.

About this time, the doctors in California had diagnosed that chest pain as something quite different from what Doc Val Scroggie suspected: they called it angina pectoralis and told me they thought I should quit racing. Angina is the result of insufficient blood getting through to the heart along the coronary arteries. This results in a condition where the muscle becomes part blue (where it's starved of blood) and remains part red (where the blood supply is normal). The way the doctor explained it, if I remember correctly, the heart muscle becomes a kind of "battery" because the difference in potential between the affected and unaffected parts creates a current of sorts, and that's what causes the pain. The nitro pills quickly dilate the coronary arteries so the blood supply returns to normal, and then the pain goes away. However, what I had going for me was the EKG, which still didn't show anything abnormal. So, because of this, it was hard for the doctors to talk me out of driving. And besides, they should have known better. Doc Val Scroggie knew better!

So the next one I went for was the big race at Castle Rock in Denver, Colorado, June 27. And I won it, too. But since I haven't until now quoted a single newspaper clipping about that guy, Shelby, let me do so here:

Carroll Shelby, king of the sports car drivers, got a chariot worthy of royalty, Sunday, and smashed all the Continental

Divide Raceway records before 9,283 fans. The 37-year-old racing veteran from La Mirada, California [I'd moved there in the meantime], piloted the magnificent Scarab No. 2 of the Meister Bräuser racing team in a wire-to-wire victory in the 100.8 mile Colorado International.

Shelby wheeled his blue and white steed home in 1 hour, 20 minutes and 42.2 seconds for an average speed of 74.9 mph. His performance smashed the old CDR course record of 74.29 miles an hour set by Jim Hall of Dallas in a Birdcage Maserati, last May 7. Shelby also established a new one-lap record of 2:09.68, or 77.73 mph, on the second lap, cracking Hall's 2:12.6. Shelby qualified in 2:08.32 (79 mph) in the morning.

Decked out in his striped bib coveralls, a familiar Shelby trademark, the 1959 Le Mans champion attributed his easy victory to the tremendous acceleration of the Scarab.

"The acceleration got me through the corners without having to slow down or brake," smiled Shelby, who pocketed $1,920 in prize money for his winning effort. "The Scarab probably would be a better car with disc brakes, but everything went real well despite a couple of sour spark plugs. After I got a 35-second lead, about two-thirds of the way along, I slowed down. I just poked along the last four or five laps."

The writer went on to say that I rated the Birdcage Maser, in which I had beaten the Scarab at Riverside in April, as about equal to Reventlow's creation, and he was right about that. The *Tipo 61* Birdcage Maserati, so-called because of its fantastic, spaghetti-like network of thin tubes which made up the frame, was a very light and well-designed racing automobile, fast as a hare and with all the scat a driver could use and the kind of roadability that many designers dream about but don't quite succeed in putting across.

Okay, so that was the little story of the Continental Divide Raceway at Denver, and with that win I got a lot closer to the USAC (United States Auto Club) championship, which eventually did fall into my lap for 1960. The clipping also said that I was going to run at Elkhart Lake, Wisconsin, July 31, "following a vacation in California," but there the guy was blending fact with fiction. My return to California was no vacation, you can lay on that. It was more of a great big headache, and I'll tell you about it in a moment. The headache was in trying to get the right parties together to help me build that all-American dream sports car, and in trying to do it with little or no money, and run a race drivers' school at the same time, plus getting the Goodyear distributorship on its feet, plus straighten out my own personal affairs, plus decide whether or not I was going to quit at the end of the season because of this heart thing. If you want to call that a vacation, you're welcome!

Before we go on, here's another clipping in which the writer makes a prophet out of Carroll Shelby, and the Texan string-bean turns out not to be so far wrong, after all. In an interview with Jim Graham of the Denver *Post* I told him that sports car racing as we then knew it would be a thing of the past within three or four years. The Gran Turismo machines would replace racing type sports cars like the two-seater Ferraris, Maseratis, and Aston Martins. To be sure, those makes would still race, but in a GT or production-car form, rather than the very costly sports-racing jobs. I could see GT racing with Corvettes, Ferraris, and Porsches, and I could also see a lot of Formula 1 and Formula Junior stuff coming up. Not so far wrong, either!

"Do you realize," I told Graham, "that Mercedes-Benz spent five million dollars in one year on their cars alone?"

That year (1960) I passed up Le Mans to run in the Continental Divide shindig which was a USAC-sponsored race. I had turned strictly pro and was after the title of "U.S. sports car champion." With two wins under my belt (the April race at Riverside also was a USAC affair), I stood a good chance of getting the title if I could finish near the top in at least one more race.

"I feel I was lucky enough to win Le Mans once," I said to Graham, "so there is no sense in going back again. There are too many slow cars along with the fast ones on the track, and along with night driving it's just too dangerous. My aim this year is to win the USAC pro sports car championship."

Then came the inevitable question: "What does it take to become a race driver?"

"Do you mean amateur or pro?" I asked. "There's a whale of a difference."

I explained it this way: "The amateur should never take the chance of getting hurt. He should always hold between zero and fifteen per cent of his speed in reserve." (Many amateurs would still be alive, or would have avoided serious crashes had they done this!) "If you want to race professionally, you need years of experience plus a competitive spirit. And you will never become a good pro driver until you've been hurt. A pro driver never takes a chance where he thinks he will get hurt, but he has to drive as fast as he can, and so he will get skinned sometime."

I could speak from hard experience, looking back only a few years. I'd shattered my elbow in that first crack-up during the Mexican road race in 1954; then, three years later, I had broken my back at Riverside when the Maserati crashed and had not even known it. Three of my vertebrae were completely fused, according to X-rays.

I rounded off the interview by saying, half jokingly, "My ambition is to build a race track in the Los Angeles area. After you get skinned and cut up enough, you begin to look around for another kind of business."

Well, I've yet to go into the race-track-building business, but my purpose in going to California was clear to me beyond any doubt. This thought of turning my dream car into a reality was bugging me more and more, until I couldn't think of anything else. I knew that California was about the only place where you might find the type of people who not only could work with their hands but also understood high-performance machinery. There are probably more people in this area dedicated to the ideal of speed on road and track than anywhere else in the world. And there's a good reason for it. They grew up here, and went to college and got their engineering degrees, and their hobby is cars and their first love is cars, but there's no place else in this country where such enthusiasts could exploit their hobby. Those who did move had to turn to the aircraft industry and gain experience there; but thank heavens my thinking was right. California has a great surplus of manpower that is capable of working on the kind of projects I'm interested in, so this is probably the only place in the world where I could do what I am doing for the amount of money I have to put into it. Although wages are high, you get a lot of productivity from people out here.

When I first came to California, I hadn't yet formulated the plan of the AC chassis and the Ford engine. I was thinking in terms of any V8 engine. At that time, it didn't make any difference to me what I used, but after I took a second long look at the Ford V8 I got to thinking that it was narrower and very little heavier than even the Buick aluminum engine, and since it was made of cast iron you didn't have any of the problems associated with aluminum, where a modestly priced production car was concerned.

As for the chassis, I've already mentioned that I had in mind something along the lines of the Austin Healey, but built with tubes. When the AG became available, this of course helped me a whole lot because it meant that we didn't have to sit down and weld our tubes together and build a fiberglass body. But I'll have a lot more to say about this later.

Meantime, I didn't have much of anything but big ideas when this whole thing began. I had sold out my share of Carroll Shelby Sports Cars to Jim and Dick Hall, back in 1958, but had agreed to let them go on using my name. This created a good tax situation for Jim because he could go racing and use the business (which was operating on a cash basis) to carry forward any tax loss. Anyway, from then on I had nothing more to do financially with Carroll Shelby Sports Cars, although I remained fairly close to the operation and on friendly terms with these people.

Talking about staying on friendly terms with people reminds me that I never did finish that business about Harry Schell, the merchant in Hong Kong, and the check on the Swiss bank that Harry stopped payment on. All through that season of 1959, every place we went racing there would be a telegram from that little man to Mr. Schell. "Please send my money. I'm bankrupt and my children are hungry!" and so forth. Finally, at Reims I believe it was, or some such place where Joe and Harry and I happened to be, we had one final big laugh about it all and Harry decided it was time to pay the man. The poor guy seemed to have suffered so much it must have taken ten years out of his life. Anyway, Harry Schell sent along the five thousand bucks he owed the guy and that was the end of the squawking.

* * *

To get back to my story, however, I still had a few more laps to go before I finally decided to hang up my hat and gloves for keeps. The next one on the calendar that I was slated to drive in after Denver was the 200-miler at Elkhart Lake, Wisconsin, the USAC-FIA Road America meet which came off about five weeks later on July 30-31. It was the first professional sports car race run on this circuit and there were a lot of names in it—people like Jim Jeffords, Skip Hudson, Billy Krause, George Constantine, Roger Penske, Jim Hall, Bob Holbert, Rodger Ward, Loyal Katskee, "Honest" John Kilbom, Peter Ryan from Canada. . . . Boy, am I dropping names! While I'm at it, I might as well give you the whole slate. It's right there in the clippings. Don Sesslar, Jack Ensley, Harry Heuer, Bud Gates, Don Skogmo, Lloyd Ruby, Charlie Kolb—heck, I'm getting out of breath and there were still a few more. Anyway, you get the idea. Not only good driving competition but a lot of good machinery as well. Oh, I nearly forgot Augie Pabst, who put up a fantastic qualifying time of 2 minutes, 41.82 seconds, in the Meister Bräuser Scarab with its engine punched out to 5.7 liters (348 cubic inches). And Carroll Shelby who stopped the watches in 2 minutes, 43.12 seconds, driving "Old Yaller II," Max Balchowsky's ugly but amazingly potent creation.

No one could have summed up this strange machine any better than Dan Gurney after he tried it for a few laps at Riverside one time. "This is as good as the finest car I've ever driven," he said, "and as comfortable as a baby buggy!"

That was the way I felt about it, too. Just for kicks, let me quote from a local paper called the Sheboygan *Press.* "Shelby's Still Having Fun Racing," it was headlined.

In this piece, the writer went on to describe Old Yaller:

"The car is strictly a home-built creation with parts of readily available stock items that aren't too expensive. Its styling is strictly for speed, rather than looks, and its aluminum skin is stretched over what Balchowsky calls a 'distributed load frame' of tubing.

"Of the two vitals—brakes and powerplant—Buick has furnished the components. The big, husky brakes are stock 1958 Buick stoppers, while the engine is of same make but, of course, souped up and topped by six potent Stromberg 97 carburetors. These still give about 7.2 miles per gallon, compared with the five that many hot Corvette engines deliver. The power unit provides 401 cubic inches of displacement, and a four-speed Jaguar transmission is used. All told, the car weighs in at 1,940 pounds with ten gallons of fuel. This famed Old Yaller is the second of its kind, the original one now having gone to another owner. Both were impressive winners and contenders in West Coast races—and with Shelby in the cockpit it could be a real dark horse. This is the car's first Midwestern appearance."

If you ever rode in a well-kept steam car, you'll have some idea of what it was like when you pushed down on Old Yaller's throttle. I've driven all kinds of cars, many of them pretty powerful, but the torque from this Balchowsky Special had them all beat. It was almost unbelievable. I don't know what the gearbox was there for. You could have started in high and stayed in that one gear all day. As a matter of record, I used only third and fourth gears in that race—while the car lasted—and it hauled me around the thirteen turns on each lap of the Road America course with a brutal, adhesion-busting power. Another thing, the mechanics who towed Old Yaller from the West Coast for this race became bored around Grand Rapids, Iowa, and took the car off its trailer. Then they drove it the rest of the way to central Wisconsin. It was a perfectly tractable street car, providing you trod that gas pedal *softly*. Otherwise, you were liable to find yourself sideways at short notice, or maybe with no notice at all!

Along with my car, another equally rare tire-spinner arrived from California. This was Billy Krause's very hot D-Jag with a 320-cubic-inch V8 Corvette mill under its hood. But on this occasion the engine just wouldn't run right and mysteriously lost power despite a careful pre-race tear-down and an item by item checkout. Krause got madder by the minute as grid time drew near, but his mechanics never did find the trouble.

The Belle of the Ball, so to speak, was a *Tipo 61* Birdcage Maserati driven by Jim Jeffords. This was a special model built for Camoradi and equipped with a long windshield and a long tail; Masten Gregory had driven it at Le Mans that year, and proved it the fastest car along Mulsanne Straight with a timed speed of 170 mph. He had also set the fastest lap around the Sarthe circuit in 4:03—nearly 124 mph—before blowing up the engine. And Jim Jeffords was no slouch, either, believe me. In fact he ended up by winning at Elkhart Lake, but not before I gave him and the others a good run for their money.

Dallas and Carroll Shelby Sports Cars were pretty well represented by a couple more of those three-liter Birdcages, one of them driven by Jim Hall, the other by Bob Schroeder. There was still another Birdcage, this one handled by Loyal Katskee, who was also running the pro circuit. Talk about safety in numbers!

Old Yaller, however, wasn't in the least put out. When the flag dropped I shot into the lead and started pulling away from Augie Pabst at the rate of about two seconds a lap. Red Byron, who later came to work for me, called the race pretty well when he said, "Much as I'd like to see Shel and Max [Balchowsky] get a win—not this time, please. I can't believe that yellow thing will last."

But that was before the start. Old Yaller whirled away happily, without any challenge, earning me $50 a lap and stretching our lead out to forty seconds by the thirtieth of that fifty-lap race. At that point Pabst, who was still second, held a 13-second advantage on Jeffords with the Birdcage, while Jeffords had a hard time of it staying ahead of Hall and Krause as they took turns filling his rear-view mirror. Krause's Chevy-D-Jag had mysteriously found its speed, after all, as the engine settled down to a tough job. It wasn't engine trouble that finished Krause but a bad bearing in the Halibrand rear end of his car. And it wasn't engine trouble that finished me, either; it was a big bang when I reached for fourth gear on the thirty-first lap and the main transmission shaft let go.

Man, I really thought I had that one in the bag. It was so easy I felt like a kid getting paid to eat candy!

But in spite of my disappointment, I guess it might have been worse. I still came away with about $1625 in qualifying and lap prize money. Not as good as the jackpot but a helluva lot better than nothing.

As I said, Jeffords won it, Hall was second, and Katskee third. What you might call a "Birdcage Day"!

About this time, the angina pectoralis began to get pretty rough and those pains in my chest kept coming back, so that I had to practically live with a nitro pill under my tongue. The doctors insisted that I ought to quit and I began to ask myself if, maybe, they weren't right, after all. I was thirty-seven and I'd climbed to the top the hard way, not sparing myself anywhere along the route. Maybe those crashes had taken something out of me that I didn't even know? It was hard for me to really believe that because, in spite of the discomforts and the skinnings, this was the sport that I knew and loved and had lived with all my life. My reflexes, I knew, were still pretty sharp, and if I was put to it I knew I could still hold my own in any company. But this heart thing was another matter. If I was really serious about building the car I had so long dreamed about, it would be smarter not to spread myself out too thin—not to try to do too many things at one time. Something had to go so that I could conserve my energies and build up strength, and racing was the most logical activity to give up, even if it was the hardest thing to do.

Still, I wanted to be sure of winning that U.S. sports car championship, and so as to nail it down beyond any question I decided to go for some extra points at Laguna Seca on October 8 and 9 of that year. This was the Pacific Grand Prix for Sports Cars—a USAC-sponsored race of two hundred miles which carried good money, and I decided to accept Frank Harris's offer to drive his *Tipo 61*, three-liter Birdcage Maserati. I liked the course, which I knew about as well as my own backyard, and I liked the car, too. But the opposition was tough this time, and I found myself directly up against three of the hardest pushers in the business—Stirling Moss, Augie Pabst, and Billy Krause, the latter a hugely aggressive driver with some pretty good skill to match.

Moss had a Lotus 19 with a four-cylinder, twin-cam, 2.5-liter Coventry Climax engine that could chum out 239 brake horsepower at 6700 rpm against almost no weight. Pabst had his Scarab with its gobs of power, while Krause s mount was also a Birdcage Maserati. Moss held off Pabst to win handily enough, despite the Scarab's 5.5-liter Chevy engine; he also held off a strong attack by Brabham, the Aussie World Champion, and after the eighth lap no one could come near him. To give an example of Krause's aggressiveness, he was determined to dislodge Hall from third spot, but didn't have quite enough speed to get by. So he nerfed Hall right off the course and made it that way. I finished fourth without any trouble but without too much excitement, either. I didn't feel especially good that day, and in that company you couldn't afford to be anywhere but right on your toes.

Where do you stop? Which is the last lap? Hindsight is the cheapest luxury in the world because it doesn't help worth a durn. Who needs it? It's *beforehand* that you have to try to guess if you're going to do yourself any good. After Laguna I decided to quit racing, but I must have had some mental reservation—like the guy who decides to quit smoking but isn't quite ready yet. So maybe I shouldn't have started in that CSCC race at Riverside on December 3 and 4; maybe I should have stuck to my decision. But the fact was that I *liked* driving in races, despite all the discomforts that I hid even from those nearest to me.

And this one was the last big event of the season—the Third Annual Los Angeles *Times-Mirror* Grand Prix for Sports Cars. Some title, any way you pronounce it. During practice, a forty-mile-an-hour wind kicked grit into our faces and everyone was hot to trot. There was a lot of prize money—about $25,000 worth—and an "officially estimated" crowd of eighty thousand fans. I don't know when I ever saw such a mob at a U.S. sports car race.

The main event was a 203-miler and I had second fastest qualifying time of the Maserati Birdcages after Krause, who eventually won. He had a brand new Type 61 entered by the Maserati representatives of California and in topnotch tune. Still, it was Moss who took the lead and held the pack by a length in his green Lotus 19 at the start of the first lap. Gurney got by him before the 3.275 miles were completed and led at the end of the first lap in his red Lotus 19. With 240 brake horsepower and about a thousand pounds to haul around, these babies were hard to beat. Doc Thompson was third in a Sting Ray Corvette, working hard. Moss regained the lead on lap two but lost it again to Dan on the sixth as those two played tag. Meantime, Krause got by Thompson into third. On the tenth lap

Moss quit with the usual troubles—transmission and clutch. Gurney blew a head gasket on lap seventeen and that was when Krause took the lead. Bob Drake with Balchowsky's Old Yaller II grabbed second spot, while Jeffords's Birdcage, Pabst's Scarab, Phil Hill's Ferrari, Doc Thompson, and I got into a swinging battle for third spot. But this was not my day. Halfway along my engine seemed to lose power and I couldn't hack the same lap times any longer. Pabst eventually took over third, Jeffords was fourth, and I finished fifth.

And that was it. I went home, hung up my hat, and quit for good.

What was I trying to prove by going on with a bum ticker? You win one and lose one, but it's a downhill battle. I'm sure, now, that I made the right decision.

But the great question, of course, was what to do next? I mean for groceries and such. I was now thirty-seven years old, a little short of health, and more than somewhat short on real money. I had a dream, a hope, and a lot of experience, but no one seemed likely to buy the dream unless I could translate the hope into something more tangible. That was where my long driving experience came in real handy. I remember that when I started racing I wasted at least a couple of years in getting to learn things about motor racing that an intelligent and qualified instructor could have taught me in a few days without any "blood, sweat, toil, and tears," to paraphrase the late Sir Winston Churchill.

Why not pass the benefit of this experience on to aspiring (and often perspiring!) race drivers and, at the same time, make a buck in the process which would enable me to get a few steps nearer what I really wanted to do—build a medium-priced, high-performance, American-powered automobile that would blow off the foreign competition?

That was how S.H.P.D. came into being. Sounds like a lot of mysterious symbols, but actually it's just an abbreviation for the Shelby School of High Performance Driving. What did I mean by "high performance driving"? I meant smooth driving; confident driving; a basic but thorough understanding of why a driver does certain things under certain conditions at speed; how he can get the most out of any car without tearing it (and himself) apart; how he can learn to evaluate his skills, pinpoint his own limitations, and generally come out a much better driver—whether he intends to drive in competition or not.

There's so much to be written about this subject that I could easily fill an entire chapter with details about the technique of good driving, either on the road or on a race course; but I've decided to save this for another time, and another book. It's enough to say here that S.H.P.D. turned out to be such a tremendous success, that it marked the turning point in the financial side of my life, and that a $90 ad, telling about the school and inviting prospective students to send a buck for some literature, brought in fourteen hundred replies, each with a dollar bill!

For all practical purposes, the school opened its doors in 1961 at Riverside track, which not only had all the topographical features needed to put novice drivers through the hopper, but also was conveniently located about an hour's drive from Los Angeles.

The school started, of course, after I moved to Santa Fe Springs, California, from Dallas, and Dean Moon had offered me a nice little speed shop from which we would be able to operate when the first Cobras started coming through. I'm using the term "we," here, with plenty of good reason: because the other half of this enterprise (and also the other irons I had in the fire) was a brilliant young stylist and designer named Pete Brock, who had worked on the Sting Ray project but just didn't care for big corporations. Pete, a born driver himself, felt the same way that I did about the need for the kind of school I had in mind. It had to break completely new ground and although it wasn't by any means the first of its kind in the world, we intended that it should be the best.

Pete Brock, as I said, had several different talents and later on, as Shelby American grew larger, he became one of my key men. At this time, however, his abilities as a driver and designer were just what I needed because he was articulate enough to explain to students just what the school was trying to do for them and at the same time could provide a useful graphic background by means of sketches on a mobile blackboard which could be easily transported to any given point on the Riverside course. I've never had much patience with details, but Pete was soon able to run the school from a prepared curriculum and do much of the actual instructing. Of course we had discussed the whole thing in some detail over a period of weeks before opening up, and I'd given Pete a fairly clear outline of my philosophy on the school and how it should be run, but from then on he picked up the ball and ran with it. I then devoted more and more time to the Cobra project, to my growing Goodyear race tire distributorship, which often required our making actual track tests of some new product under racing conditions, and to Champion spark plugs, which I also handled.

Well, to cut short a long and interesting story, S.H.P.D. succeeded beyond our most optimistic hopes. We had made arrangements to rent Riverside Raceway on a weekly basis for a special rate because we intended to be out there for quite some time. In fact, our curriculum was based mainly on the idea of teaching one pupil at a time for a week at a time, either with his own car or with one supplied by the school, in which case, of course, the rate would be higher. But we didn't work set hours so much as with a definite objective—to bring every promising student to a given standard of proficiency within a week. Pete Brock was so devoted to this phase of his work that he actually rented a house almost on the very edge of Riverside track so as to be as close as possible to his work!

Since, as the old saying goes, "the proof of the pudding is in the eating!" I'll end by saying that in the first American Road Race of Champions held at Riverside last year, six or seven of our former pupils won their respective Divisional SCCA class championship and were invited to compete in the finals.

And we've had them from all walks of life—not just would-be Fangios. A chef on a transpacific liner; a guy who bought an E-Type Jag and wanted to learn how to drive it; men who, through our S.H.P.D., became master at handling just about everything from the heavy and cumbersome Corvette to the fleet and dangerously fast Lotus 7. And more than one good-looking girl driver, too!

And we certainly shouldn't forget John Timanus, a noted West Coast driver who joined our school as an instructor when things got way beyond the handling of just Pete and myself and who has done a great job as a first-class instructor ever since.

-16-
THE DREAM COMES TRUE

THE THING IN life that spells "success" is to take advantage of the right opportunity, I guess. The right opportunity, so far as my dream car was concerned, occurred when I got news that the Bristol Aeroplane Company in England had gone out of the business of building automobile engines. Some AC cars had been put into production with a British Ford Zephyr engine—a small six-cylinder mill that went pretty well—but the drop in sales did not seem to justify continued manufacture of the old and honorable make of AC under those conditions. Suddenly I saw the light. The light, strong, tubular AC chassis was the ideal medium for an American V8. I decided I had better get going, but quick, before the AC factory decided to close down altogether. So I airmailed a letter to Thames Ditton, near London, England, in September, 1961, suggesting that with some not-too-extensive modifications to the AC chassis we might drop an American V8 into it and get really terrific performance for a low initial cost, plus the kind of flexibility and day-to-day reliability I had in mind. I mentally thanked the Bristol Aeroplane Company for their decision and kept my fingers crossed that the backbone of the AC firm—the Hurlock brothers—would go along with my idea. Primarily my letter was addressed to Charles Hurlock of AC, but his nephew Derek also had a finger in the pie. In this letter I didn't mention Ford specifically, or in any way, because what I had in mind was a Chevy engine, maybe, or a Buick aluminum engine, or something from Oldsmobile. Another reason why I didn't mention Ford was because I had not yet heard of their new lightweight cast iron block, but oddly enough the seed had already been sown with Ford.

On July 4 I had met Dave Evans of the Ford Company at the Pike's Peak Hillclimb, where he represented Ford while I was the Goodyear representative. Dave, a short, intense type of man with a razor-sharp mind and the ability to look ahead, was in charge of the Ford stock car racing program and the engine end of this program. I did not, at this time, mention to him what I had in mind regarding a V8 powerplant to go into a lightweight, sports-type chassis, but we got to know each other and that was a start that proved far more useful than I ever dreamed possible.

At this time I was operating from a small office and space I had in Dean Moon's speed equipment shop in Santa Fe Springs, working up my Goodyear distributorship and the Champion spark plug business, and, of course, directing S.H.P.D. from there as well. I had moved to Santa Fe Springs because that was conveniently near my place of business, and along in October I heard of the new Ford casting process which had enabled them to produce a lightweight V8 engine at much reduced cost, with none of the complication of the series-produced aluminum job. Meantime a favorable reply had come back from Charles Hurlock in England stating that he would be interested in my plan if a suitable engine could be found and tested in one of his AC cars.

So the moment I heard about the new Ford engine, I wrote a letter to Dave Evans and told him I was going to build a versatile type of sports car and needed a competitive engine, and asked whether Ford had any racing plans for their new lightweight cast iron job which was going into the Fairlane.

Evans didn't waste any time in writing me back. He picked up the phone from Dearborn and got through to me with characteristic speed of decision.

"Carroll Shelby?"

"You've got him."

"This is Dave Evans of Ford. I just received your letter and I think you might have something. That AC chassis may be just the thing for our new engine."

"Yeah," I agreed, "it sure might."

"Tell you what we're going to do," Dave said. "We're sending you a couple of these new engines. Play around with them;

put them in your chassis and see what you come up with. Let me know."

I tried to sound casual—you know, the so-called Texan drawl and such—but inwardly I was really hipped up. Now I had both a chassis and an engine and it was just a matter of putting the combination together. I wrote Charles Hurlock another letter and told him of this development and that we were going to soup up those Fairlanes a bit before dropping one into an AC chassis. I gave him the dimension of the Ford power unit and the weight, which was little more than that of the Bristol engine—a good but obsolete design derived directly from the prewar German BMW 307, with transverse pushrods and absolutely no low-speed torque. I suggested that Mr. Hurlock might come up with some ideas for basically altering the AC chassis to absorb the power and torque of the Ford mill. I also came up with some ideas of my own, which I sketched in a general way as a start.

Meantime the Ford engines arrived somewhere about November and we started playing with them right away. Here, Dean Moon's help proved invaluable in hopping up those two Fairlane units, increasing valve size, porting, balancing and such. We also played around with carburetion and ignition. One of the first things we learned, though, was that this 221-cubic-inch engine was as strong as a horse and so husky at the bottom end, with five main bearings of ample size, that it could stand a lot of hopping up and was therefore an excellent candidate for racing.

But Dave Evans had another trick up his sleeve. Soon afterward he called me up again with a "get ready for this one!" tone in his voice and said, "By the way, we have a high-performance version of this engine in a 260-cubic-inch size which might be just the right thing for you. So we're sending you a couple of those as well. Try them on for size."

Needless to say I was delighted and at once got off another letter to Charles Hurlock to let him know of this new development. Negotiations with AC were well advanced by then, so I scraped up what money I could and flew over to England to finalize the details which would enable us to bring the first AC chassis and the first Ford engine together as a complete car.

The Hurlocks, who own the AC business and are certainly not hurting for cash, proved extremely helpful. They worked closely with me when we found we had to make a lot more changes to the chassis than had at first appeared necessary, or that most people might think. For instance, we needed a whole new rear-end carrier assembly to cope with the vastly increased torque. We also needed to beef up the front suspension, which was basically a transverse spring. But against this we had some pleasant surprises. The Fairlane engine fitted right into the existing compartment and we didn't even have to relocate it or move it farther back because, surprising as it might seem, it was only about fifteen pounds heavier than the Bristol.

However, as might be expected, there were other problems. The Bristol gearbox would stand but about 90 foot-pounds of torque, which was completely useless for our purpose. But we had the Ford gearbox to fall back on, which could absorb up to 400 foot-pounds and weighed only eight or ten pounds more and, in addition, had synchromesh in low as well. So that suited our needs perfectly, more so because it didn't have to be matched to the engine. It already was.

Added weight with the Ford power unit and transmission never became a problem and we had all the room we needed. Where the wrinkles came in was that we were throwing much heavier loads on the car's components in starting and stopping and going around corners at any sort of speed. This became apparent when we began tests with the front end of the AC chassis. The car had worm and sector steering and very small frontwheel spindles, and when we started hitting bumps at 135 mph with parts that had never before been called upon to withstand more than 100 mph, the trouble began. We started knocking some of the suspension and steering hangers loose and soon discovered that the stub axles were not equal to the job. All this testing and modifying took time and patience, of course, and it wasn't until February of 1962 that the first car was completed as a unit and ready for evaluation. At that point, although everything was not perfect, we *knew* we had the basis of what I had so long dreamed about and that the car would do what was expected of it.

When the first car arrived in Santa Fe Springs, although it bore the designation CSX0001 (Carroll Shelby Experimental) we already had the name for it. While the machine was on its way from England a strange thing happened. One night I had a dream in which I saw the name "Cobra" on the front of the new car. I woke up and jotted the name down on a pad which I kept by my bedside—a sort of ideas pad—and went back to sleep. Next morning when I looked at the name "Cobra," I knew it was right. This had to be it. But when I decided to call my car the Cobra, we ran into an unexpected problem while getting the paperwork ready to apply for a copyright. It suddenly turned up that years before Crosley had built an engine which they had called a "Cobra," though for very different reasons.

The little Crosley overhead-camshaft mill had been COpper BRAzed—get the idea? Fortunately, however, it had passed through nine different companies with the engine, rights, and patents, etc., changing hands each time, and not one of those nine successive firms had ever used the name "Cobra." It therefore turned out that the name Cobra no longer could be considered as a valid trade name insofar as Crosley was concerned, and we were able to copyright it.

The name that had come to me in that dream went over so well that Pete Brock already had the name badge designed when CSX0001 arrived in California. However, it was still some time before we were able to use that name by itself, for reasons I'll explain in a moment.

CSX0001—the future Cobra—was flown in after I had spent some time in England at the AC factory getting the necessary chassis modifications carried out and testing the car; and now the next step was to do a hard-selling job with Ford. If I could convince the Ford people to let me have some engines on credit, then it would not be too difficult, I thought, to convince the Hurlock brothers and nephew to do the same with the AC chassis, until I could get the ball rolling and production started.

So I called Dave Evans in Dearborn and told him what I had and asked whether he'd be interested in discussing things further.

"How does the car look to you?" he asked.

"Pretty good," I said. "Not perfect. It needs some more development work, but I firmly believe we have something worthwhile. The performance is fantastic but the handling needs to be improved here and there."

"You think it's practical?"

"No problem there. I'm convinced it's feasible and I want you to see it."

"Bring the car to Dearborn, then, and lets take a look."

"I'm on my way!"

It was characteristic of Evans that he took one look at the car, drove it around a bit, and said, "I'd like you to come in and talk to Don Frey, who's in charge of planning for the Ford Division from an engineering standpoint. He knows all about what you're trying to do."

"Fine," I agreed.

Mr. Frey turned out to be an academic, college professor type of man with glasses, but he was another of the "heads up" group at Ford Division and he didn't miss a trick. In fact, to my mind, he's probably the most knowledgeable racing executive in the world.

I told him briefly what I had in mind and he listened and nodded. I got the impression he kind of liked the idea. He's a young guy—only about forty years old—for the position he holds today, that of general manager of the entire Ford Division, but he's also a hunch player where something makes sense to him.

"I drove an old Allard when I was in the Army, back in 1950," he smiled, "and I know what you mean about that kick in the seat when you put a lot of torque into a lightweight chassis. Matter of fact I don't mind admitting I've been a sports car buff for quite a while."

Well, he, too, had a look at the car and then we came back to his office and talked some more, and after a while Don said, "You know, I think you may have something there."

Then he excused himself and left the office for a moment and I guess he must have talked to some other people and told them, "Let's play along with this fellow's pipe dream for a while. You never can tell."

Don had to take this attitude, I guess, because most of the people at Ford, as in any other automobile company, have a problem in common: they just *don't* like cars! To them, cars are just a job—something to be treated in the same way that you treat an icebox or a washing machine or a TV set. To their way of thinking, any man who *does* love automobiles, the way I did and still do and always will, is a nut. He's a freak, not quite right in the head. Because in the industry to enthuse about automobiles simply isn't done.

But, thank God, Don Frey is cast in another mold. He liked cars and didn't think of them as "just another product that you make and sell." He gave the idea his blessing, which meant that he gave me the chance to put something together and I was able to get engines from Ford on the cuff till I could sell some cars. When Charles Hurlock got this news in England, he sportingly went along, too, and offered me the chassis on credit. What he asked in return for this financing wasn't much, really. He agreed to the name "Cobra," as did Ford, but asked that we use the name "AC" as part of the car's designation. Of course we agreed to this. Ford, in the beginning, were not sure that they wanted their name associated with my project, so there was no problem on that score, but they did insist on my name being used, too. So we started off with the "Shelby AC Cobra," later we went from there to just "AC Cobra" and, finally, to "Ford Cobra" when we had become a success.

Well, now that I had the cars and the engines, the next thing was to find some place to put them together and continue development work. Let's face it, CSX0001 was a hunk of dynamite, all right, but compared with today's Cobra you wouldn't be too far off in calling it a dog. Then there was this matter of installing equipment and storing cars and engines. We started looking around right away and came up with a pretty good answer. Lance Reventlow was getting out of business and had decided to quit building Scarabs and his place was available. He'd had all the fun out of it that he wanted, so he had made up his mind to move out. There was a bunch of wonderful machinery available and (we then thought) more room than we would ever need. So we made a deal with him and moved in during June of 1962.

It was then that Don Frey's counsel and guidance proved of tremendous help, since I had no actual business education. Don assigned to us a brilliant businessman who held a master's degree in business and who was also a lawyer. His name was Ray Geddes and he was then in the business and control end of Ford—a young man with dark hair and keen eyes that missed nothing. It's thanks to Ray that I was able to plan and guide the financial end of the business to where it is today. In fact I would say that if any two people deserve credit for getting my company to its present state of success, they are Don Frey and Ray Geddes. However we also got a lot of help from Dave Evans and Jacque Passino. This team worked marvels whenever we got bogged down for one reason or another and saw me through all the hard spots that you just can't escape when you're starting a new enterprise—especially one of this kind.

Derek Hurlock also deserves much praise for doing a large part of the initial testing for me while I was busy on this side, most of the time working on engine development. Following the 221 engine that we sent over to start with, which included a four-speed box, we sent the 260-cubic-inch high-performance engine. The difference between these two was merely the size of the connecting rods, the increased bore, solid lifters, and different pistons. Otherwise it had the same cast iron crank and all the other features of what's probably the world's best pushrod V8.

During those early 1961 days when I had the drivers' school going and the big project was taking shape, Pete Brock actually lived beside Riverside Raceway, just to be as close as possible to his job. He was a truly dedicated enthusiast, only about twenty-three years old at the time, but just to give you some idea of his ability, when I talked to him, one time, about styling a body for a car, he said casually, "Yeah, I have some drawings here—some sketches I did of a car that General Motors was going to build when I worked for them."

"General Motors?" I stared at him. "I had no idea you'd worked for them."

"Yes," he said. "I worked for them for about a year, but they're too big and bundlesome and I don't like to work for a big company. Not one that size, anyway."

"So you quit?"

Sure thing, Pete had quit and come out to California, broke, and gladly taken on the job of instructor at S.H.P.D. when I offered it to him. Do you know what those drawings were that he showed me? They were sketches of the Sting Ray. That was what he had already accomplished when he was only twenty-one or twenty-two.

Anyway, he helped in many different ways—not only at the track. For instance, when I put on a couple of enduros for Corvairs, he was on tap, ready to assist because we had been talking about doing some business with them, engine-wise. At the same time, Pete was driving his own Lotus in races. He was a very good driver and still is. To this day he gets all steamed up when I tell him he's too valuable to us to be a race driver, but he still gets in a lick whenever he can. Recently we were out doing a movie and Pete came by to run through his scene, and of course he had to get in just one more lap, as fast as he could go, in this Mustang. He actually wore out a set of tires where he should have used about one millimeter of tread.

In a way, the trouble is that I have too many people around my place who can do just about everything, and Pete Brock is about the best example of this. He did the body design of the now famous Daytona Coupe, about which I'll have more to say later. In all, I think he must have designed probably as many as fifteen Specials that are now running around the country. He designs all of our letterheads, too, and the Cobra T-shirts. He also laid out the first Cobra ads. He's chief instructor at our school; he used to run the accessory department, which does quite a volume of business; and of course he has this unusual driving ability. So you can see how versatile the guy is. In fact, if I were going to pick somebody to drive on the team, I'd pick him as quickly as I would some of our name professionals.

So you can see how our little organization was put together from the beginning. Pete was the first employee I had. Well, that's not quite right either. I started off with a telephone answering service and Pete was the second employee.

On the mechanical end, there are the people in Dean Moon's shop—men such as Larson, who built the first headers for the first Cobra. It took us two and a half years to come up with a better configuration, which we finally did about three months ago. I've had from fifty to seventy-five people working in the engine shop. And who was the first driver I had for the Cobra—Billy Krause! He did a lot of the track testing and then drove the Cobra in its first race, a three-hour enduro at Riverside, where the new Sting Ray also competed. We had a four-barrel carburetor and the 260 engine, but the Webers were not yet completed—at least the manifolding wasn't. Billy led the race for about an hour before a stub axle broke.

The next race that Krause drove in for us was at Nassau in 1962, and there the front end fell apart. Bolts started coming adrift from the worm and sector steering mounts and that was the end of the day. It was also the end of the worm and sector steering. We had been thinking about rack and pinion and that decided us.

At about that time Chevrolet was fixing to get into a big program of Corvette racing and Mickey Thompson came to Billy and offered him a lot more money than I could pay, so the poor, unlucky devil signed the contract. He discussed it with me first and I told him to go ahead because it was an offer he just couldn't afford to turn down financially, and I'll be a son of a gun if within a couple of weeks they didn't decide to withdraw from racing! But I'd like to have Billy driving again for me this year if Shelby American runs any factory entries with the Cobras. I don't know what happened to his contract. It was none of my business—just something between Krause and Thompson and General Motors.

But to get back to our beginnings, after I got the first car race-tested by Pete Brock, Billy Krause and I built another car and sent it to Dearborn for evaluation. Looking back, I guess I got away with a lot in starting out as an automobile manufacturer, but even so I put up about $40,000 in developing the first car to the point where it was a salable item. I wasn't exactly broke when I quit racing, although my assets in ready cash amounted to little or nothing. But I had other things going for me—a few little assets lying around and a lot of credit from a lot of friends. There were many people without whom I could never have put the first Cobra together. These people didn't have much money but they did have a lot to do with the automotive world and that helped no end. Names that come to mind are *Road and Track* and Petersen Publications and people like Dean Batchelor, Wally Parks, John Christy, Dean Moon, and a lot of others.

The second Cobra traveled in style to Dearborn. We flew it out there, and although this might sound like a lot of expense, with deferred rates it's cheaper to fly a car than carry it on a truck. Deferred rates simply means that the vehicle doesn't have priority of transportation, so it might take a day and a half to fly a car from California to Michigan, but it only costs about a couple of hundred bucks. Anyway, Ford flies all their racing cars because they figured long ago it was cheaper that way.

When Cobra No. 2 got to Dearborn, Engineering took it over. I think Dan Jones was in charge of the project and he did a pretty thorough job. We talked on the phone every day, discussing each problem as it came up—evaluating the electrical system, steering, instrumentation, you name it, the same way they would evaluate any Ford. By this time, Phil Remington, one of the finest practical engineers in the automotive business, had come to work for us. He was one of the original hot rodders, along with Stu Hilborn, Frank Koons, Jim Travers, Wally Parks, Vic Edelbrock, and many others who started the hot rod movement back in the thirties. What Phil doesn't know about an automobile, I don't think anybody in the world knows; so you can forget it. He was working very closely at this time with the Ford Engineering people, evaluating the second Cobra that we built. There's one thing, however, I want to make clear: Ford didn't help me build that car; what they did was to sell me engines on credit and, of course, transmissions. They also offered me the valuable facilities of their engineering and sales departments, or any other department where I might get help when I need it.

Since then, when I've needed financial advice Ford has been there to help me; or when I've had need of public relations advice they've also provided that kind of assistance; but they haven't financed the cars or anything like that.

Anyway, about the middle of 1962 along came a customer and I sold my first Cobra. By the end of that year I had sold between seventy-five and eighty cars, but the ratio of race car to street car sales was (as we had expected) very low—only about 10 to 15 per cent. That's how few of the people who buy my cars have any idea of racing them. This figures; it doesn't bother us at all. In fact, we like it that way because the Cobra is just as good on the street or for going to and from the supermarket and the railroad station as it is dashing around those mad curves of the Targa Florio or bowling along the banked track at Daytona. It can wear pretty much any kind of hat its driver wants.

We're still in the Reventlow building as this book is being written, but we'll shortly be moving again, this time to much larger premises vacated by North American on the perimeter of Los Angeles airport. This, too, I'll have more to say about later.

As regards that wonderful word "homologation," which seems to have been invented by the FIA or one of those learned European bodies, we quickly proved that we had the components ordered and were building cars at the rate of so many a day; and that happened to be at just about the time Signor Enzo Ferrari was building eight or ten cars—lo and behold!—getting *them* homologated, too. So we didn't have too much trouble. No sir. Luckily the rules have now been tightened up a little bit so that a person really has to build a hundred cars to get a homologation certificate for a particular model and move out of the Prototype into the GT class.

By the end of 1962 we already had the Cobra homologated as a regular Grand Touring automobile, but although the Ford company allowed us to use their dealers, I had to go around and contact them myself. However, after the buff magazines road-tested our car, it was the Ford dealers who contacted *us*. We currently have about 175 dealers but are planning to cut back to 100 because, since we build a limited production automobile, we're primarily interested in dealers who have the knowledge and capability of merchandising the car. Discount artists don't really belong in our organization. They have enough scope in the mass-production market.

So, by the end of 1962, you could say that we really were in business and producing automobiles. Despite an oversized quota of headaches, we had at least seventy-five cars sold and delivered over here and something like another hundred chassis built and on the water. And we had only begun producing the Cobra in March. Not a bad start when you consider that it takes something like five weeks to get the chassis and bodies across the ocean.

-17-
ANATOMY OF A COBRA

I THINK ONE of the most startling things about the Cobra is that there is very little difference between the street machine and the racing car. This was one of the objectives I had in mind from the beginning; it was how I visualized the Cobra before ever it became reality; and we are continuing this philosophy in our new 427-cubic-inch version for 1965. In fact, other than a wider tread and more horsepower, there was at first virtually no difference between the new Cobra and the 289-cubic-inch version.

If you want to go racing, of course, there are certain things you must do to make the car competitive, but they are mainly in the performance department; they have little or nothing to do with safety and roadability. You need a rollbar, naturally, because no car is allowed on the course without one, but outside of that it's things like brake scoops to keep the brakes cool, slightly harder brake pads, which wear longer, magnesium wheels with wider rims that provide a lighter rolling mass and space for tires better suited to racing and better able to "absorb" more horsepower, and a so-called bigger engine, meaning more horsepower than is available from the stock 289-cubic-inch Ford Fairlane engine. (I've already mentioned the 427-cubic-inch mill being installed in our production cars.) On the competition 289 job we add Weber carburetors, change the manifolds (intake and exhaust), put in solid lifters instead of hydraulic ones, and rework the cylinder heads extensively to provide better "breathing." With the changes we can get up to 385 horsepower from the 289-cubic-inch engine and *that's* what you might call a big stableful of horses!

One other thing: we do install adjustable shock absorbers, but we don't monkey around with the standard spring rates or suspension or anything like that. You get exactly the same suspension in your street Cobra as we use in the race cars, and essentially the same automobile as we assign to the best-known pro driver. Naturally the zero-to-sixty acceleration figure depends on the way the car is geared. Most of the races we run are the USRRC (United States Road Racing Championship) events, and on the majority of these circuits we run a little bit higher gearing than you would normally run on the street, but zero-to-sixty is still within the four- to five-second range.

I am convinced that one of the most important factors contributing to the Cobra's success is the tremendous over-the-counter availability of practically any part. We don't use crankshafts machined from steel billets and costing $650 apiece; we don't use specially forged connecting rods or exotic cast pistons or any of that stuff. It's all standard 289 high-performance equipment, right from the factory.

I'll tell you precisely what happens when an engine arrives from Dearborn. We open the crate and as a routine procedure disassemble everything and check it over carefully. Then we rebalance the moving parts, just to make absolutely sure there's no problem. This we regard as our *own* insurance. It's not that we're afraid the factory engine might be faulty or anything, because even if it were, the normal warranty would take care of this. But even where a customer gets a new part for nothing, it wastes his time and our time and it does nothing for the goodwill we want to build up. Of course, it's always possible that some mistake *might* creep in with a mass-produced engine, especially where machines take over most of the work; but we've found mighty few, if any, errors so far. We use all the stock parts, but we drill a couple of holes in the block to let the oil go back down faster into the crankcase. That's because at the high rpm's we use, the engine tends to pump a lot of oil up into the top—more than is really needed.

Until a little while ago, believe it or not, we were even using the stock Fairlane valve springs and camshaft; but in the end, the search for more power finally decided us to switch to a slightly hotter cam and this was bound to entail stronger valve springs. The reason for this change was the development work we did on the engine—the original development work—gave us so much horsepower at the bottom of the range that we were breaking loose too quickly and tire adhesion had become quite a problem when you tromped the throttle. Since, as you know, a cam limits your rpm to a certain range where you get the most out of the engine, what we did was to go to a different camshaft configuration which gave us more horsepower at the *top* end. To achieve this, we planned on losing a little at the bottom, where we could well spare it, and this in turn made the car much more controllable.

In a word, this was exactly the opposite of the development work we had done in the first place, with a view to increasing *bottom end* power of the car. Our approach proved to be right and gave us a more balanced engine performancewise and an easier car to drive. On our latest Cobras you can no longer put all the power on the ground at once, even if you stomp the throttle, so the car doesn't go sideways anymore. Putting it another way, the engine as it comes from the factory in stock form is a nice blend of low-end power and maximum speed but start playing around with improved porting and cylinder heads and you find yourself with an *excess* of low-speed torque, unless you switch to a different cam, one which is designed to shift the power and torque peak much higher up than normal. The other modifications still leave you all the torque at the low end that you can use with any degree of safety.

Get the idea?

As for parts availability and service, why heck, if you can't find what you want at your local Ford dealer (I mean any dealer who advertises high-performance equipment), all you need do is call us and we can get anything you need to any part of the United States or the world in less time than it might take you to recite Kipling's "If!" Well, for me that would be easy because I can't recite the durn thing, anyway. But it doesn't much matter whether you need a wristpin or a complete engine, you get the same attention.

Everyone who first walks in the door to buy a Cobra asks the same question, funnily enough: "What can I have for an option? What have you got that'll make this car *really* go?" It just seems to be a standard American phrase and the guy feels that he simply has to ask the question. Of course he's curious, too.

Well, we know there's no way that you can talk people out of this notion, so the first thing we do is to hand them the keys of a stock Cobra and say, "Here. Try this one. Be our guest. Then come back and we'll discuss options. Okay?"

So they take off with a lead foot and when, after a while, they come back, they say, "I guess I really don't need any of those speed options after all!"

The standard car comes with a limited slip differential and that's one of the things that amazes many people—all the extras we deliver standard on the car, which normally would cost a small fortune in options. The limited slip, a four-speed, all-synchromesh gearbox, disc brakes, full instrumentation, racing-type multiple-spoke wire wheels—all these things are standard in our automobile. You don't have to pay a dime extra for them. Not a cent.

Yet the fact remains that everyone who drives a Cobra is an individual in himself; an entity apart, just a little bit different from the next person. So you can't very well build a car by the IBM process, where you punch a card that triggers off certain operations and exactly the same automobile comes down the assembly line, just because market research shows that X number of people are going to ask for the very same thing. It doesn't work that way. In fact, I think one of the most enjoyable things about selling a Cobra is the knowledge that each person who buys one is a little different from the next person. Almost anyone who comes in is somebody that you would like to talk to and I think he's precisely the type of guy we built this car for. He's an individual who knows and appreciates fine machinery and who falls for a beautiful thing when he sees it. Not only that, but he knows how to use it and as a rule he's a pretty good driver.

It's surprising, you know, how many Cobra owners are people who first bought other high-performance makes like Jaguar and Sting Ray, then one day came down and took a look at the Cobra and asked for a demonstration. They were quick to spot the areas where we lacked a few things, like roll-up windows and all the other fancy stuff—yet they couldn't wait to turn around and get out and go and sell that other car so as to get together the price of the Cobra.

"This is a *real* automobile!" is their usual (and gratifying) comment.

The original worm and sector steering we used on the first Cobras was an exact copy of what had been fitted to the British AC chassis for years—the AC Ace and Ace Bristol; but as we began to add more horsepower and push the speed up, the front-end geometry became a critical factor. In any case, the geometry of those early worm and sector steering setups wasn't exactly the best. You could, for instance, jack up the front end and it would go from toe-in to toe-out—a kind of crazy transformation. Again, the change we made here, to rack and pinion steering, was a development that stemmed from racing—something that we found necessary for safety and controllability. So as soon as we got the Cobra version on the road, we began making changes to the steering, where necessary, that eventually led to the rack and pinion system. Phil Remington went over to England and worked with the people at AC and they designed a completely new front end featuring the rack and pinion. This had two important advantages: first, it lightened the steering and made it much more pleasant to handle. Secondly, and by far the most important, it put the correct geometry on the front end so that with that one change alone the car was two seconds a lap faster around Riverside when we tested it.

Phil Remington is our chief engineer and probably one of the most indispensable people in the company. He not only has a unique basic understanding of automobile engineering, but he's also one of the finest craftsmen in the world and it was he who was responsible for some of the Scarab cars that Lance Reventlow built and sponsored. Phil can sit down with the tools in the shop and build a car from the ground up that—constructionwise—is second to none in the world. He's also a valuable asset in the managerial end of the business. I think one of the main reasons for this is that he commands the complete respect of all and has the same kind of respect for the people who work for him and they know this. They know more than this: they believe, as I do, that Phil is the best man in the business.

As I said, by the end of 1962 we had made a good start toward the production of the first hundred cars and by January, 1964, some four hundred Cobras had been built and sold. I think we're well over the six-hundred car mark now, including the last series that the factory undertook to build for English distribution only. AC contracted to build a few cars, complete but for the engines, and to bring some engines over from the States and finish the job in England, just for their own area. There seems to have been a tremendous demand for Cobras in England, despite duty and price problems.

At this time we are no longer producing the 289 Cobra; we are well into the manufacture of the 427 model with the bigger engine and a completely new and different chassis. The total of six hundred that I mentioned a while back does not include these new models.

Perhaps a word about the latest Cobra chassis would not be out of place here. It retains the two husky parallel tubes of the earlier cars, but the suspension geometry is much more sophisticated because it is a so-called computer-designed suspension that was developed by a brilliant and very articulate suspension designer named Klaus Arning, who works for Ford engineering. It was Klaus who developed this "four-link" suspension that can be programed into a computer which spits out a little book, about half-an-inch thick. You run through this book and select a bunch of numbers to locate your points for the suspension geometry and this is put on paper. That's the only real way a suspension can be designed nowadays. As you know, when you run through arcs in geometry, there is no way to plot them on paper unless you want to keep doing different projections. If you run through, say, six inches of suspension travel you will find yourself with a room, probably as big as your living room, solid with paper from top to bottom. Only by the time you had run through all of that paper would you know what you had started out to get.

What the computer does is to give you all the variables that you can conceivably come up with. It does not actually design the suspension; it does not create anything. But it has a fantastic and instantaneous "memory" for any information previously programed into it, and the answers—*all* the answers—are there, waiting on tap. It's therefore still up to the suspension designer to pick out the variables that are necessary in order to achieve what he has in mind. You get the idea? You still have to go back to the computer to pick out which suspension layout or configuration you want and the way you want to achieve that result. Then it will tell you precisely what to expect. But obviously there are so many thousands of combinations and compromises that you would end up in a padded cell trying to figure them out in your head.

With the possible exception of "cut and try," which in some instances can be as good as a computer *if* you have the correct basis from which to start and *if* you have a good engineer and a good test driver, there is no other way to come close. What we now have in the new chassis is a series of eight unequal A arms (two at each corner, top and bottom) where before the AC chassis used transverse leaf springs. The term "A arms" actually is not quite correct. Its what we call a "four-length" suspension with adjustable arms that go forward and backward and, in fact, are great, long, adjustable triangles. What's more, they are not parallel to the direction of the chassis. They run off in different directions so that the arcs through which the wheels travel—those roll and steering characteristics which, as I said, are plotted beforehand—give you the best possible combination of wheel adhesion.

In redesigning the Cobra frame, although, as I mentioned just now, we still use a pair of main parallel tubes, the wall thickness has been increased slightly along with the diameter of the tubes. By going to a four-inch tube instead of the former three-inch, the stiffness of the chassis has just about been tripled. That's a pretty good safety margin in anybody's book. The AC factory at Thames Ditton, England, still builds the chassis for us, but they now do so exactly to our requirements and measurements. They, in effect, have become subcontractors to Shelby American. The design is laid down over here and the chassis is then built over there according to those specifications. We have found that for a limited production run it actually is cheaper to have the cars built over there than to do so here. Tooling, also, is less expensive.

The new model is to be called the "427 Cobra" and long before this book appears in print we will have one hundred or more cars built. In fact, this quota should be completed within about a week of this estimate being recorded on paper. The Prototype 427 was completed in England in October, 1964, and the initial testing took place at Silverstone. Presently planned rate of production is two to two and a half cars a day. Usually, at the beginning, things go a little slower because the fellows have to learn about the car and its components and develop a certain assembly routine. Just like any other production, it takes a while to get into the swing of things, but as soon as the routine has been established the rate of production goes up considerably for a given time. Of course our new facilities will allow us to put things together a whole lot more easily. It is not intended at this writing that the whole plant should move to our new North American building at the same time, but the entire shift-over will have been completed long before the end of 1965. We have two large hangars at the new 12½ acre premises, totaling 30,000 square feet of floor working area. However, if you add to that the office and storage spaces in those two hangars, we come out with 96,000 square feet. The parking area alone is large enough to run a full-size drag strip.

For the information of those who might be seriously interested, the address of the new Shelby American location is 6501 West Imperial Highway, Los Angeles 9, California, and as I mentioned further back it is located on the very fringe of the airport—most convenient for sending out and receiving shipments by air. Since it is located on actual airport property, you will be able to see our new assembly plant even at night as you fly into Los Angeles International Airport.

Well, now that we've talked a bit about the 427 chassis, I think a word about the body would also be in order. The rear fenders of the new body have been flared out to accept the wider rims and tires which are required to absorb the extra power, while the nose has a much more oval opening to admit the greater quantities of air required to cool the big 427 mill. There is also an oil cooler built directly underneath this opening but basically this is very much the way it was in the earlier cars. I'm talking about the team cars, since an oil cooler is not standard equipment on the street version and is not really required.

Naturally, all this means progress, more power with less effort, more performance with minimal stress, still better handling, and so on. We keep looking forward to the future, as does any manufacturer in this business; but that is not intended to sell short in any way the 289 Ford engine or the pre-427 chassis. That 289 V8 is still a fantastic engine, tough and reliable as a workhorse, easy to maintain and repair, and about the best power unit for its displacement and weight on the market—to say nothing of the price. The Cobra we've been selling in the hundreds also is still a wonderful automobile—a sports car or a racing car at will; but of course it's difficult to beat a good "big" one with a good "little" one, and those extra cubic inches tell their own story. Even so, we feel that we are now going to have to begin development of the bigger engine all over again so as to compete successfully in 1966, and so on. Some of the fastest European GT machines are again creeping up past four liters (like Ferrari, which, as a matter of fact, built a highly successful, if brutish, 4.9-liter car several years back that Gonzales drove so brilliantly at Le Mans in 1956; and like Maserati, which has gone up to a 5.5-liter V8, and so on).

With the 289 we felt that we had just about reached the limit that we could get out of it with the existing suspension and overall design of the car. The new 427 Cobra not only handles better but has a much more comfortable ride. It's an extremely smooth automobile to ride in—in fact about as smooth as the average passenger car. I think any of the truly modern sports cars, if you take a run in them—machines like the Lotus 19, or the Ford GT or any of these cars—are actually a very comfortable ride. Far more comfortable than any casual observer might be led to believe, and without a trace of that harshness that used to be the hallmark of the "real" competition car in the old days.

Transmissionwise, we will definitely continue with four speeds for obvious reasons. The existing transmission, which is very good, is quite capable of handling even the 425 horsepower of the 427 street version engine, but you can see why we had to beef up the chassis so extensively. During the 1964 racing season our competition engine put out only about 385 horsepower, which is quite a bit less. That's why we will be up to 9½-inch rims at the rear and probably 7½ inches at the front on the racing versions.

Well, so much about the anatomy of the Cobra, past and present, but on looking back I find that I have really said very little about our earlier cars and I would not want the reader to get the idea that the apparently simple business of dropping a Ford V8 engine into an AC chassis was what the British would call "a piece of cake." It wasn't. When we started that project we bought ourselves a whole truckload of headaches—and aspirin wasn't enough. We needed quite a bit of ingenuity and patience and that's where the unique group of fellows working with me came through like real troupers.

Let me go back to the beginning and run through this thing real fast and catalogue some of the problems we had to tackle and overcome.

Funny as it may seem, when CSX0001 (our very first car) arrived in Los Angeles by air, there was no way to get it to the shop at Santa Fe Springs! None of us seemed to have thought of that little detail, but luckily we had an S.H.P.D. student who owned a Ferrari and was also a good sport. Naturally enough, he owned a trailer to carry the Ferrari around, and we didn't have to ask him more than once.

"Go ahead," he said. "Be my guests."

So we hooked the trailer to one of Dean Moon's pickup trucks and made a rush for the airport where the car awaited us. It looked a bit sorry, standing there unpainted, plastered with big stickers that said FOR EXPORT ONLY. There were other labels that said NO WATER IN THE ENGINE and ADD OIL BEFORE DRIVING. The interior of the machine was fully trimmed in the best AC manner, but when we lifted the hood there was no engine there. Just a big empty space. Not even a rubber band!

Well, we put this baby on the trailer and towed it back to Dean Moon's shop and right away his whole staff pitched in to install the awaiting engine, which was an early Ford V8 of 260 cubic inches. Believe it or not, on the same day that we unloaded the car it was actually driveable! The engine was in place, properly mounted, and even the unpainted body had been shined up so the aluminum skin looked like silver. As it happened, we were lucky in one respect. There was so much under-the-hood room that the weight-distribution problem solved itself. It worked out just about right, first time off.

How this prototype handled was something else, and here I think that Pete Brock, my earliest test driver, summed it up pretty well: "That season I was racing a Lotus, and the difference in handling between my featherweight job and that Cobra was really something! You could take the Lotus around a corner, *any* corner, at speed with a mere flick of the wrist—a movement of two or three inches. You sat in my car low and relaxed, with your fanny almost touching the ground, and you had to work like the devil to get it to break loose. But that Cobra! There you found yourself perched on top of a couple of frame rails trying to keep a tight rein on a V8 that bellowed and howled and at the same time you had to worry about excessive lean because, in that first one, we didn't even have a sway bar.

"Sure, it went like a runaway train, but even though I was willing and anxious to make every allowance, I found it pretty hard to think of Carroll's creation as a modem automobile. Yet, in spite of all this, it seemed eager to do a job and it moved mighty fast. And then a funny thing happened. That car began to grow on me. Each time I took it out for a new test, I wanted to drive it a bit farther and a bit faster until we came to a point where, more than anything, I wanted to run that Cobra in a race! You try to explain it."

Oddly enough, CSX0001 (and 0002 as well) had precisely the same effect on other test drivers. During production of at least the first thirty-five cars things were constantly being changed and improved, of course, and not the least important detail was that we finally learned how to put the top up! The original car had arrived without any instructions on this seemingly trivial point and we found ourselves with a collection of collapsible bows, some prestitched canvas with a rear window, and mysterious fittings that were supposed to secure the top to the upper edge of the windshield. Well, the "one-man top," as the British so casually put it, produced something like a ten-man hassle without any practical results. No one knew how to put that durned top up and secure it so it wouldn't blow away until I finally found an AC Ace owner in Southern California who showed us how to put the thing up properly.

Then other little things quickly turned up. Like your feet got roasted by the engine because no provision had been made for ventilators and we had to install these in a hurry. Soon after, we found that people who bought Cobras and drove them up north complained bitterly because there was no heater! Strange, we hadn't thought anyone would ever need a heater in the car.

The next thing that bugged us was the rear-end ratio. The first 125 cars we built had a ratio of 3.54, which was a bit too high with the existing engine to provide the required degree of scat from the lights. So we went to a 3.77 ratio, which was a marked improvement and yet still gave the car a maximum speed of about 140 mph— certainly as fast as the average street driver would want to go!

With the 126th Cobra we also switched from worm and sector to rack and pinion steering, which improved the handling at speed on turns to an unbelievable degree. It got rid of the dead spot in the swing between one lock and the other, when the car tended to wander a little and had to be "steered," and it also gave much lighter control.

For a while there, on the 260 engine, we tried a number of fairly radical cams, different carburetion setups, and varied ignition timings, but for the street car the stock product as turned out by Ford— which was the outcome of compromise—appeared to do the best job.

CSX0002 made its racing debut at Riverside in October, 1962, driven by Billy Krause, but we'll come back to that later. The next three cars, which arrived in a group, had to be assembled immediately, tested, then prepared and painted so that they could appear at an exhibit held in Dearborn, Michigan. The paint problem was another headache when we found that the cars were the wrong shade because our Shelby American painters worked under fluorescent lights while the Dearborn exhibit would be held under incandescent lights. So they had to be done over again, completely.

We began serious production of the first hundred Cobras in December of 1962 and completed the last of that batch about April, 1963. Of these, probably the first thirty were assembled and finished in Santa Fe Springs, where limited space and facilities kept our output down to two cars a week. Then we moved to Venice, California, and things improved quite a bit. We were able to work on as many as five cars at a time and production soon rose to this figure weekly. We also had a shed in which to store spare engines until they were required. The added space meant that we were able to hire more people, so that soon after we moved into the expanded premises at Venice, we had thirty-five people working for us, including some racing mechanics.

For the record, the first seventy-five Cobras we built had the 260-cubic-inch V8 engine. Then the 289-cubic-inch job came out and we immediately switched to that because it gave an additional

25 or 30 horsepower without any measurable weight increase. For a while after the change was made, an occasional customer would show up and ask us to switch the 260 engine in his car to the new 289 job. We always tried to accommodate these people, of course.

Meanwhile, when the 289 appeared, we started fooling around with Weber carburetors for our own information and for customers who happened to be competition-oriented. Phil Remington, our chief engineer, designed a set of ram tubes and a manifold for those Webers, which immediately boosted engine power by some 75 brake horsepower. Unfortunately, the sidedraft manifold we fabricated was too bulky and took up too much room under the hood, so that we were not able to offer it as an option, good though it was. But after a while the first downdraft Webers arrived and that changed the picture radically.

I would say this gives what you might call a broad-brush treatment of the anatomy of a Cobra. Perhaps the most gratifying thing in connection with the normal growing pains we had to experience was the fact that we got very few customer complaints. The only serious gripes came from owners who got no more than they deserved because, despite careful warning, they insisted on over-revving the engine. We not only write it all down in a booklet but, whenever possible, I would personally tell the customer: "There's no need to baby this car. Drive it as hard as you like and as rough-and-ready as you like, *but don't over-rev the engine!* Seven thousand is the limit. Get that firmly into your mind. Go over seven grand with this mill and you'll drop a valve."

Then, just in case the customer might not be too clear as to what was meant by dropping a valve, I'd explain it. "The valve springs just won't take more than seven thousand rpm. You can get up there, but they won't take it. They begin to float. That throws your valve timing all out and the next thing you know you've put a valve through a piston. You just knock the piston all to hell and then you've got a basket case on your hands. No kidding."

Of course you always get a small percentage of smart-alecks who know it all and give you the smiling nod and go out and try to turn 7500 rpm and that's the end of the engine. But I don't remember that we ever lost any engines or ever had any serious trouble, except for that one thing. Every other part is so strong, so overde-signed for the job that you'd have to devise some new torture test to break it.

I'm not talking about racing, now, but about day-to-day use. Racing is a very different matter. If the customer wants to race we do all kinds of things to safeguard his investment. Principally, we modify the engine and drive train with options that anyone can buy over the counter and we change the wheels and stuff like that. But the price goes up quite a bit. We've held $5995 as a base price for the street Cobra since the beginning, but once you decide to race you may spend up to $9000 if you want all the trimmings. We do turn out a pretty good competition automobile for about $6150, but naturally you don't get all the goodies for that kind of money. Rac-ing automobiles is just about the most expensive sport you can fool with, after polo ponies. So there's no use kidding oneself about that.

To wind up this chapter, I feel we should also talk a little about the anatomy of the Tiger and the anatomy of the Mustang. They're also very much a part of our business.

The idea of dropping a Ford engine into a Sunbeam Alpine chassis was a project that originated in the minds of Bill Carroll and Ian Garrett, who is the West Coast representative for Rootes. Ian was so excited about his first ride in a Cobra that he at once asked himself the question: "Why can't we do the same thing with a Sun-beam Alpine?" What he had in mind was a sort of cheaper version of the Cobra, and Bill Carroll at once agreed to do the development work on the car, along with Ken Miles. Ken now works for us as competition adviser, test driver, and sometimes race driver as well. But not so long ago he had a shop of his own and that was where one version of the Sunbeam Tiger originated. The other version was put out by us and was perhaps a bit more sophisticated. We added rack and pinion steering and made some other changes to minimize the effect on weight distribution. Ken, on the other hand, didn't bother with such finesses. He kept the standard steering and this forced him to install the engine farther forward than in our version, so that it wasn't as well balanced. There were some other details that we also looked into pretty carefully and so, in the end, it was the Shelby American installation that got the nod from Rootes. Soon afterward it became the prototype for the production version of what is now known as the Tiger. Nowadays everything is put together in England, but during the development stages it was Shelby American that did the testing.

At the present time, after the car is completed in England, with the engine mounted and all the basic details taken care of, we supply the high-performance components, including the aluminum manifold, four-barrel carburetor, valve cover, and such. The finished product looks pretty nice, if I do say so. It's been a big seller, not only in England but over here, too. In fact, Rootes have ordered another twelve thousand engines from Ford, which, by the way, creates rather an amusing situation when you consider that Chrysler Corporation has just acquired a large slice of Rootes!

I think that if the figure of speech about the shoehorn ever applied to anything, it surely did to the tight squeak in getting that 260 Ford mill into the Sunbeam engine compartment. There was a place for everything and a space for everything, but positively not an inch to spare! Still, the Sunbeam Tiger is a lovely road car, well mannered, fast, and zippy. The finish is excellent, too, all the way through. Pretty much as in the case of the Cobra, the Tiger allows you to do anything you like because there's so much power to spare. The car, oddly enough, has a tendency toward high-speed oversteer, but you can neutralize this by standing on the throttle. It's all up to the skill of the driver. Initially, of course, as you might except, the Tiger is a low-speed *under*steering car. It has to be because of the forward-weight bias, but you can do wonders by applying the throttle at the right time and in the right amount.

The Mustang—at least, the Shelby American version of the Mustang, which we now call the G.T. 350—is a truly fantastic machine, measured against anything at any price. That's a broad statement to make, maybe, but you have to consider the origin of this car; the price and quality objectives coupled with a versatility never before achieved in a low-cost production automobile; and what we have been able to achieve by tweaking and modifying it here and there.

Certainly by the time it leaves the Shelby American shops the G.T. 350 Mustang is one of the most enjoyable and forgiving automobiles you could ever hope to drive. And it goes, too. I mean it really goes. Don't get any wrong ideas about that.

What we do with this automobile is to order the two-plus-two fastback version of the coupe, but stripped of many components. In fact, these cars are sent to us from the San Jose factory in what might be called a semifinished condition, and we go through them from end to end to achieve the result we have in mind. Basically, what we do is change the front-end geometry to improve roadability and we add radius arms that we developed specially to hold the rear end in place as well. Then we add some horses by using a high-riser manifold and a specially developed center-pivot carburetor which allows smooth, uninterrupted power even in a tight turn at speed. But that's just the beginning.

Actually we produce two versions of the Shelby Mustang—a street version and a racing version. The racing version has a completely "gutted" interior, which means the absolute minimum of trim and the elimination of all nonessential geegaws. Special bucket seats have been designed to provide unusual comfort with complete back support, and we also replace (and greatly improve) the entire instrumentation. Then we fit a rollbar, shoulder harness or seat belts, and design and install our own fiberglass hood with special scoops in it. We've designed ducting that goes to all the brakes and we install much tougher racing pads on the front disc brakes and metallic linings to the rear drums. The reason why we have kept drum brakes at the rear is that maximum braking force is normally absorbed by the front wheels when you really stand on the "binders," and that is where disc brakes are most needed.

There have been, I know, all kinds of rumors about independent rear suspension on Mustangs and statements that Ford would build a thousand cars so equipped for special customers, and all the rest of it. None of this is anything more than the fanciful hopes of enthusiastic automotive writers. The swing axle (I.R.S.) is strictly on the development program at this writing, and although we feel it is something which will eventually have to come in the future in order to make the car competitive in terms of the latest thinking, there is right now no definite date set for the introduction of independent rear suspension. What has happened at this time is that we do many testing programs for Ford in the arena of practical experience and this type of rear end is just another of those programs. You must bear in mind that Ford has to cover a much wider market than does Shelby American with its specialized products, and unless an improvement gives a manufacturer a significant jump over the competition, or unless it can be introduced without prohibitive tooling costs and production changes, there isn't too much point in going ahead with that change. This is not to say that someday Ford might not decide to go to independent rear suspension, but the fact remains that the present live axle does its job pretty well for all normal purposes.

It's very much the same kind of thing with the antisway bar we fit to the front of the Mustang. This is just about twice as thick and tough as the regular sway bar; but then the average owner is more interested in a soft ride than he is in worrying about whether that soft ride is going to end up by having him corner on his door handles! He doesn't take turns that fast, anyway.

Then there are the wheels. We don't use the standard Ford wheels but fifteen-inch jobs with wider rims and a much lower-profile, wider-section tire that puts a lot more rubber on the ground. In general, we find it hard to say what's better, because that depends solely on what you want the car for and how you are going to use it. There's no question that the Shelby American version of the Mustang is much superior in the handling and the get-up-and-go departments, but, on the other hand, we couldn't hope to sell one-tenth as many of our cars as Ford does of the regular Mustang. Not one-thousandth as many. Certainly not of our racing Mustang, anyway, for this comes with straight-through headers, no muffler, and virtually no luggage space since the spare tire is bolted flat to the floor behind the two front seats. The minute you get in, turn the key, and get into gear, you know you're in a living, firebreathing machine, and it's beyond doubt one of the most exciting and easiest driving cars that I have ever handled. It's a completely predictable machine at all speeds and therefore offers more scope for flat-out, fourth-gear, drift-type driving than any fun car I ever drove before. I think "pure pleasure" describes it best in the fewest words.

Actually we market two versions of the Mustang: the racing version I have just tried to describe, and a high-performance job that's not nearly so stark and maintains most of the usual trim and soft interior and cute ornaments and all that stuff. In fact, the chassis on both models is identical; it's just that on the racing version we put more handwork into the engine to get some added horsepower, and we trim stuff down to reduce unnecessary weight. Suspension, brakes, tires, wheels, steering, and the like are all the same on both versions of the G.T. 350. But while one is a full touring version with real glass that rolls up and down and all the comforts inside, the other has plexiglass windows (all except the windshield) and is strictly lightweight.

The price of the race car is somewhere in the neighborhood of $6000, while the hopped-up street version is about $4,500. You can tell our cars by the blue stripes which run over the roof and along the hood. We're kicking off with a production of about one hundred cars a month. Things are humming in our present facility, but they'll move along a lot faster when we're installed in the new plant. We'll have a special production line for Mustangs, with a pit which will allow us to run into a real production schedule. At this writing the best we could do was get two cars up at a time on the racks and hand-build them, then back them out and move them over to another area. Our new factory allows us to run right down the line with them. The basic car enters at one door and the finished car exits through the other door, complete, painted, and ready for testing.

In 1964 we had several test Mustangs running long before the fastback version was announced to the public; so we've been testing them for quite a while—a necessary step before we could get the modification program geared for action.

It's almost unbelievable, but we can now take a G.T. 350 around any circuit where we test it faster than the best Corvettes in full racing trim! You just can't very well accept that fact, I know, until you drive the car.

Well, so much for anatomies and why we do what we do with Ford or Ford-powered automobiles.

–18–
THE COBRA STRIKES!

I THINK THE title for this chapter is an adequate heading, but it certainly would not be a complete chronicle if we listed only our 1964 successes, when we came within a hair's breadth of winning the International GT Championship from Ferrari. It was certainly not all sugar and spice from the beginning, and I propose here to give you some of the rough as well as the smooth patches. Don't think we had it easy because just the opposite was the case. If ever a designer came out with a competition automobile that was dead-right from the very first time out, that had no bugs or problems, that revealed no defects and suffered no setbacks, either that designer is a fabricator of fairy tales or he deserves, when his time comes, to be immortalized in a wax museum. It just doesn't happen that way. Mathematically the odds are so stacked against you that you would have a better chance of making a dozen straight passes shooting crap!

As I mentioned in the previous chapter, the very first time a Cobra ran in a race was at Riverside in October, 1962, when Krause drove good old CSX0002 on its initial public appearance. This machine had a mildly tuned version of the 260-cubic-inch Ford V8 and ran on nothing more potent than a single four-barrel carburetor. We took a lot of trouble preparing the car, so that it certainly looked one of the cleanest jobs on the starting line, but we didn't notice any spectators doing a backward flip or rushing up to place orders.

"Cobra?" they asked each other, casually. "What the heck's that? Something Carroll Shelby dreamed up?"

"Guess so."

"Well, it looks nice, but you know how it is with those backyard Specials."

Sure, sure.

Everyone knew how it was with those backyard Specials. They knew it even better when the late Dave McDonald (who later drove very successfully for me) took off in a hot Corvette as though a charge of dynamite were about to explode under him at any moment. By the end of the first lap McDonald was half the length of the straightaway ahead of everyone else; but the Cobra caught him after a couple more laps and went away as if the Corvette was tied to a pole. Then, of course, it had to happen. Some time later, with the race seemingly in the bag, an overstressed left rear hub snapped at Turn Nine and that was the end of Krause's ride. However, the day was not lost. By the time we got the car towed back to the pit area, a mob was ready to rush us with an avalanche of questions.

"Cobra, eh? Going into production with it? How much does it cost? Boy, that thing can sure go." And so on. One fellow even remarked that it looked a lot like an Ace Bristol.

Four days later Phil Remington had a new hub designed and some forgings made and we were ready to go again.

The first really big one we tackled was Daytona, in February of 1963, four months later. Ford asked us to test out some new aluminum block engines for them, set up with very loose tolerances, and as a result they gulped oil like a drunk would down a fifth of whiskey. FoMoCo wanted an evaluation of this oil consumption thing, plus information in actual racing which they hadn't had time to get on the dyno. Well, we ran three roadsters, driven by Dan Gurney, Dave McDonald, and Skip Hudson, in the Three-Hour Continental, which was run on the 3.81-mile road course with a goodly portion of the blanked track. Dave turned a practice lap at 101.35 mph, but it was not his day and his ride ended in a crash that put the car out of action.

Dan Gurney's car ran into trouble when a Welch plug blew out of the engine shortly before the start and the water pressure disappeared. Dan's mechanics did a wonderful job of replacing the ruined engine in ninety minutes and got him off only half a lap after the race had started. For quite a while it looked as though

Gurney were going to pull it off. He made up the handicap and pulled ahead and seemed to demonstrate that the Shelby-Ford Cobra was the fastest machine around, production or otherwise. Then on the forty-eighth lap he was sidelined for good with ignition trouble. Not daunted, Dan busied himself giving Dave McDonald pit signals. Skip Hudson's crash was due to a disintegrating flywheel on the fifty-fourth lap when he was way up with the leaders and left him with not only a busted car but also a badly fractured ankle.

Dave, meantime, had worked up to second place behind the Rodriguez GTO Ferrari until the forty-fifth lap, when he pitted to replace a radiator hose and looked as though he might never get going again—until I had a brainwave. I bridged a faulty starter solenoid with a fifty-cent piece and Dave took off again to finish fourth overall. Corvette got the best of it that time with a third overall by Dick Thompson, but it was a near thing and the name Cobra seemed to take on a new note when people mentioned it. Could be that guy Shelby might have something, after all.

But, man, our troubles were only just beginning. At Sebring just about everything that could possibly go wrong or drop off did go wrong or drop off. For us it was more a practical, and rather infuriating, education than an actual race. I'd teamed off the late "Fireball" Roberts with Dave McDonald, Dan Gurney with Phil Hill, and Ken Miles with Lew Spencer. The first crew was to make the pace; the second was to keep within striking distance of the leaders, if needed; and the third car was to finish the race, regardless of anything else. The cars had the new rack and pinion steering which had made them go two seconds faster around Riverside in practice, but in the actual race it was another story. While in seventh spot after only an hour's running, the Spencer-Miles car made the first of several pit stops that finally sidelined it for keeps. First the oil pump pickup shook loose and starved the bearings. Then a rocker arm broke, and finally four attachment bolts holding the rack and pinion steering assembly sheared off. They turned out to be regular hardware bolts instead of aircraft quality. Scratch one.

The Roberts-McDonald car, which was running eighth, disappeared when a rear oil seal let go. Phil Hill, meantime, ran over a road marker and damaged the brake caliper assembly of a front wheel while in fifth spot after two hours. The cooling scoop was shoved up against the disc and so reduced the flow of air that the brake severely overheated. After that the car ran into a bunch of electrical troubles but managed to keep going with Gurney sweating out Hill's problems every time Phil drove, and Phil doing the same for Gurney. We'd brought twenty-three mechanics and a lot of stuff, so I won't attempt to describe my feelings when, on one occasion, all three of my team cars pitted at one time! Two privately entered Cobras never really joined in the hunt, but the Hill-Gurney car, hanging on by its teeth, managed to win the class and finish eleventh overall.

And that was that. So far, nothing to get excited about, yet more and more people were talking about Cobras and more and more people came in to try to buy them. Oddly enough, while I was out at Dearborn making arrangements to get distribution of the car through nationwide Ford dealerships, people were knocking at my door, first in Santa Fe Springs, then in Venice, with the money in their hot, sticky little hands!

Well then, of course, we had to go to Le Mans, with some of the racing world's toughest company. I entered two factory roadsters: one driven by Bolton and Sanderson, and the other by Hugus and Jopp. Both were GT cars, but in addition there was a Lola Ford Prototype GT driven by Hobbs and Attwood, who had bought one of my spare engines.

Le Mans 1963 was nothing too much to brag about, either: the Bolton-Sanderson Cobra spun like crazy on an oil slick, through no fault of its own, when MacLaren blew the engine of his Aston Martin and scattered parts and lubricant all over the road. By some miracle the Cobra avoided a crash and went on to finish seventh overall. The Hugus-Jopp Cobra blew its engine and the Lola Ford suffered all kinds of trouble with its shift mechanism and got delayed a long time. Finally, at dawn, when it looked as though things were sorted out, the car jumped out of gear while going through the Esses at a pretty good clip and did what the British call a "shunt." It clobbered the earthworks and was too badly damaged to continue.

Though we had not yet "set the Thames on fire," as they say in England, we were getting the message over, all right. My mental image of the Cobra as a tough, very fast, easily handled, easy-to-service sports car, capable of wearing as many different hats as its owner might require, was going over pretty well. It *would* do all of those things in an honest, simple fashion, and as time went on it did them a little better and a little more dependably and comfortably each month.

Back from Le Mans we looked around a bit and there was this National SCCA meet at Lake Garnett, July 7, which just gave us time to get three Cobras ready and really get in there and mix it with the Corvettes. Already, at club meets, our boys were up to all kinds of tricks; they would dig a mock grave at the trackside with a big show and a ceremony, and then they would put up a grave marker that read "Here lie the Sting Rays" and stuff like that. Well, it was fun, of course, and it rattled the opposition. It's not enough, however, just to wave the big stick and beat the drum. You also have to deliver the goods and once in a while, at least, show the opposition a clean pair of heels.

I sent three Shelby American Cobras to Garnett, Kansas, plus the usual bunch of mechanics and troops, plus the "bad man" himself—that's me—or at least the guy wearing the "bad man's" hat—a black tricorn with a leather band that seems to have become my trademark. In fact, I'm rather superstitious about it and wouldn't think of going to a race without that hat, any more than I'd go without my cowboy boots.

Garnett was a real road course, snaking pretty tightly around the contours of Lake Garnett, with some nice uphill and downdale sections and about 2.8 miles per lap. It was a driver's course and it kept the drivers busy; but it was also fast and rather fun to get around.

This was to be a real "Corvette versus Cobra" thing, and naturally the interest rose to a keen pitch and about 60,000 fans turned out to see the "battle of giants." Driving for me were Bob Johnson of Columbus, Ohio, (the late) Dave McDonald of El Monte, California, and Ken Miles, of Hollywood, California.

Pitted directly against us was the famous Grady Davis Corvette team, with some fast, well-tuned, well-prepared, and well-driven cars, chauffeured by guys like Dick Thompson, Washington, D.C., Don Yenko, Canonsburg, Pennsylvania, and Davis himself, from

Pittsburgh. They brought along a couple of A-Production Sting Rays and a B-Producti on Corvette, and just to make things a bit more interesting, they threw in a C-Modified Corvette Grand Sport.

Naturally the sixty-four dollar question was what would happen between us and the Sting Rays as we diced around the 65-acre lake!

There were actually two separate races: one for A, B, and C Production cars, and another for C through G Modified. The first race started a few minutes after 1:00 P.M. and I'm not likely to forget the sight that greeted my anxious gaze. In less than half a mile the three Cobras were showing their tailpipes to the rest of the field, with Johnson, McDonald, and Miles in that order, and that was just how they finished. The Corvettes picked up the next three slots with Thompson, Davis, and Yenko.

Now a funny thing happened. Before the start of the production race, someone had protested that Ken Miles's Cobra was "modified"— because it was fitted with an oil cooler. Our mechanics quickly removed the offending oil cooler before the flag fell, and then no one had any gripe or excuse. But after the race Miles and I got to figuring this thing out, and we agreed that if the removal of that oil cooler had turned the Cobra into a "production" car, then if we were to put the cooler back the Cobra would once more become "modified."

Wasn't much the officials (or the protesting guys) could say about that. They couldn't have it both ways and they were hoisted with their own petards by all this brilliant logic. So we went out again, and this time Miles ran away from the "modified" field and drove a real fine race, averaging better than 85 mph to win the Lake Garnett Grand Prix overall in 45 minutes. Harry Heuer in a Chaparral followed him home, a lap back Hinkle was third with a Cooper Monaco. Dick Thompson, whose Corvette Grand Sport d.n.f'd when something let go, was our closet threat, running second for quite a while. But that race did more to boost our team morale and prove a point than almost anything that had happened until then. We had a fast car and a reliable car and a good-handling car that could outspeed all the available opposition. And each time we went out we learned something new—and made good use of the lesson learned.

I'm not going to run all through the 1963 calendar, although there are some events I've left out, of course, like the Dodger Stadium races in March, when Dave McDonald won handily, followed by Ken Miles in another Cobra. Or Laguna Seca, in June, which turned out to be a sort of Cobra benefit where our cars took first, second, and fourth, and exotic machinery like GTO Ferraris didn't look so good.

What I want to talk about in greater detail is 1964, because that was when the Cobra really struck. This time we weren't kidding; we were after the big time and the FIA International Manufacturers' Championship for Grand Touring Cars, and if the people at Monza hadn't pulled the rug from under us, there's no question but that we would have won it—Ferrari or no Ferrari. But I'll tell you more about *that* incident at the proper time and place.

By October, 1963, we had become a power to reckon with among GT cars. No one called a Cobra a "hot rod" any more. In fact, where our drivers went, people started asking for their autographs.

Ole Shel, the "penniless" driver—the has-been who had been forced to quit because of heart trouble—had come up with something pretty good by way of a sports car, and the further we progressed, the more interested Ford became in our activities and plans.

Anyway, by October of that year we realized that if we were really going to go into this racing business in earnest, on an international basis, that if we had serious designs on the Manufacturers' Championship, which seemed to have become Commendatore Ferrari's exclusive property, we had better do something about it and get going, like now.

Our most pressing need, we realized (and Pete Brock had pointed this out some time back), was a much more streamlined body than was provided by the original AC roadster body which we were still using on our Cobras. We had to have this in order to compete with those sleek GTO Ferraris on high-speed circuits, and there wasn't any use kidding ourselves about it. So Pete went to work at once on a suitable body design—a coupe which became known as the Daytona—while Ken Miles worked on stiffening the chassis even further and repositioning some of the components within the body skin.

Meantime, John Ohlsen worked on a full-sized "buck" of the new body—a plywood former that was intended to determine the final body shape. The chassis we used for the mockup former was the one of the roadster that Skip Hudson had crashed at Daytona, early in 1963.

Now came a little episode which I think is worth telling. When Pete Brock had the body drawings almost completed, I happened to drop by his office with a leading aerodynamicist from one of California's largest airplane manufacturers. He took one skeptical look at the drawings, asked some wise questions, produced a slide rule, and promptly shook his head.

"You might as well forget it," he said. "It'll never go. With this design, you're going to need at least 450 hp, and maybe more than that, to go 160 mph."

"How come?" I asked.

"Well," said our expert, "it's like this. . . ." And he plunged into a whole bunch of equations that sounded a bit frightening to me, because he might as well have been talking Czechoslovakian. "So you see," he concluded, "why you'll be smart to drop the whole thing!"

To Pete's eternal credit he never said a word. He didn't interrupt or argue or make any remarks in defense of a job of work which I knew had cost him many hours of burning the midnight oil to get done on time. I don't even remember whether he asked that guy any questions at all. When an "expert" comes along and pulls the skids from under you with a slide rule and a truckload of equations, and you never even went to college, this kind of a guy has the jump on you. But I had too much faith in Pete to say anything then, and in any case it was too late to scrap Brock's design and make a fresh start—not if we were going after that GT Championship.

But later on, when this guy had gone, I rushed back to Pete's office, first chance I had, and asked him in private, "What the hell's goin' on, here? Is this man right or is he nuts?"

"I don't think he's right," Pete smiled, "but I don't think he's nuts, either. Some of these brilliant guys live on a cloud of equations. You can't get them down to earth, Carroll!"

"Well, he's got me worried," I admitted. "We've just about run out of time as it is."

"That's your privilege," Pete nodded, "and I can't say that I blame you, Carroll. But I just want to ask you one question."

"Shoot," I said.

"Did I ever let you down before?"

"Nope."

"Okay. Suppose you leave this thing to me and see what happens."

I had to laugh. "Guess I don't have much choice," I agreed.

"You don't have any choice at all," Pete said. "But let me do the worrying."

"He gave me a long spiel about the high tail and straight roof of that coupe being the main points of the problem," I said.

"That may be," Pete shrugged, "and I'm not going to argue the fact that we could have reduced the frontal area a bit, but that would have been at the expense of a lower roof line, which in turn would have upset the airflow over the roof. And that's one of the things you need to maintain stability at high speed."

"It's all yours," I decided. "But it had better work!"

"Leave the headaches to me!"

And that was the way it went. Within four months we had a complete car with a body which became known as the Daytona Coupe, because that was where it got its first real outing—during the 2000-kilometer Continental at Daytona Speedway in February of 1964. Meantime, we took the car out for its first test at Riverside on February 1, and it showed a 25 per cent better gas mileage and 15 mph more top speed, even on this relatively short circuit. Even the brakes ran cooler. With this encouragement, we decided to go ahead and run the car in the Continental at Daytona. The drivers I assigned to Brock's coupe were Bob Holbert and Dave McDonald, and the car easily led the race for the first eight hours against the best, fastest, and newest of the GTO Ferraris. For a body design that "wouldn't work," it held 160 mph and better on the outer banked track whenever needed, and both drivers called it "stable as a rock." Pete must have had a big laugh, and I don't blame him!

Why the car didn't finish, but was sidelined and badly damaged by a serious fire, had nothing whatever to do with the body design. The electric fuel pump which we had installed for the oil cooler on the rear end failed when the points stuck. This caused such critical over-heating that the oil seal burned out, allowing hot grease to escape. This caught fire while the car was being refueled and that, whatever else may have been written about it, was exactly what happened.

Well, despite a setback which probably cost us the race—because, frankly, I don't think any of the GTO's had a chance to stay with us for long—we still managed to finish three cars in the first ten. Johnson and Gurney drove their Cobra into fourth place; Butler and Rainville into seventh spot; Hitchcock and Prince Tchkotoua in tenth. Our Daytona coupe recorded the fastest lap in 2:08.2 or 106.989 mph—not bad for a design that "wouldn't work," according to an expert and his slipstick.

We took five Cobras to Sebring for the Twelve Hours in March and, I think, did well enough in finishing five cars out of the first ten and winning the GT class. Actually, we took fourth, fifth, sixth, eighth, and tenth spots, and the only stuff ahead of us was a trio of Prototype Ferraris. Our highest-placed car was, of course, the Day-tona Coupe, all the others being roadsters. Once again, Pete Brock made his point. I flew in on the day before the race with my chief engineer, Phil Remington, and a couple of Ford representatives, and the press had much to say, seeing me move around in a wheelchair be-cause my leg was bothering me. But we had sent a dozen mechanics on ahead and plenty of spares, and in our huge transporter we held fifty or sixty tires in reserve, just in case we might need them. Guess who interviewed me when it was all over? None other than Stirling Moss!

Well, at this time, I think even the hard-nosed Ford executives (who judge everything by one criterion only—results!) were satis-fied. At all events they said they would help us "a little" with the next leg of the Championship grind, so we got some of our own money together and some Shell Oil Company money and decided to pursue this Manufacturers' Championship merry-go-round to the bitter end. Right up until Sebring, despite our serious efforts, we maybe had some reservations at the back of our minds; but now there would be no turning back. It was going to be all or nothing.

This decision gave us just three weeks to be in the mountains of Sicily for the Targa Florio. Hardly what you might call time to spare. Yet thanks to a lot of help that we got from Ford of Italy,

Belgium, France, and England, and all the companies over there, acting on their own, who jumped in and gave us wonderful cooperation throughout the year, we were able to make it.

We had no mechanics of our own over there. We couldn't very well send our Cobra mechanics because we also had our U.S. Manufacturers' Championship to defend. But despite a lot of problems, we seemed to be doing right well at one time in the Targa Florio, which is without a doubt the toughest road race in the world. We were actually running one-two-three, but the course, being as rough as it was, didn't lend itself at all to our type of suspension. It was altogether too rough for our leaf springs, which lacked the more sophisticated qualities of shock-absorbing found in the newer designs. So, despite a really good start, we gradually banged our suspensions to death. Dan Gurney, however, did manage to finish eighth in the overall picture and first in GT-3; therefore we picked up some more points. *And* we came in ahead of two Ferrari GTO's!

The next one was at Spa, in Belgium, probably the fastest road course in Europe. This road race was held May 17, for GT-2 and GT-3 cars and we sent the coupe with Phil Hill as the No. 1 driver in this three-hour grind. We also sent along several of the roadsters, but they didn't have nearly enough speed on a circuit where 170 mph and better is commonplace. I wasn't there, but I do recall that Phil put up fastest time in practice and then, during the race, lost five laps when he pitted with clogged fuel filters. Still, he got back in the race and actually made up one complete lap on Michael Parkes's GTO Ferrari! And Parkes is no slouch, as everyone knows. So it proved that we not only had the faster car but also one that could be run pretty hard for a long time. At Spa, by the way, we had besides Hill, Bob Bondurant, Innes Ireland, and Jochim Neerspach.

Our next European venture was the Nürburgring, and I don't have to describe that course all over again. But I made it a point to use drivers from practically every country.

For the forty-eighth Targa Florio we had Dan Gurney and Jerry Grant (from Seattle); Masten Gregory and Bob Bondurant; plus two Sicilian drivers—one named Arena and the other Coco.

In Germany I had Arena again, where he crashed and hurt himself pretty badly; and I also had Bondurant, Neerspach, and

Innes Ireland. Two drivers shared each car and we wrecked all our Cobras, either during practice or in the first few laps of the race. During practice, oddly enough, a privately entered Cobra of Hitchcock and Thiele made seventh fastest time, but the things that happened to us after the flag dropped were beyond belief. Jo Schlesser tagged onto Parkes's leading GT Ferrari in the class, until a coil wire broke. Then, when a replacement was found and Attwood took over, the accelerator fell apart and he had to waste twenty-two minutes in the pit. Olthoff's Cobra caught fire and lost five laps cleaning up the mess. Bondurant broke a shock and finally an oil line, while Hitchcock, through no fault of his own, had a head-on collision with Sutcliffe's spinning Jag. It was just one of those days when you begin to wonder if you ought to have your head examined for getting mixed up in this motor racing business.

At Le Mans, in the Twenty-four Hours, things picked up somewhat. We had two coupes, with Gurney and Bondurant in one; Neerspach and Chris Amon in the other. We lost the second car with a dead battery, but the Gurney-Bondurant Cobra finished fourth overall, despite the fact that the engine ran twelve hours without an oil cooler and the oil temperature was often at 300°F! We also beat Ferrari for the GT honors, which was what we had set out to do, regardless of anything else. Those beautiful Prototypes of the Commendatore's were absolutely useless on the open market, whereas anyone could buy our car.

After that there was the Tourist Trophy, held no longer on the dangerous Ards circuit but at Goodwood, and there we again beat Ferrari in the GT class, with Dan Gurney taking the honors. Actually we finished third (Dan Gurney in the same lap as the two Ferrari 330-P and 275-LM Prototypes); fourth (Jack Sears); and fifth (Bob Olthoff). The best a Ferrari GTO could do was finish sixth, Innes Ireland driving. So the twenty-ninth Tourist Trophy was our dish, at all events as far as GT was concerned, and I think at this point Signor Ferrari ceased loving us altogether. For a bunch of upstarts, we were doing altogether too well, stealing most of the candy in the GT class.

There was more to come. Bob Bondurant won both the Sierra Montana and Freiburg Hillclimbs for us, stacking more GT points on our side of the ledger. But then came the payoff, and if I do say so, it was one of the dirtiest moves that I have ever seen in any kind of motor racing. Just because our coupes had proved superior to the Ferrari GTO's in speed and endurance all year, and we were only about three points behind in the Manufacturers' Championship, the Italian Automobile Club and the gentlemen of the FIA decided to pull the rug from under us and leave us on a nice, slippery floor. We had entered three Daytona Coupes for the Three-Hour Coppa de Europa, when suddenly the boys at Monza got a real brainwave. They told the FIA that if the FIA did not at once homologate (as GT cars) the 250- and 275-LM Ferraris (of which only about ten had been built!), the event would be called off. On the face of it this looked like a "sporting" move, designed to ensure that everything was "fair and aboveboard," and that everyone got a proper chance. In fact it was nothing of the kind. It was a face-saver to prevent the GT Ferraris from getting beaten by our Cobras, which they richly deserved and which they could not possibly have prevented. Of course the FIA went along with this farce and did *not* homologate the Prototype Ferraris and so the Monza race was canceled. Imagine that!

In my estimation, and this is not to be a cry-baby, the skul-duggery that went on between the Italians and the FIA cost us the World Championship for GT cars in 1964, beyond any doubt.

On top of this, we fell into another trap neatly laid out for us, and this was the Tour de France, a high-speed drive of more than one thousand miles across France, which includes a run at Mont-lhery track, another at Le Mans, the famous Mont Ventoux hill-climb, and God knows what else. Everything from soup to nuts. We should never have entered that one, as we had absolutely no experience of this type of event and didn't even know the right places to arrange for spare parts and service for our cars. We also made some terrible blunders in the preparation of the cars, mainly due to lack of personnel, because most of our mechanics were busy getting other Cobras ready for Bridgehampton, the clincher of the year. After the Coppa de Europa was called off, our only chance of winning the GT championship was to win both the Tour de France *and* Bridge-hampton. We fell into that one pretty neatly, because all three of our entries failed in the Tour de France, and after that Bridgehampton couldn't possibly save us. We won Bridgehampton like a pack of fleeing bandits, taking the first four places in the GT class! However, as no make can score more than once, we would have been skunked even if we had taken the first ten GT spots! The dear old Commendatore sent only one factory Ferrari to Bridgehampton and he didn't even have to do that. It was just a token entry. He had it sewed up on the points system, taking those five events during the year in which he had put up the best performance—or rather, his cars had.

So that about analyzes the Cobra-Ferrari battle for the 1964 Manufacturers' Championship, and you can be the judge as to whether or not we were given the run-around. As I mentioned much earlier in this book, American drivers (according to many Europeans) don't know how to race; and an American manufacturer not only has no business trying to win an international championship—he has one hell of a nerve even thinking that he might be able to do so! But that's the way it goes, and not even FoMoCo has the kind of pipeline and direct wire to the FIA that has been available to the Commendatore from Maranello. No sir. He has had only to snap his fingers and the officials jumped. If some rule was not to his liking, it had better be changed, but quick, or heads would fall. Everyone seems to live in a kind of perpetual fear of displeasing Signor Ferrari. He has only to threaten to pull his cars out of a race, and the officials blanch and tremble. *What?* A race with no Ferraris? Why, that's unthinkable. Scrap those rules and rewrite them at once! *Pronto!*

"*Si,* Signor Ferrari!"

"*Non,* Signor Ferrari!"

"But certainly, Signor Ferrari!"

"At once, Signor Ferrari!"

This was how it was for all too long. Now that is slowly changing, I'm happy to say.

But that stunt they pulled at Monza—boy, that was a lulu. Those officials from the Italian auto club deserve full credit. I can even think of a few Hollywood movie tycoons who'd be happy to have "yes men" like that around.

However, don't get me wrong about one thing. I think the Ferrari—*any* Ferrari—is a mighty fine automobile. I think those

Italian engineers are also artists, and what they don't know about fine machinery and sizzling performance, you can throw into the trash can with last week's old newspapers. The Old Man has done a great deal for the sport of motor racing, both GP and GT, since those early days when he bought up the Alfa Romeos which the Milan factory no longer wanted to race and formed his own *Scuderia* . . . and when he put two Fiat four-cylinder engines end to end, made a small eight out of them, built a chassis, and let "Silver Fox" Taruffi drive the very first Ferrari to run in competition.

All this is true and more than true. Neither Dempsey nor Tunney underrated each other in the ring, or out of it. They had more sense. But, by heck, I think we can break the monopoly of those sleek red cars on the roads and tracks of the world, and I think we can do it for a lot less money, with automobiles that are within the reach of a hundred times as many buyers as Ferrari can ever scare up. And that's the whole point. The average Italian may dream of a Ferrari; he may touch one and talk about it; but he'll never own one. The average American who likes sports cars can own a Cobra with very little help from his bank.

That's the whole difference.

-19-

THINKING ALOUD

I'VE USED THIS title for the chapter because that's exactly what I'd like to do for a bit, if you'll bear with me.

Winning the 1964 U.S. GT Championship was something else again. We just didn't have any real opposition any more. We had been clobbering Corvette Sting Rays so badly for the past two years that people were beginning to lose their enthusiasm for them, at least in competition. Certainly as an everyday, all-American sports car it's a fine effort and it seems to be selling in greater numbers all the time. But I'm talking, now, about competition and racing. However, GM has come out with a new 396-cubic-inch version of their V8 for 1965, and if—despite all their protestations that racing is of no value in improving the breed, and all that stuff—this is not the basis of a really good *racing* engine, I'll eat my black hat with oil and vinegar!

So equipped, the Sting Ray will be a much faster car than ever before and we may yet see some really good battles on the race courses in this class between Cobra and Corvette. I'm afraid that spectators may have become a little bit tired of seeing the same make winning all the time, although we shouldn't forget that the Corvette also won for years, didn't it, until we came along. And so did Jaguar and Mercedes in their day, and that's just the way the wheel turns. Maybe I'm wrong here, but I naturally hope that my Cobras are now in for a winning spell that'll also last for years. We've backed the U.S. Manufacturers' Championship because we think it's a good thing. It doesn't necessarily mean a lot of prestige, because not very many people know about it yet; but we're hoping it does build up into big time over the coming years.

By the way, I told you how some of our boys dreamed up that little gag about the Sting Ray epitaph and all that bit—well, here's another that was a bit more subtle and, I would say, good promotional stuff. One of our biggest Cobra dealers, Coventry Motors of Oakland, California, hit on a bright idea. They dug up the names of all the Sting Ray owners in the area and sent each of them a snake bite kit!

Still, there's one thing I want to make very clear in this rivalry between the two best all-American sports cars: none of this is to be construed in *any* way as a criticism of Zora Duntov, who has rightly earned the title of "Mr. Corvette." He has done a wonderful job of development in spite of, and not because of, General Motors, which for years has expected him to perform miracles with one hand tied behind his back. Nobody is poking fun at Zora for a minute. In fact, everyone loves and respects the guy and anybody who knows anything at all about sports cars also knows what a great job he has done, starting with almost nothing and working with next to nothing. I just hope those boys upstairs have the good sense to untie his hands before long so Zora can really get at it the way he wants to. If they ever do, it's going to be a rough day for us, but we'll welcome it and we'll certainly rejoice for Zora Duntov. They don't come any better than this guy.

Two questions that seem to pop up the most often in connection with motor racing are these: Is motor racing the most efficient testing ground and does it sell more cars than you can through conventional advertising? My answer is this: While there's probably no substitute for a race course as a testing ground—even a short race is the equivalent of taking ten thousand ordinary road miles out of the life of a car—it does not necessarily follow that racing is at all times and under all conditions the best advertising and sales medium.

I've already expressed my opinion about the valuable sales rub-off that comes from racing, but I should perhaps specify that this view applies especially to sports cars. It all depends on what you're trying to sell. Obviously, to state a ridiculous case, the man who's in the market for a station wagon could hardly care less whether the make of car he has in mind won the Targa Florio or not; but I would say that even in stock car racing you consistently find a marked increase in local sales for a given make immediately after one of its models has won a local stock car event, such as a sedan race. Dealers report this time and again, far beyond the bounds of coincidence, and it happens, as I say, usually in the city nearest the track where the event was run. And you can't very well argue against figures—or can you?

My own explanation for this is that the average buyer of a family sedan *identifies* more closely with the performance of that car on a race track, especially when it wins, than he can possibly identify with the performance of a Ferrari, Jaguar, Maserati, Cobra, Sting Ray, and so on, unless he happens to be a sports car bug. And we know from experience that the ratio of buyers who race their cars is very small compared with the overall sales of any given sports model. So it *has* to be this identification thing. It makes the family-car buyer feel good that he can buy and drive an automobile that belted the opposition off the local track. Perhaps unconsciously, if he has any red blood in him, he would like to do the same thing.

Perhaps this whole philosophy of racing or not racing to boost sales could be summed up in this way: if you *win* and advertise, you're going to sell many more cars of any type than if you just advertise. If you lose consistently, then advertising (and racing) doesn't help you a bit. In fact poor performance in competition can do your sales enormous damage. No amount of fine talk and slick phrases can get around this basic fact. And that, I guess, is just where the element of gamble—businesswise—comes into motor racing.

We could get into quite an argument, here, about the direct relationship (or lack of it) between motor racing and automobile sales, but I think you already know my own views about that—certainly insofar as they apply to Cobras and cars of that type. Sales and results surely tell their own story. In 1964 we did $7.5 million worth of business, some $5 million of it in the sale of Cobras and speed equipment. We also employ fifteen graduate engineers, five of them with doctorates. But first, of course, you have got to have a quality car to sell. That's for sure. It's interesting to recall that whereas the Ford Safety Campaign of advertising fell flat on its face a few years back, now that the company is knee-deep in racing it is selling more cars than ever before; yet FoMoCo does not rely solely on racing as an advertising medium. Not by any means. There's stuff like the LTD model being quieter than a Rolls-Royce, and such, but there is another factor we haven't yet mentioned. A few years back, at about the time of this Safety Campaign bit, Ford seemed to de-emphasize quality and began taking shortcuts here and there in the finished product. Nothing very big or important, but a bunch of little details that all added up and did not escape the prospective buyer. Because it's really a strange thing, you know, but the average automobile buyer may not know a piston from a carburetor or a flywheel from a spare tire, yet you just can't fool him. He has an unerring *instinct* for quality, in much the same way that a homing pigeon has an instinct for getting back to where he came from. It's not a reasoning process at all. It's just, well, a kind of flair, hard to define but seldom wrong. You can sell the public one dawg if you turn on enough colored lights and cheesecake and brass bands, but you'll never sell him another.

And I think Ford was quick to realize this and did a complete turnabout and started once again to put a premium on the *quality* of what they were selling. There was another factor which, I believe, hurt Ford sales at that time, and that was that—besides not doing any racing, which makes a strong appeal to the constantly growing youth market—they also slanted their advertising clear away from that direction.

Market analysis and sales evaluation and public opinion polls can help you really put together a winner—like Mustang—or a dawg—like the Edsel. The market research people are walking a tightrope all the time, with a billiard ball balanced on their noses while they twirl a baton in each hand! I don't envy those guys their job. But the whole business can perhaps be summed up in this way: there's a point of no return in highly and consistently successful racing over long periods, and when you reach that point you're in danger not only of boring spectators but, because of this, of also hurting your sales. Believe me, it's just as dull for the fans to reach a point where they no longer ask themselves, "Who's going to win this one?" but instead, "Will this make grab the first three or the first four slots?" Mercedes-Benz was quick to recognize this danger and that was one of the main reasons why they pulled out of racing.

There was just nothing left for them to win; and if they had gone on and done the same thing all over again the following year, and spent another five million bucks, so what?

We, at Shelby American, are well aware of this snag, and if, as I hope, we do succeed in winning the 1965 International GT Championship* then we will have to watch out that we don't overdo this winning business. What I have in mind beyond that point is to continue racing in a small way, say like Jim Hall does with the Chaparrals. But for me to continue fielding teams of cars all over the world at huge expense, just to do the same thing over and over again, would be completely ridiculous. Not only is this racing game very costly when you run it on a properly organized basis, but it gets costlier every year. I would say that if we did win the Manufacturers' Championship in 1965, this would be good advertising rub-off for the next three or four years. Then we would change our policy completely.

One thing, however, is certain; we will have plenty of time to devote to the needs of private customers who want to race Cobras, and to help them with our accumulated store of technical and practical experience. At the same time, we will be able to concentrate on developing an even better automobile. This racing business, you know, is a double-edged sword from the standpoint of that valuable 15 per cent of private owners who buy our cars to race them. If the factory wins, the customer invariably says, "Well, what did you expect? Naturally Shel is going to keep an ace up his sleeve every time. A factory *never* gives a private buyer—just a Joe like myself—the very latest equipment, no matter how good he may be. Factory cars are always just a bit faster, a little bit better!"

This is only a half-truth. While some firms positively do *not* like to have their factory teams beaten by private individuals driving the same make, I take rather a different view. I *like* to see customers win; in fact, we all do at Shelby American, and I guess it's because we have some sporting blood around in our veins. A customer win is another form of advertising that you *don't* pay for but that can still bring you valuable returns. Sure, you have to be a bit selective as to whom you sell the hottest race product you can put together,

---

* Editor's note: Shortly after this writing the Shelby American Cobra clinched the 1965 FIA International Manufacturers' Championship for Grand Touring cars.

because a poor driver, even as a private entry, can make you look pretty bad—in fact much worse than any good independent driver who's smart enough to beat the factory team.

But as I say, there's this one important provision: you *don't* indiscriminately put into the hands of the first Joe who can write a check a car that's going to end up killing him because he has no idea how to handle it. With this one reservation in mind, we make it a point to sell the owner-driver exactly the same car as we field on the factory team. You can believe that, or not, as you choose; but it happens to be the truth. If we *do* hold anything back, it's not because we think we have something better, but because we're not sure just how it's going to hold up under the stress of racing and we don't want it to break, for a lot of pretty obvious reasons.

It's a funny thing, really, this business of selling race-prepared cars to private owners. You just can't win. If you prepare an exact replica of a works team job for him, he doesn't believe you. If you hold something back, then it's because you have sinister motives and don't want the "little guy" to win at the expense of the factory. There's no convincing these buyers. The best that you can do is play it by ear and play it square, and the truth does come out sooner or later. So far as I am concerned, I can only repeat that we *like* to have independent drivers do well. We will sell a responsible buyer any piece of equipment he can afford and we're not in the least concerned that the works team might get clobbered by Joe Blow from Oshkosh, Indiana. All the more power to his elbow.

As to the future, and I'm constantly asked about this, I think that in terms of production and real sales we're just getting started. We have the 427 Cobra; we have the new Mustang G.T. 350 in a Cobra version which may well wind up with that name—Mustang Cobra— if the buffs take a fancy to the idea; that or perhaps "The Skunk" because of its two stripes which go down the back! We have, as I've said, our new all-American chassis way past the drawing board, and within the next five years we intend to have a real all-American product—body and chassis as well as transmission, brakes, and tires.

On the other hand, for the next couple of years at any rate, I'm not particularly interested in getting into expensive Formula 1 racing—at any event not with Shelby American products. Our primary interest is in becoming an organization that can quickly update its models and get into production, not only with GT cars but also with ordinary street versions of our products. These, after all, still outsell about seven to one any kind of competition automobile we might build and sell, for either races or rallies. What I am trying to do is to build a car for a very special class of automobile buyers—the kind of car that instantly appeals to the man who, when he sees one like it, says, "There goes the hottest all-around setup your dollar will buy you. It may not have the fanciest roll-up windows and push-button top and so forth, but—you know—you'd better not try to fool with that one, Jack!"

Another thing we do, which we hope to have more time to devote to in the future, is to act as consultants to people seriously interested in getting into the racing car field and Formula 1 racing. As we continue to add to our wonderful and highly efficient group of dedicated enthusiasts at Shelby American—people who can handle the regular production and sales and do a better job of it in the future than ever I could—we shall have a little more time to spare for the kind of advisory activities I have in mind.

This whole thing, as you know, began as a dream—an idea—without any of the details filled in. Much water has flowed under the bridge since those days, but one thing, I believe, remained constant. I just knew the way this thing had to go, along general lines, because I happened to be the guy who had spent a lot of time trying to find out how other manufacturers rang the bell of success, and when they failed, *why* they did so. But now that we've got a real going business, I hope my main interest will be concerned with product planning and future development.

Incidentally, and this will answer the question asked by many potential buyers of Cobras, yes, we do plan to market a coupe as opposed to a detachable hardtop which we already have. As a matter of interest, I have a new top under development by Pete Brock, one that has been patented for a number of reasons. It combines all the internal comfort and security of a coupe, yet is completely collapsible and allows the car to be used as a roadster when the mood takes you. Possibly, as this book goes to print, we may be able to announce details of our new top.

Another thing I've been asked about often is what I think of the possibility of an all-American small-bore sports car. After all, I'm concerned with big-bore engines, but where does that leave the small power-unit enthusiast? The answer to that is simple. *The market place has got to be there.* Look at Porsche, for one—the huge success it has achieved over here. And sometimes a small-bore car is actually more fun to drive than a large-bore one. I feel that the price, comfort, and docility of a small sports car built over here will have much to do with whether or not it is a success. Imports in general cost a lot of money and I believe that Americans are becoming more and more conscious of the wish to drive an American car. In other words, this fetish that only Europe can build a fine car of any size or type, in whatever class, is fast losing ground. I'm convinced that an Italian can do anything an American can do; an Englishman can do anything a Frenchman can do; and an American can do anything a German can do. This nationalistic thing about cars is really like pulling for your national soccer team or your own baseball team, but for some reason we Americans have been led to believe that Europeans can build superior automobiles and too many people have taken this for gospel. I don't think it's true at all and I believe the time has come for us to rear up on our hind legs and *prove* we can match Ferrari, Jaguar, and the others, nut for nut and bolt for bolt. In fact I believe we already have with the String Ray, and I also think the Cobra, today, can match any production car in the world—and it's just the beginning. Look at what the Chaparrals have done. Look at what some of our small car builders have done. Why, heck, in many cases they've just about run the small car competition in Italy clear out of business! We're getting into it now, and we've already got the Europeans scratching their heads.

Within a couple of years, I'd say, this kind of thing will be history. Take Ferrari as a prime example. Already there's no longer any one class in which this great car can show any decided superiority. In Formula 1, it's just about even with the English. In the GT class, I think we've already got the edge on the Italians. And in price as related to comfort and performance, we make a lot more sense than those overpriced products from Modena and elsewhere.

To sum up—and this book has got to end somewhere, I guess—we have already taken some great strides forward and it's just a matter of letting the public know about it. A word about overhead-camshaft engines wouldn't be out of place here, either. The new Ford 427 is available with an overhead cam, and the Indy versions were tested on the 289 with four overhead camshafts. But for my part, I'm going to stay right along with pushrods because this type of engine costs so much less, is easier to service, and does everything one could reasonably expect of it. We don't really need overhead-cam engines at this time against the European product. I think we've proved that. An easier, cheaper way is to punch them out a little bit more, and you find yourself with just about as much power as can be gotten out of all that hand-machine work they have to put into an overhead-cam engine.

I'd better counter any arguments about my philosophy right now by saying that I'm well aware Europe has far more experience in terms of actual time at building cars than we have; and time is something you can't really buy, not even with all the millions in the world and all the computers. Another thing is that European labor is cheaper by far than ours, so it's possible for them to build some really exotic machinery for a lot less money than we can—but always thinking in small numbers, in limited production runs. It's true that, say, a Ferrari or a Maserati costs much less in Modena than we could ever hope to build them for, but don't forget the huge tax bite that the Italian government has on cars. This literally means that, for instance, a little 1500 Fiat ends up costing as much as a Ford or a Chevy does in this country.

It's also true that, because of the labor situation, they can build an overhead-cam engine over there far more cheaply than we ever could; but *we* can build a pushrod job that weighs no more and we can run it off the production line for $300 or $400—and that's thousands, even hundreds of thousands a month. Our engine will do the same thing as its sophisticated cousin from Europe and it weighs about the same. So think that over.

To wind up on this thinking-aloud session let me say this: What I really want to do and enjoy doing is to produce the fastest son of a gun I can for the least money, and in that department I don't think any country in the world can compete with us.

CARROLL SHELBY has been a major figure in my life since 1954 when he was driving Maseratis in this country and I was a mechanic working for the Maserati Corporation of America. Of course now as sports car magazine editor, I have to keep even closer track of his activities. Knowing this, Carroll entrusted me to add the last two chapters to his book bringing it right up to date in typical Shelby fashion. "You know what we've been up to these past few years. Say anything you want." Maybe I won't do justice to this trust, but I think it's just as well that someone else tells at least part of the Carroll Shelby story. He'd underplay the tremendous influence his energy, enthusiasm, and success have had on the sport. Carroll Shelby is now pretty big business as well as a household word. Certainly he's more experienced, but otherwise unchanged. The brief philosophical sentences he'd come up with a few years ago—and many of us wrote them off as being a little too homespun to be true—have been borne out. Shelby may be one helluva salesman, but he believes in what he's selling; and if he says he'll do something—no matter how fantastic it may seem at the time—you'd better listen closely, because it'll happen before you know it.

—*Jerry Titus, Editor, Sports Car Graphic Magazine*

-20-

1965: GROWING PAINS

THE YEAR 1964 closed with Shelby American showing signs of maturity . . . *and* severe growing pains. The small Venice, California, plant was bulging at the seams and mechanics preparing race cars were falling over mechanics building G.T.350's and vice versa. Although things were going full blast, everything but the engine shop had to be immediately moved to the Los Angeles Airport plant before they became strangled by their own activity. Also Carroll had taken on another project: the Ford GT. The GT, as you probably know, is a sophisticated prototype designed and built by Ford, with former Aston Martin engineer Roy Lunn as the project head. The first chassis were fabricated in England by Ford Advanced Vehicles. It was really an Anglo-American effort. Eric Broadley, of Lola fame, was assigned to head up the fabrication because of his experience in semimonocoque, or frameless, construction. Theoretically it was a fabulous machine, but they had run head-on into Ferrari's years of practical experience in high-speed distance racing. To understate it, they'd come out second best. Shelby's crew, on the other hand, had proven they could screw together a car that would stand up to a 12-hour or 24-hour grind. It was logical that Ford would call on the race-ready bunch to pull their pet iron out of the fire. The GT project now had three bases: Dearborn, England, and Los Angeles. With the 2000-Kilometer Daytona event, the Continental, practically upon them, it was panic-button time trying to ready two of the sleek-but-heavy coupes for this endurance test along with a complement of four race-proven Daytona Cobras.

There were three categories listed for the Daytona race: GT, Prototype, and SCCA Sports-Racing (later recognized by the FIA as Group 7). The last, without any minimum weight restrictions like those governing prototypes, should naturally be the fastest and, thereby, the race leaders. Before the race, rumors ran strong that Ferrari would make a major effort out of it. He'd seen the potential of the Cobra and knew he was in trouble. If he could catch the Ford effort unsorted and squash it early in the season, he might thereby discourage their coming to Europe for another challenge. Thus the entry of Dan Gurney's potent Lotus 19 (now sporting a 289 engine enlarged to 325 cubic inches) became strategic in the American defense. Dan and co-driver Jerry Grant could obviously set a blistering pace. If they won, it would steal Ferrari's thunder. Short of that, they might tempt some of the red cars to chase them and—hopefully—break down in the process.

Shelby had selected the late Ken Miles and fellow Texan Lloyd Ruby to drive one GT, with Bob Bondurant and John Whitmore in the other. Ferrari's effort turned out to be strong, but not as fierce as it could have been. John Surtees and Pedro Rodriguez were teamed in a new quad-cam P2. It was the most threatening of the bunch and managed to log the fastest prerace lap time. Bondurant was next quickest—2 mph slower. Gurney was having sorting problems and was 10 mph off the pace during practice. This was corrected by race time and Dan went into an immediate lead, tagged closely by Surtees. To everyone's surprise the four Cobra coupes were next in line, while the Ford GT's held a seemingly leisurely pace.

All the strategy proved unnecessary, however, as first the late Walt Hansgen lost twenty laps with his single-cam P2 Ferrari (barely averting a crash from a blown tire) and then Surtees went through the same agonizing gyrations, losing an equal number of laps before Pedro could return the car to the fray. A third 3.3-liter Ferrari was already limping with a slipping clutch. Privately entered, a lone GTO was soon the only Ferrari in contention and the pressure was off the Ford-powered boys . . . for a while.

By the seventh hour, fate had flicked a finger at the Shelby pits. Gurney turned his race-leading Lotus over to Grant and it holed a piston before the latter's stint was up. The Bob Johnson-Tom Payne

Daytona coupe had already blown an engine, and Bondurant's GT refused to start after its scheduled pit stop, necessitating a plug change and carburetion adjustment. No, it wasn't their race just yet. The GTO was holding down a worrisome fourth overall, and, as always, there was a brace of fast Porsches running like trains and picking off any of the big-bores that sickened.

Miles and Ruby were meanwhile running the race like computers, with everything going right. They brought the Ford home for its first win. The Jo Schlesser-Hal Keck Cobra nailed down second overall and the Grand Touring win and Peter Clarks GTO was third, followed by John Timanus and Rick Muther in the second Daytona coupe. One of the Porsches managed to slip past the Allen Grant-Ed Leslie coupe to finish fifth.

Carroll and his hard-working crew were quite happy with the Daytona results but well aware it had only been a partial test. They had proven the Ford GT could be made to finish a race and again proven they had the fastest Grand Touring car in the world. Yet Sebring was just around the corner and slippery old Enzo Ferrari might just have some surprises waiting for them there. As it worked out, he had his games to play, but they were more of a face-saving move than anything else. He decided to take exception to the fact that Sebring's organizers were also allowing the sports-racing cars to run. It was already known that Jim Hall would have a pair of his Chaparrals there and Ferrari, claiming they might steal the overall win and attendant publicity, promptly announced he would withdraw his factory teams (SEFAC, NART, and Maranello Concessionaires). On the surface this appeared to be a firm stand, but a private team (Ferrari Owners Racing Association) showed up with the latest cars, the factory drivers, and the factory mechanics.

Shelby wisely decided to concentrate on the GT category, and to make sure they didn't goof it by spending all their effort on the Ford GT's. There had been a raft of modifications they'd found necessary to make on the latter, based on the Daytona race, and it was still a much less reliable weapon than the well-sorted Cobra. Shelby had four Daytona coupes and four Cobra roadsters under his wing for Sebring, the two Ford GT's, and assistance for the Gurney Lotus.

Sebring '65, as you may recall, was the Year of the Floods. A literal wall of water moved onto the circuit some five hours into the race and stuck around for two more. It nearly turned the event into a fiasco. Mechanics had to chase floating tires down the pit lane and one nearly drowned when he dived beneath a Ferrari to check its suspension. As predicted, the Hall-Sharp Chaparral moved into an early lead and was chased for a while by Gurney's Lotus. But the latter dropped out with a broken oil-pump drive. The Rodriguez-Graham Hill Ferrari moved into second spot. When this happened, Carroll decided to risk one of the Ford GT's and ordered the Richie Ginther-Phil Hill car to join the chase while the Miles-Bruce McLaren GT was held to a predetermined pace. The Fords were exhibiting far more of their potential in this event, turning quick laps and sounding strong. The Bondurant-Schlesser Cobra had the GT class in hand, but in the freak rain anything could happen. Well into the race Ginther's GT broke a suspension mount, leaving Carroll with only one car in the Prototype category. But the Ferrari effort was already turning sick.

At the end of the twelve hectic hours, the Chaparral still held its race-winning lead. Shelby, however, had taken both the Prototype and GT wins. The team now had a firm lead on both the categories and it was a green light to prepare for the Le Mans effort. If things were hectic back at the "Snake Pit" before Daytona and Sebring, it was a tea party compared to the preparation that started immediately afterward.

Meanwhile, the G.T. 350 was at last smoothly rolling off the assembly line of the new plant and it had, in terms of volume, supplanted the Cobra as the mainstay of the company. The racing version had been accepted by SCCA and classified in B-Production in competition with the E-Jaguar, the older Corvette, the Sunbeam Tiger, and others of roughly the same performance potential. Ken Miles gave the G.T. 350 a sensational racing debut at Green Valley, Texas, early in the year, nearly whipping the quickest sports-racing car in a combined event. It was about that time that Carroll made one of his occasional visits to *Sports Car Graphics* office and, during a casual conversation, asked me if I thought it'd be fun to race a G.T. 350. I tried to reply just as casually that it would. "O.K!" was his retort, and the subject was closed.

Carroll had agreed with the SCCA officials that it wouldn't help the sport if he swamped the opposition in amateur racing as he had when he took his team on the USRRC tour. The Cobra effort had been turned over to his customers, who were successfully upholding its honors. The G.T. 350, however, was a new car and he felt it wise that he at least keep a close eye on one of them. A few weeks later he called to ask if I'd be running at a forthcoming Pomona regional. I had a Modified ride there, but nothing going in the Production events. It was still somewhat of a surprise when Lew Spencer, then manager of Hi-Performance Motors and a partner with Carroll in the dealership, showed up with a G.T. 350 on a trailer and told me I had a ride in the Production events, too. It turned out well and I wound up in a ding-dong battle with Dick Guldstrand for the overall win, taking it by a car length. Dick's A-Production Sting Ray was as hot as they came, and it almost looked as though the Mustang had been underclassed by the SCCA.

Things got tougher as the season progressed, however. By the time the National schedule was under way, Merle Brennan's E-Jag had gotten full support from the importer, and Hollywood Sports Cars fielded an out-to-the-limit Sunbeam Tiger with Jim Adams at the wheel. Thanks to Carroll's watchful eye, the advice of Lew Spencer, and the help of Chuck Cantwell—an ex-GM development engineer now heading the G.T. 350 project—I managed to win the Pacific Coast National title and, more important, went on to take the American Road Race of Champions run-offs at Daytona that year. My biggest competition in that race came from other Mustang entries that had been equally successful in their own section of the country. Mark Donohue, Bob Johnson, Chuck Yaeger, and Brad Brooker were the quick ones, I remember. Mark, especially, *really* made me earn the win.

It is of interest to point out that anything we developed on the "factory" car was immediately fed to other competitors around the country and that every racing G.T. 350 to come off the line was identical to ours. To buy a completely race-ready production car for under $6500 in this day and age seems just about an impossibility, but that's what Carroll was offering.

An example of this came about early in '66 when Carroll asked me to drive a Mustang at the Green Valley, Texas, regional. Dallas is his home town and he likes to help the region's effort by providing them with an entry each year. Pedro Rodriguez had showed up without a ride, and at the last minute, a local Ford dealer agreed to bump his own driver and put Pedro in the car. To make a long and embarrassing story short, Pedro outjumped me at the start and, driving as wild and hard as I could, I never did catch him. We finished three car lengths apart. A G.T. 350 sold indiscriminately to a south Texas dealer had proven to be every bit as quick as the factory's own. That was my final ride in this car. Carroll, as he'd done with the Cobra the year before, turned the racing entirely over to his customers.

To return to the international racing scene, Shelby American readied cars for Le Mans while Ford of England fielded sparse entries in the Monza, Targa Florio, and Nürburgring events. Ferrari mopped up in all three as far as the Prototypes were concerned, but the Cobras still held the GT lead going into Le Mans. When at last his cars were ready, Carroll held an impressive Open House at the new plant. It was climaxed with the machines being loaded on a jet freighter pulled right up to the door. Everything looked great . . . except that the mechanics were still working on the cars as they were being loaded. About the only Shelby employees who had been getting a full night's sleep during the first six months of that year were the security guards. They work shifts.

Ford's "secret weapon" for Le Mans was the 427 engine installed in two of the GT's (designated as Mark II's) that were under Shelby's care. It made the already-heavy cars a little heavier, but the added torque and power was more than enough to compensate. Exhaustive dyno tests had indicated these engines would live for the grueling 24 Hours *and* provide the GT's with the necessary top speed down the long straights. The 7-liter cars were backed up by two 325-inchers and two "old reliable" 289's. There were five Daytona coupes readied for the fray. Ferrari, too, made a full effort for Le Mans with three P2's and a 2-liter Dino. He had assistance from "private" entries to the tune of eight more cars; two of them also P2's, one a new GTB, and the remainder 275-LM's. The 7-liter Fords proved their potential when Phil Hill put up a new lap record during practice. Gurney posted a new GT record in a Cobra. But the 325 engine in the GT's turned sour and were replaced by the 289's. In the race, Bruce McLaren and Chris Amon swapped the lead with their Ford GT's, easily heading the Ferraris of John Surtees and Jean Guichet. Bob Bondurant was harassing the latter pair, while Dan Gurney was actually chewing at some more Ferrari prototypes with his Cobra a bit farther back.

By the end of one hour, the race speeds were over six miles an hour faster than at any previous time, but by the end of the third hour the Ford dominance was already fading. Bondurant's car blew a head gasket. Miles took over the leading McLaren car and the ring and pinion gears failed soon after. Phil Hill's 7-liter had failed to fire up at the start and joined the race some 96 miles (11 laps) behind. Within six hours the car had passed half the field, but its gearbox also packed it in by the end of another hour. Into the night it began to look like a Ferrari rout, but then they too began to disintegrate as gearbox and brakes started failing. By morning a pair of 275-LM's held the lead. All the P2's were either out or far behind. The remainder of the race was mainly a parade of cripples, but Ferrari was leading it. The Cobras had had their problems too, and the GTB led them to the wire for the GT victory, with the Sears-Thompson Cobra getting some all-important points for second place in class. Both Ford and Shelby American had been whipped in this event, but to those in the know, the handwriting was on the wall. The potential was there and only minor development was needed to put the cars in shape to sustain the terrific pace of which they were capable. Carroll would have well repeated the famous phrase he'd uttered a year before at Sebring: "Next year, Ferrari's ass is mine." But with the GT championship pretty much in the bag, he refrained. Bondurant and Jo Schlesser brought a Cobra home first in the Reims 12-hour soon afterwards to squash any hopes of Ferrari catching them for the Manufacturers' Championship. The trophy now reposes in the reception office at Carroll's plant, soon to be joined by another for the 1966 season.

By fall of 1965 the prototype '66 Cobra was already being tested, with a 427 Ford as its powerplant. And Carroll was involved in another deal that would soon excite the racing world: the formation of All American Racers with Dan Gurney as his partner. It's long been the dream of both Carroll and Dan to field a U.S.-built Formula 1 car and this was one of their major goals with the new firm. The other was equally ambitious—a three-car team for Indianapolis. They would use Ford twin-cams for the Indy race, but the formula car would start out with a Climax four-cylinder engine while awaiting a V12 design to be completed by Harry Weslake in England. While Goodyear Tire and other sponsors were behind the AAR effort, it should be noted that no car manufacturer was involved. The pair could probably have gotten all the help they wanted from Ford, but they weren't asking. This left them free to develop their own powerplants or modify any existing one they might choose. This was no rebellion against Ford but a desire for complete flexibility and indicated the intensity behind their thinking. Furthermore, as much as they wanted to carry the American banners, an Englishman was chosen to design their engine and another was hired (Len Terry) to come up with a dual-purpose chassis. Obviously AAR was to be a get-the-job-done organization.

The season closed in mid-December with the Ford First Annual Performance Banquet in Dearborn, where Carroll and other contributors to Ford's successes during the year were honored. Roy Lunn unveiled his latest creation, the "J" car, an aluminum honeycomb successor to the Ford Mark II he hoped to have ready for Le Mans in 1966.

–21–

1966: LE MANS SUCCESS

THE WINTER MONTHS gave the Shelby team some time to catch its breath. At a steady, more "casual" pace they prepared a strong entry of Mark II's for Daytona, Sebring, and Le Mans. Miles headed a corps of drivers running through programed tests, and many improvements were incorporated to make the cars more durable as well as quicker. In prerace tests at Daytona it became apparent that a set of brake discs wouldn't last the full twenty-four hours it was scheduled to run in 1966. So "quick-change" discs were an innovation the Shelby crew came up with. Ford, meanwhile, had improved its high-performance 427, making it lighter and more reliable. Lunn was busy with the "J" car. It showed lots of promise, but could only be considered an experiment this first year. At best, it could set a pace at Le Mans and take the heat off the proven Mark II's.

There were five Mark II's ready for Daytona. Two of them had been turned over to Holman and Moody. This performance firm, with a well-established reputation in Ford stock car and marine preparation, had been in on the Mark II development since the beginning of the year. One of their cars was equipped with a new automatic transmission that Ford held high hopes of debugging before Le Mans. I've never asked Carroll about Holman and Moody's participation in the sports car effort. Obviously it was a Ford Motor Company decision, and while the two teams cooperated with each other for the good of the program, it was equally obvious to an insider that there was a good deal of competition between them. Miles and Ruby were teamed in one of the Shelby cars and Gurney and Jerry Grant in the other. McLaren and Amon took over another car for Ford Advanced Vehicles, while Bucknum and Ginther drove the automatic for Holman and Moody and Walt Hansgen and Mark Donohue teamed in the second Holman-Moody car.

Ferrari P2's driven by Pedro Rodriguez-Mario Andretti and Lucian Bianchi-Gerard Langlois represented the hot segment of Enzo's effort, but there were eight 275-LM's, the fastest of these driven by Don Wester and George Follmer. Porsche debuted their new Carrera 6—a single entry—but brought along five 904's to back it up. Hall's two new Chaparral D's, driven by Phil Hill and Jo Bonnier with Jim and Hap Sharp in the other, were the only Group 7 cars of consequence, but Miles skated them out of the top qualifying time by two-tenths of a second.

During the race it quickly became obvious that the Miles-Ruby car was to play "rabbit" for Shelby, and that the Hansgen-Donohue car had orders from Holman and Moody to keep them in sight. Gurney laid back at a respectable pace, as did McLaren. The Ginther-Bucknum car had brake troubles right from the start (the parking brake had been left partially on) and the automatic transmission was already running into overheat. The Chaparrals had teething trouble that soon put one out of contention and out of the race, the other lasting some thirteen hours before the suspension broke. But the P2 Ferraris were staying just close enough to be worrisome. At six hours the Bianchi P2 retired with a blown engine, but Rodriguez was doggedly hanging on to his position.

Before morning both Chaparrals had retired, the Ginther-Bucknum car was out with transmission problems, but Miles, Hansgen, and Gurney were running one, two, three. The crews had been watching the brake discs all night and decided to change them in the early morning pit stops. It took five minutes for the Miles-Ruby car to make the change, but some fifteen to get the Hansgen car out of the Holman-Moody pit—a delay that dropped them almost a lap behind the Gurney-Grant car into third. I watched the change on the Miles car and the crew moved incredibly quick, having carefully rehearsed the handling of the hot discs and unbolting of the calipers. There were apparently a few tricks they'd learned that the Holman-Moody crew hadn't. From there on it was a tour for

Ken and Lloyd, while Gurney and Grant made sure they kept the "cushion" ahead of the Holman-Moody car without hurting their chances of finishing. Round One of the '66 Ford-Ferrari battle went decisively to Ford. High hopes were held for Round Two at Sebring because Ford had already run some highly successful tests there during the month or more spent in Florida.

Sebring was looked on by everyone as the real test for Le Mans. It was harder on equipment than Daytona, even though it was only half as long. Also expected was that Ferrari would field even more P2's and possibly the newer P3 at Sebring. The Chaparrals would be more sorted out than they were for Daytona. Ferrari *did* get a P3 to Sebring, but it was otherwise a relatively weak entry for the Black Stallion team. Parkes and Bondurant drove the P3 while Rodriguez and Andretti had their P2 spruced up from Daytona. A new Dino 2-liter driven by Bandini and Scarfiotti was amazingly fast and proved to be the machine to be reckoned with.

Ford-powered entries dominated the entry list and subsequently the race itself. There were four Mark II's—two for Shelby, two for Holman and Moody. A. J. Foyt replaced Ginther in the Mark II he and Ronnie Bucknum had not tried to finished in at Daytona. It was an automatic again. Miles and Ruby tried an automatic in theirs, but it didn't look reliable enough and they switched back to a standard four-speed. Gurney and Grant were ready to charge this time around, and when Parkes lowered the track record to an unheard of 2:56.6 in qualifying, Gurney went out and knocked exactly two seconds off that with his inimitable grin in evidence. Like "*Adios,* Enzo." Gurney was logically selected to be the rabbit for this show, but things got a bit screwed up when he flooded the car at the start and lost almost two minutes!

There were thirteen Ford GT's in the race, making it look like Dearborn had changed one of the Mustang production lines over, but most of them were GT40's powered by the reliable-but-small 289-inch V8. The Canadian Comstock team had a pair, as did Alan Mann from England and Essex Wire, a semiprivate team. These could be counted on as back-up cars only. Even the swift Chaparrals were having trouble getting under three-minute laps, so the show was strictly between the Mark II's and the Ferraris.

The Dino got away first at the start, but Graham Hill had one of the Alan Mann cars in the lead by the end of the first lap. Parkes soon took over, with Miles coolly keeping him in sight while Gurney threaded his way up through the pack as quickly and cautiously as he could. It was twenty-five laps from the start before Gurney passed Parkes to take over the lead. One of the Chaparrals was already out, the other fading. Hansgen had to pit early out of third spot and dropped way back. A. J. Foyt soon brought the automatic in for the first of many stops, so both the Holman-Moody cars were quickly out of immediate contention.

Routine pit stops around the three-hour mark provided the next drama. Dan had a healthy lead and Miles was chewing at Parkes' tail. Gas stops for this pair reversed their order, and Dan had to make a second stop to get his door closed, putting him barely in front of them. As Parkes pitted, Miles moved up to challenge Gurney. Now Just a damn minute! Everyone in the Shelby pits, including Carroll, was open-mouthed at this routine. The lap times dropped almost ten seconds and Dan cut one only two-tenths off his record—with lots of gas on board. Shelby solved the problem of their ignoring the pit signals. He grabbed a brass hammer, and standing atop the pit wall, made like he'd toss it right into their cockpits on the next go-round if this foolishness didn't stop. The lap times immediately came back to normal and Miles was about four car lengths behind on the next run past the pits. Everyone admired the display of swiftness, but Carroll was a little grim for a while; they weren't here to play games, no matter how relaxed the competition might be. The end of the race was a long way off.

The P3 never regained a threatening position, but lasted some nine hours before it retired. In the night, Andretti looped the P2 and clipped Don Wester's Carrera 6, knocking it off course and into a warehouse. It hit and killed four people who were standing in an unauthorized area. Mario got the Ferrari back to the pits, where it caught fire there from an electrical short. This moved the tiny Dino into third, a number of laps behind the leaders. It finally retired with shifting problems. Gurney was coasting now, almost a lap ahead of Miles, with only a few minutes of the race left. Then his engine blew on the backstretch, only a half mile from the pits!

Excited, he tried to push it in, and this resulted in his disqualification as Miles sailed by to take the checker.

Since Ken is no longer with us, perhaps it's all right for me to betray a confidence. Weeks later he told me, "I knew we had it pretty well in the bag and that Dan had orders to lead until he broke. If I could get him to dice with me, I figured he might bloody well hurt it just enough to make it sick. Rather close, wasn't it?" You have to remember that Ken was a master at psychological games and he might just have been playing one with me when he told that tale, but I don't think so. As at Daytona, he knew exactly what a finishing pace was at Sebring. And he knew those Fords, every nut and bolt of them. He could get away with such a delicate trick without blowing the show.

The Le Mans trials were next and Ferrari was noticeable by their absence. Enzo was crying he was being steamrollered by Ford and appealing to everyone for more funds to combat the invader. The "J" car debuted at the trials and Chris Amon took it around only one second slower than the lap record for the fastest time of the prerace tests. Miles was next, in a Mark II. Walt Hansgen, lapping faster in a rainy practice session than anyone had ever before attempted, got just a hair out of the dry groove and lost control. He tried to snake the big 7-liter down an escape road but it was blocked by a sandbank and he impacted at over 125 mph. Walt died some twenty-four hours later from his injuries. His passing was felt deeply by everyone in the sport, and Ford's management debated withdrawing their Le Mans entries for a while, before deciding that it would be the last thing Walt himself would have wanted to see happen as a result of his death.

By mid-March, All American Racers was already testing their first completed Indy car and it looked good. Named the Eagle, it was closely patterned after the Lotus 38's but brought up to U.S. standards of materials and fabrication. Five of the Indy cars were getting the finishing touches and two Formula 1 cars were well under way. Three Eagles were sold to other Indy entrants (one for Lloyd Ruby, one for Roger McCluskey, the other for Jerry Grant), and the remaining two comprised the AAR effort, to be driven by Gurney and Joe Leonard. Carroll had already moved his public-relations manager, Max Muhleman, from Shelby American to AAR full time to act as coordinator, expediter, and just about everything else that could be considered a loose end, while Dan did the testing and Carroll tried to hustle up enough sponsorship to finance the tremendously expensive venture.

As you know, the Indy race turned into a first-lap debacle that wiped out Dan's car and flat-spotted the tires on Leonard's. His magneto later failed. Lloyd Ruby *almost* brought an Eagle home first, but was black-flagged out of the lead with an oil leak. Mc-Cluskey, too, went out with loss of oil. Only Grant finished, after losing over a half-hour in the pits with magneto problems. Dan was bitter and Carroll was about sick after the many months of hard work and planning they'd devoted to the Indy attempt. They'd counted heavily on it kicking off their Formula 1 project nicely, with both money and publicity. But these are determined guys, and it wasn't long before things were moving ahead again.

Nürburgring was the curtain-raiser for Le Mans. Hall's Chaparral coupe won it overall. A single Mark II Ford was loaned to Alan Mann, and Ferrari sent a lone P3. It was a bit like sending out advance patrols before the battle. The P3 was extremely quick, besting the Mark II in practice and then even more so in the race, where it proved less effected by a strong crosswind that blew up. The rumor was that Enzo would have pulled his Le Mans effort completely had it not been for this prototype victory over the Ford.

After much feinting, Enzo sent three P3's to Le Mans and backed them up with four "independent" P2's. There were also some 275-LM's and GTB's. Three Dinos had their own work cut out for them against a full Porsche team and the rapid Matra-BRM's in the under-2-liter class. Ford elected to leave the "J" car home, so there were three Mark II's handled by Carroll's team, three by Holman and Moody, and two by Alan Mann. Miles teamed up with Denny Hulme; McLaren and Amon were in the second Shelby car; and Gurney and Grant drove the third. Paul Hawkins and Mark Donohue shared the first Holman-Moody car, Ronnie Bucknum and stock-car pilot Dick Hutcherson the second, Bianchi and Andretti the third. Graham Hill-Muir and Whitmore-Gardner were the Alan Mann chauffeurs. Parkes and Scarfiotti handled the No. 1 Ferrari,

Bandini and Guichet the second, with Rodriguez and Ginther in the third P3. Phil Hill and Bonnier had a lone Chaparral entry. Backing the 7-liter Fords were five GT40's in the hands of capable drivers and independent teams, but they like the P2's had little hope of running up near the leaders. Gurney showed what the pace would be like in practice when he lowered the lap record by three seconds for an *average* speed of 142.99 mph. Ferrari just couldn't hack that kind of lap time . . . at least they didn't try.

The race started with Ferrari thinking they had one advantage— an ability to run some twenty minutes longer between fuel stops than the Fords could. It was enough to keep them from trying to directly challenge the pace set by the Mark II's, figuring the greater number of pit stops over the twenty-four hours would balance out their superior speed. It was a mistake the Shelby and Holman-Moody crews played up as prudently as they dared, and the race was well over an hour old before the Ferrari team realized they'd been had; the Fords were able to match them pit stop for pit stop. A fairly old trick in distance racing, it none the less demonstrated the team had things well enough under control to play this kind of game, and it was this aspect that Ferrari underestimated. They were dealing with a mature and competent opponent, a fact they were well aware of by the time the race had ended. Graham Hill set the early pace, trailed some five seconds back by Gurney. Miles had to pit to get his door shut and Hawkins twisted off a drive axle.

Two hours into the race and the Gurney-Grant and Miles-Hulme cars were swapping the lead. The P3's were still very much in the race, however, with Parkes and Rodriguez staying in contention. Parkes was leading before midnight, but the two Fords took it away easily. The Rodriguez-Ginther P3 moved up to challenge, trailed by the McLaren-Amon Ford. Before dawn both of the Alan Mann Mark II's were out of the race, but Scarfiotti crashed his P3 into a smaller car and the Rodriguez-Ginther car dropped a gearbox. By morning all the Fords had to do was finish. At 11 A.M., however, Grant came in with a blown head gasket. It wasn't over yet! The leading Mark II's spent the remainder of the race running nose-to-tail at a drastically reduced pace. Toward the end the order went out for the McLaren car to take the checker. Why the decision was made, I don't know and I don't intend to ask. It could have been punishment for Miles' dice with Gurney at Sebring. It could have been to give McLaren and the British segment of the effort proper recognition, or they may even have figured the publicity Ken would gain by winning Daytona, Sebring, and Le Mans in a row would overshadow the Ford victory. Whatever it was, Carroll made sure he disappeared for a couple of hours. He didn't want to face a disappointed Miles until things had cooled down.

Deservedly, the Shelby and Ford people had themselves a wing-ding. It had been a terribly long grind to take home a Le Mans victory. They'd had to learn the game from scratch and beat the recognized master of endurance racing—Ferrari. The party continued from Le Mans to New York and gradually tapered off on the way back to the West Coast. The Dearborn troops went home thinking perhaps they could forget all this madness of twenty-four hour racing, but there was a nagging remembrance that Mr. Ford himself had told everyone after the race that they'd be back next year. Performance budget approval for '67, signed some four months later, did, indeed, include another Le Mans effort.

A new circuit sprang up in 1966 that offered yet another outlet for the Shelby American talents: The Trans-American Sedan series. FIA Group 2 rules governed the circuit, meaning one thousand identical cars had to be produced for a model to qualify. A limited number of options and modifications are allowed to make them more raceworthy. In Carroll's employ for a number of years were the Pike brothers, Don and Gary. Their hobby had been sedan racing in local amateur races with a well-prepared Falcon. Their enthusiasm for it infected Carroll and he was well on top of it when the Trans-Am came into being. Their Group 2 notchback Mustang is only fractionally slower than a racing G.T. 350.

The early races started in the East and gradually worked their way west, ending with Riverside in September. There were strong Dodge and Plymouth teams, but independents like Chuck Yeager and Brad Brooker brought their Mustangs in first often enough to keep Ford in the points standings. By the time the series got to Green Valley, Texas, Don Pike had traded his Falcon for a Mustang and was dominating West Coast sedan racing, so Carroll sent him down to Texas to see if he could swing the points balance in Ford's favor. It was a nasty six-hour event, run partially at night and in the rain. Don was black-flagged out of the lead with shorted taillights, but Brooker went on to win and tie things up with Plymouth.

A week before the final Riverside Trans-Am, Carroll called me to ask if I'd like to team with Don in another Group 2 they were just finishing off for a customer in Mexico City. He got the friendly price for our using the car and it was to be put back in top shape after the race. I said, "Yup!" again, but I'm getting ahead of my story. . . .

Immediately after Le Mans, Roy Lunn began work on a sprint version of his "J" car. It was constructed entirely by Lunn's group in Ford's Dearborn plant and, when it was completed, Ken Miles was borrowed from Shelby to test it. Strictly by accident, I'd dropped into the Ford Public Relations offices to say hello, while I was back in Detroit for some car tests. They told me Roy was bringing the "J" car over to the proving ground for Ken to take it on its first outing and would I like to see it. It was a beautiful machine, one of the most professional from both design and fabrication standpoints that I've ever seen. It was equipped with a lightweight 427 and two-speed automatic transaxle. Ken dragged it up and down for a while, then took a couple of laps around the tiny handling course. The major portion of the testing would be moved to Riverside. While they reloaded the car, Ken and I made small talk. He was enthusiastic about it, but even more excited that he'd just been told Ford was presenting him with a Lotus Cortina for his part in the victorious Le Mans project. It was the last time I ever saw him.

Some weeks later Miles was testing the "J" car at Riverside and had completed a goodly number of laps when, braking down off the long back straight, something appeared to lock one wheel, spinning him into the inside of the course. The car tripped over a haybale and started flipping violently down a thirty-foot bank. It broke in half; Ken was thrown out and killed instantly. I can't describe the shock I felt at the news, but it must have been minor compared to the way Carroll must have been hit by it. Ken had been a personal friend of long standing and had become practically indispensable in the Shelby American organization. Ken knew no peer as a development driver and he could race with the best in the world. I too considered Ken a personal friend, but the greatest shock was in realizing that, even with his uncanny ability to be on top of any situation and remain in control, he had died in a race car. Certainly no driver can save the one situation we all fear: mechanical failure at an intolerable moment, but with Ken it was still unbelievable.

At any rate, when Carroll offered me the Group 2 ride, the press put two and two together and figured I was taking Ken's place in the car. The idea didn't sit well, so I squashed it as quickly as I could. Ken is gone and someone else will ultimately be doing his work. But replace him? Never!

Two days before Qualifying we tested the new Mustang and it was a beaut, sound as a dollar and just one of those cars you can feel taking all the heat you can generate without even breathing hard. Subsequently I set a new sedan record with it at Riverside and managed to win the race going away despite two goofs: flooding the carburetors at the start and getting away almost dead last, then hitting a loose tire marker near the midway point that broke the oil filter and dumped all the oil. Imagine: I drove it back to the pits a full two miles with absolutely no oil pressure, figuring that'd finish it. But Carroll's guys jumped on it, fixed the filter, threw in oil, a tank of gas, and had me back on the track in a little over two minutes! After the race they checked the engine. The compression was still up to spec and the bearings looked like new! It's pretty hard to lose with that kind of equipment and preparation. Don took over the lead when I lost my oil and would have won it. When he pitted, however, the starter jammed and the delay blew his chances. So Lady Luck must have been riding with me.

It was late into the Formula 1 season before AAR got their new V12 into an Eagle. Dan, meanwhile, had been doing an admirable job with a 2.6 four-cylinder Climax. He debuted the V12 car at Monza, where it went out with fuel problems. The next race was Watkins Glen, where he turned the 2.6 over to Bob Bondurant and tried further sorting out of the new engine. But blow-by problems put him out here, detonation the suspected cause. Bob tangled with bodywork that came off Pedro Rodriguez's Lotus and left the road early in the race, bending the suspension and retiring the car.

The two Eagles were taken to Mexico, where Dan swapped cars with Bondurant when the V12 began acting up early. Bob was soon out with boiling fuel (due mainly to the altitude), but Dan worked the Climax up to fourth spot behind Ginther and eventually finished fifth in this last GP of the season. While the Eagles have made a somewhat inconclusive showing, the winter months should provide them with the time to sort out the many problems. Next season may be an entirely different story.

You've undoubtedly seen Shelby American's offerings for 1967. The G.T. 350 is even further removed from the production Mustang than it has been in the past, both in appearance and performance. The G.T. 500, powered by Ford's 427, can only be described as Something Else! They are fine products and, considering all their features, offered at an amazingly low price. The Cobras have only detail changes and Carroll tells me this will be the case for at least another model year. There are some race car plans that I can't talk about without checking with him and he's been too busy bouncing all over the world these past few weeks to get an okay from . . . which is why I'm writing these last two chapters instead of Carroll telling it in his own words.

There's little doubt that Mr. Shelby, who only a scant six years ago was eating off the brochure profits from his School of High Performance Driving, is now a long way from worrying about where his next meal is coming from. And he's worked damned hard for every penny of it. But financial gain is strictly a side effect for Carroll. He loves cars and automobile racing and wants more and more people to share his interest. He is happiest doing exactly what he's doing and pours his tremendous talent and energy into it unceasingly. He'd do the same if it only kept him in hog jowls and chili. There is no doubt that his efforts have greatly increased both the stature and growth of the sport . . . and that the lot of the automotive enthusiast is a much happier one because a former Texas chicken farmer, turned racer, had an idea about putting a Ford V8 in an AC chassis.

APPENDIX 1

SPECIFICATIONS OF THE 289 COBRA

ENGINE:

High-performance Ford Fairlane V8 with pushrod operated valves.

Bore & Stroke: 4.00 × 2.87 in.

Piston displacement: 289 cu. in.

Compression ratio: 10 to 1.

Basic carburetion: Single four-barrel downdraft carburetor.

Output: 271 bhp @ 5800 rpm.[*]

Torque: 269 lbs/ft @ 4800 rpm.

[*] With the 289 cu. in. engine, a variety of options and extras is available for performance increase, which will produce up to 370 bhp. These options are chiefly for use in racing and include solid valve lifters in place of hydraulic; different camshaft configuration; different ignition curve; multiple Weber downdraft carburetors with special manifold; oil cooler; tuned intake and exhaust systems, etc. Prices on application.

DRIVE TRAIN:

Four-speed, Ford all-syncromesh transmission with floor shift. This is known as the "Sebring Type" gearbox, and is standard equipment. Gear ratios of transmission:

> First: . . . . . . .2.36 to 1
> Second: . . . . .1.61 to 1
> Third: . . . . . . .1.20 to 1
> Fourth: . . . . . .Direct drive

Differential ratios (with limited slip fitted as standard equipment):

4.56 = 110 mph at 6500 rpm with standard equipment
4.26 = 115 mph
3 .77 = 132 mph
3.54 = 140 mph
3.31 = 150 mph
2.72 = 180 mph

Clutch: single dry plate with hydraulic actuation.

CHASSIS AND SUSPENSION:

• Tubular-type chassis based on two parallel main members.

• *Front suspension:* independent by transverse spring with lower A-frame and upper arm consisting of transverse leaf. Adjustable shocks and concentric springs.

• *Rear suspension:* independent by transverse spring with lower A-frame and upper arm consisting of transverse leaf. Adjustable shocks and concentric springs.

BRAKES:

• Girling 12-inch disc on all four wheels. Dual master cylinders.

• Brake pad swept area: 550 sq. in.

STEERING:

Rack & pinion. Adjustable steering wheel.

GENERAL:

12-volt electrical system with alternator.
Wide-based, 72 spoke wire wheels for better handling.*
Knock-off hubcaps.
18-gallon gas tank.

* Selection of magnesium knock-off wide based rims for competition, as optional extras.

WEIGHTS & MEASURES:

Wheelbase: .... 90-in.
Overall length: .... 167-in.
Overall width: .... 61-in.
Tread   (front) .... 53.25-in.
         (rear) .... 52.75-in.
Height (top of windshield) ... 45-in.
Ground clearance .... 5.5-in.
Curb weight .... 2100 lbs.
Weight distribution 49/51
Steering (lock to lock) ...... 3 turns
Turning circle .... 33 ft. 3-in.
Tire size (front & rear) ..... 735 × 15

STANDARD ROAD EQUIPMENT:

• Full instrumentation.
• Safety glass windshield.
• Folding top and side curtains.
• Turn indicators.
• Genuine leather upholstery.
• Aluminum hand-formed body.
• Choice of colors. (Red, maroon, white, black, bright blue, princess blue and silver.)

LIST PRICE:

F.o.b. Los Angeles: $5995.00
See, also, list of optional factory-installed equipment.

APPENDIX 2

FIA INTERNATIONAL MANUFACTURERS' CHAMPIONSHIP FOR GRAND TOURING CARS 1964

February 16: **Third Annual Daytona Beach Continental (2000 kilometers).**

GT 4th: Johnson-Gurney	(Cobra)	4th overall.
GT 6th: Butler-Rainville	(Cobra)	7th overall.
GT 8th: Hitchcock-Tchkotoua-Schlesser		
	(Cobra)	10th overall.

DNF: Holbert-McDonald, due to fire on refueling. This Daytona Coupe led the race until the 209th lap.

NOTE: A Ferrari GTO was 1st in GT class and 3rd overall.

March 22: **Sebring 12-Hour Endurance Race.**

GT 1st: Holbert-McDonald	(Cobra)	4th overall.
GT 2nd: Spencer-Bondurant	(Cobra)	5th overall.
GT 3rd: Schlesser-Hill	(Cobra)	6th overall.
GT 5th: Keck-Scott	(Cobra)	8th overall.
GT 6th: Gurney-Johnson	(Cobra)	10th overall.*
GT 7th: Hitchcock-Tchkotoua	(Cobra)	14th overall.
GT 12th: Lowther-Winstersteen	(Cobra)	35th overall.

DNF: Miles, crashed Prototype 427 in practice.

* This car, while 3rd overall, was involved in an accident half an hour before the end of the race.

Shelby American took point lead from Ferrari: 18.3 to 16.5

April 26: **48th Targa Florio, Sicily. 10 laps; 450 miles.**

GT 2nd:Gurney-Grant   (Cobra)   8th overall.

DNF: Four GT Cobras, various causes.

NOTE: A Ferrari GTO was 1st in GT class and 5th overall.

Ferrari regained points lead: 30.9 to 27.9

May 17: **Spa-Francorchamps, Belgium. 500-Kilometer Sports Car GP.**

GT 6th: Bondurant-Neerspach   (Cobra)   9th overall.
GT 8th: Schlesser-Attwood   (Cobra)   11th overall.

DNF: Olthoff-Hawkins Cobra.

NOTE: Ferrari GTO's took first four places overall. Ferrari increased points lead: 42.6 to 29.2

May 31: **Nürburgring 1000-Kilometer Sports Car Race, Germany.**

GT 6th Schlesser-Attwood   (Cobra)   12th overall.*
GT Bondurant-Neerspach   (Cobra)   19th overall.**

* Defective ignition.
** Oil cooler failure.

Ferrari GTO's 2nd and 4th overall. Ferrari increased points lead: 57 to 30.8

June 21: **Le Mans 24-Hour Endurance Race for Sports Cars. France.**

GT 1st: Gurney-Bondurant (Cobra) 4th overall.*

DNF: Neerspach-Ammon, disqualified illegal restart. Bolton-Sears, crashed AC-Cobra factory Coupe.

* New GT class record of 4492 kilometers.

Ferrari points lead, 69 to 48.8

July 4: **12 Hours of Reims, International. France.**

GT DNF: Neerspach-Ireland (Cobra), defective gearbox.
          Gurney-Bondurant (Cobra), overheating.

Ferrari GTO won overall, 1st in GT.

Ferrari points lead, 73.2 to 48.8

August 9: **Freiburg Hillclimb, Freiburg, Germany.**

GT 1st: Bondurant	(Cobra)	4th overall.
GT 3rd: Neerspach	(Cobra)	
GT 5th: Siffert	(Cobra)	

NOTE: Ferrari GTO 2nd and 4th in GT-3 Class.

Ferrari points lead, 79.2 to 57.8

August 29: **RAC Tourist Trophy, Goodwood Airfield, Chichester, England.**

GT 1st: Gurney	(Cobra)	3rd overall.
GT 2nd: Sears	(Cobra)	4th overall.
GT 3rd: Olthoff	(Cobra)	5th overall.

NOTE: 1st and 2nd overall taken by Ferrari Prototypes.

Phil Hill (Cobra) finished 11th. Oil cooler failure.

Ferrari points lead, 79.2 to 68.2

September 6: **Monza Three-Hour Coppa de Europa. Scrubbed.** *

* See "The Cobra Strikes."

NOTE: This cancellation probably cost Shelby American the FLA World Championship for GT cars.

September 12–22: **Automobile Tour de France. Race including 16 separate events.**

GT DNF: Bondurant-Neerspach (Cobra) *
               Trintignant-Simon (Cobra) **
               St. Auban-Peron (Cobra) ***

* Broken crankshaft, third event. Won first two.
** Front wheel bearing burned out after Rouen, which they won.
*** Blew piston in fourth event.

Ferrari GTO, 1st overall.

NOTE: Ferrari points lead, 84.6 to 68.2. Shelby American could no longer win.

September 20: **Bridgehampton Double 500, Bridgehampton Course, Long Island, N.Y.**

GT 1st: Miles	(Cobra)	4th overall.
GT 2nd: Bucknum	(Cobra)	6th overall.
GT 3rd: Johnson	(Cobra)	7th overall.
GT 4th: Parsons	(Cobra)	8th overall.

DNF: Two other Cobras, 48th lap. Ed Leslie, broken gearshift. Charlie Hayes, ran out of gas.

Shelby American gained another 10.1 points in this event, but lost the World GT Championship to Ferrari, 84.6 to 78.3.

NOTE: Winner of FIA World Championship was rated on five best performances out of a possible eleven races.

Shelby American Cobras easily won the United States Road Racing Championship for 1964, competing in eight events between March 1 and August 30, and winning six of them. In three races (Augusta, Ga., Pensacola, Fla., and Laguna Seca, Calif.) Cobras took 1-2-3 overall. In one race (Mansfield, Lexington, Ohio) they finished 1-2-3-4. In one race (Kent, Washington) they finished 1-2. In the remaining two events (Des Moines, Iowa, and Meadowvale, Ill.) they finished 4th and 5th, respectively.

APPENDIX 3

SPECIFICATIONS OF THE 427 COBRA

(Street Version)

ENGINE:

High performance Ford V8 with pushrod operated valves.
Bore & Stroke: 4.24 × 3.788 in.
Piston displacement: 427 cu. in.
Compression ratio: 11.5:1
Basic carburetion: Two four-barrel downdraft Holleys.
Output: 425 bhp @ 6000 rpm.
Torque: 480 lbs/ft @ 3700 rpm.

DRIVE TRAIN:

Four-speed, Ford all-syncromesh transmission with floor shift.

Gear ratios of transmission:

First: . . . . . . .2.32 to 1
Second: . . . . .1.69 to 1
Third: . . . . . . .1.29 to 1
Fourth: . . . . . .Direct drive

Differential ratio (with limited slip fitted as standard equipment): 3.54 to 1

Clutch: Ford, single dry plate (11.5 in.) with hydraulic actuation.

CHASSIS AND SUSPENSION:

Tubular type chassis based on two parallel main members. Front and rear suspension: independent coil springs with parallel arms.

BRAKES:

Girling discs on all four wheels.

Front: . . . . . . .11⁵/₈ in.
Rear: . . . . . . .10³/₄ in.

STEERING:

Rack and pinion.

GENERAL:

12-volt electrical system with alternator.
Wide based alloy 7¹/₂ × 15 in. wheels.
18-gallon gas tank.

WEIGHTS AND MEASURES:

Wheelbase. . . . . .90 in.
Overall length. . . . . .156 in.
Overall width . . . . .70.5 in.
Tread   (front) . . . . .56 in.
        (rear) . . . . .56 in.
Overall height . . . . .49 in.
Ground clearance . . . . .5.5 in.
Curb weight . . . . .2150 lbs.

(Competition Version)

ENGINE:

Output: 490 bhp @ 6500 rpm.

Torque: 510 ft/lbs @ 3700 rpm.

Cylinder heads are aluminum as opposed to cast iron for the street version. Differential ratio options: 3.09, 3.31, 3.54, 3.77, 4.09 to 1.

Optional gearbox ratios:

First:. . . . . . . .2.32 to 1.
Second:. . . . . .1.54 to 1.

Third: . . . . . . .1.19 to 1.
Fourth: . . . . . .Direct drive.

WHEELS:

Wide-based alloy. (Front) 7 $\frac{1}{2}$ × 15
                   (Rear)   9 $\frac{1}{2}$ × 15

OPTIONAL EQUIPMENT:

Special racing bucket seats. Shoulder harness. Quick-change
brake pad kit. Dry sump kit.

APPENDIX 4

FIA INTERNATIONAL MANUFACTURERS' CHAMPIONSHIP FOR GRAND TOURING CARS 1965

February 28, 1965: (Daytona Beach, Fla.)

GT 1st: Jo Schlesser—Harold Keck
(Cobra Daytona Coupe)

March 27, 1965: (Sebring 12-Hours)

GT 1st: Jo Schlesser—Bob Bondurant
(Cobra Daytona Coupe)

April 25, 1965: (Monza, Italy)

GT 1st: Bob Bondurant—Allen Grant
(Cobra Daytona Coupe)

May 1, 1965: (Oulton Park, England)

GT 1st: Sir John Whitmore
(Cobra Daytona Coupe)

May 16, 1965: (Spa, Belgium)

GT 2nd: Bob Bondurant
(Cobra Daytona Coupe)

May 23, 1965: **(Nürburgring, Germany)**
GT 1st: Bob Bondurant—Joachim Neerspach
(Cobra Daytona Coupe)

June 13, 1965: **(Rossfeld Hillclimb, Germany)**
GT 1st: Bob Bondurant
(Cobra 289 Roadster)

June 19/20, 1965: **(Le Mans 24-Hours, France)**
GT 2nd: Jack Sears-Dr. Richard Thompson
(Cobra Daytona Coupe)

July 4, 1965: **(Reims, France)**
GT 1st: Bob Bondurant—Jo Schlesser
(Cobra Daytona Coupe)

NOTE: By their seven GT victories and two second places during 1965, Shelby-American sponsored and built Cobra products scored a total of 90.3 points to win the FIA International Manufacturers' Championship (displacement class III).

INDEX